Heroes
After
Hours

. . . .

David C. Forward

Heroes After Hours

. . . .

Extraordinary Acts of Employee Volunteerism

Jossey-Bass Publishers
San Francisco

Substantial discounts on bulk quantities of Jossey-Bass books are available to corporations, professional associations, and other organizations. For details and discount information, contact the special sales department at Jossey-Bass Inc., Publishers. (415) 433-1740; Fax (415) 433-0499.

For international orders, please contact your local Paramount Publishing International office.

Manufactured in the United States of America. Nearly all Jossey-Bass books and jackets are printed on recycled paper that contains at least 50 percent recycled waste, including 10 percent postconsumer waste. Many of our materials are also printed with vegetable-based ink; during the printing process these inks emit fewer volatile organic compounds (VOCs) than petroleum-based inks. VOCs contribute to the formation of smog.

Credits are on page 264.

Library of Congress Cataloging-in-Publication Data

Forward, David C., date
    Heroes after hours : extraordinary acts of employee volunteerism / David C. Forward. — 1st ed.
      p. cm. — (A joint publication in the Jossey-Bass nonprofit series and the Jossey-Bass management series)
    Includes bibliographical references and index.
    ISBN 1-55542-666-2
    1. Voluntarism—United States. 2. Volunteer workers in social service—United States. I. Title. II. Title: Employee volunteerism. III. Series: Jossey-Bass nonprofit series. IV. Series: Jossey-Bass management series.
    HN90.V64F67 1994
    361.3′7′0973—dc20
                                            94-7516
                                              CIP

FIRST EDITION
HB Printing 10 9 8 7 6 5 4 3 2 1   *Code 9463*

To my wonderful wife, Chris,
for her support and encouragement
in all the volunteerism projects
that have kept me away from home so much.
There will surely be a special place in heaven reserved for her,
but while on earth I am so happy that she is by my side.

Contents

HOW TO GET INVOLVED:
A Resource Guide for Companies and Individuals

. . . .

Foreword

All of us know we face serious social problems such as hungry school children, homeless families, and violence in our communities. In the United States, and indeed, around the world, we are at a crossroads where we must choose to address these problems and make a difference, or pass along a future of overpowering social ills to our children and grandchildren.

In this book you will find the leaders who chose to make a difference and become involved in community service aimed at solving these serious issues. These heroes who rally the support of their fellow employees for community service have made a significant impact on their own community's housing, on a school near their workplace, and in countries on the other side of the world.

Heroes After Hours is a valuable contribution that inspires and challenges all of us to ask ourselves what impact we can have on the problems we confront each day. With enthusiasm and vision, these employees serve as models for us. More importantly, they often lead their employers to make company-wide commitments to the community.

At The Points of Light Foundation we are dedicated to motivating leaders to mobilize others for community service directed at solving the most serious social problems facing society today.

We recognize the outstanding contributions made by the employee volunteers featured in this book and urge corporate policy makers to commit to establish, support, and promote an employee volunteer program that encourages the involvement of every employee and treat it like any other core business function. Inspired by these examples, every company can help its employees move from success to significance.

Washington, D.C.   Richard F. Schubert
July 1994   *President and Chief Executive Officer*
                                        The Points of Light Foundation

Preface

In the book *Words to Love By*, Mother Teresa tells the story of how she started her ministry to the sick and dying poor. She had been a high school teacher in Calcutta for almost twenty years when, in 1952, she came upon an abandoned woman lying in the street, being consumed by rats and ants. She picked up the frail body and took the lady to the hospital, but they would not help. Then she carried her to authorities at the city health department. Mother Teresa appealed to the officials to provide a sanctuary where this woman and hundreds of others who lay dying in Calcutta's streets could spend their last earthly days away from heat, filth, and danger. A city health officer was moved by her compassion and showed her an unused building originally intended as a hostel for pilgrims visiting the adjacent Hindu temple. She immediately accepted his offer and within twenty-four hours had moved other destitute sick and dying people in. Her first patient died there a few days later, but she did so in an environment of peace, surrounded by people who treated her with tenderness and love.

I often wonder whether that poor, suffering lady could ever have imagined herself as the catalyst who triggered an unknown nun to start her worldwide Missionaries of Charity movement and who has since cared for over forty-two thousand patients in that building, now known as Kalighat.

In *Words to Love By*, Mother Teresa writes:

I never look at the masses as my responsibility.
I look at the individual.
I can love only one person at a time.
I can feed only one person at a time.
Just one, one, one.
You get closer to Christ by coming closer to each
    other.
As Jesus said, "Whatever you do to the least of my
    brethren,
you do to me."
So you begin.... I begin.
I picked up one person,
—maybe if I didn't pick up that one person
I wouldn't have picked up the next 42,000.
The whole work is only a drop in the ocean.
But if I didn't put the drop in, the ocean would be
    one drop less.
Same thing for you
same thing in your family
same thing in the church where you go,
just begin...one, one, one.

Those words inspire me as much today as when I first read
them many years ago. What an appropriate challenge for people
to go into their communities and give a helping hand to someone in need.

Many people, including the speaker of Japan's House of
Representatives, have called American employees "lazy" and "un-
productive." At the same time, it is a common misconception
that America's largest corporations are greedy, avaricious, and un-
caring. *Heroes After Hours* will show that even the largest companies are made up of concerned individuals; people who, research shows, care about their communities and the needy in the
world beyond; employees who have demonstrated creativity,
compassion, and motivation.

For most of my years in the United States I have been actively involved in volunteerism projects, in my local community, elsewhere in the U.S., and around the globe. In a number of cases, my project was an urgent response to a natural disaster such as an earthquake in Italy, floods in Pennsylvania, or a volcanic eruption in Colombia. Many of the people who helped were employees who cared about the needy both at home and in the world beyond. These people went out of their way to donate their time, money, and relief supplies without question or hesitation. Some of them put aside their ethnic or religious differences to support projects in Beirut, Romania, and the Dominican Republic. When I was on the board of Trevor's Campaign for the Homeless, I was continually moved as adults and children, senior citizens and employee groups responded with fiscal and physical support for our transitional housing and nightly food runs for the homeless.

These people responded quietly, often anonymously. They did not wear badges at work the next day saying, "I slogged through the snow last night taking hot meals to the street people." They inevitably say their reward comes from the inner satisfaction of giving something back for the blessings they have received.

This book was written to answer the question, When faced with the overwhelming problems that confront us today, can one person—that flight attendant, secretary, bank employee—do anything to make a difference? Secondarily, it was written to explore the human attributes that lead to extraordinary acts of volunteerism.

My research began with a letter personally addressed to the CEOs of *Fortune*'s 250 largest U.S. companies asking for examples of their volunteerism programs and individual employees who have demonstrated commitment to their communities through voluntary service. Follow-up telephone calls were made to each of the companies that responded, and I then traveled around the country interviewing the volunteers as well as their co-workers and senior management.

Heroes After Hours will introduce you to some truly inspirational people whose accounts are moving testimonies of how ordinary American employees are helping mankind. Their stories will highlight individuals who are generally no wealthier, are no more secure in their jobs, and certainly have no more free time than the average person. They are young singles with active social lives, grandmothers with extensive church commitments, and young parents with children at home. Yet they found the time to make dreams turn into reality.

The volunteers you are about to meet are from diverse ethnic backgrounds and run the gamut from entry-level employees to senior executives. You'll meet public servants like policeman Al Lewis and employees from corporate entities such as AT&T, Chevron, and Bank of America. In some cases, the employees are essentially running one-person projects, while in others, the volunteers are motivating dozens of co-workers to participate. They have responded to needs in areas as varied as child mentoring, homelessness, environmental protection, and caring for sick children. Other projects help the elderly and victims of natural disasters. Many volunteers launched humanitarian programs in their own communities, whereas other projects span the globe. The point I am making is that the individuals you will meet in the pages ahead are ordinary, everyday people, some newly hired, others now retired, who are bound together by their love of helping others. They initiated voluntary service projects, often having no idea what the ultimate outcome would be. They just cared enough to act—and they jumped in.

Heroes After Hours is the first book on employee volunteerism. It will demonstrate that the common thread here is the corporate connection: each employer has programs that not only tolerate employee volunteerism but actively encourage it. These organizations have adopted voluntary community service as a central component of their mission. They do not necessarily need to fund such programs with a lot of money, but they urge employees to participate and publicly recognize those who do get involved.

American employee volunteerism is on the rise. Corporations recognize the value, both in internal morale and external public relations, of their workers' contributing to needs in the community. A 1988 Gallup poll showed that nearly 50 percent of respondents were involved in volunteer or charity work, compared to 31 percent in 1984. These figures are corroborated by a study undertaken by Independent Sector, a nonprofit coalition of 450 business and charitable-organization members. Their poll shows that through 1992, while financial contributions to charities have declined, volunteerism has increased significantly. Another study, by Opinion Research Corporation in 1992, illustrates that consumers are more likely to patronize a company that is seen to be active in addressing the social concerns of the community.

In traveling around the country interviewing the people featured in the following chapters, I anticipated that the diversity of age, job description, and industry would make it impossible to draw a central thread from the stories. I was wrong. There are four common themes linking every volunteer featured:

1. They were all incredibly busy people, even before their volunteerism involvement. As one person replied when I asked her how she could accomplish so much in addition to her professional, family, church, and social commitments, "If you want to get something done, ask a busy person."
2. They were all results oriented. They could see the final objective and would not let minor obstacles deter them from maintaining that focus. As Zig Ziglar says, "If you waited for *all* the lights to be on green, you'd never leave home."
3. They have the ability to motivate others. These employees are not necessarily great speakers, but by their vision and their own actions they inspire their friends and co-workers to work with them on their projects.
4. They take enormous personal satisfaction from the act of serving others. Although their companies may present them with some form of award or recognition, the real reward for them is in their service to those in need.

To these I would add one theme that not only covers every volunteer, it captures the essence of the entire book: One person *can* make a difference. As you read these moving accounts of employees who cared enough to act, I hope you feel the warmth, compassion, and love for mankind that touched my heart as I attempted to put them on paper, and that you, too, will be inspired to become involved in voluntary service to those in need.

Medford, New Jersey   DAVID C. FORWARD
July 1994

Acknowledgments

I am deeply indebted to a number of people who have given their time and advice to make this book a reality. I thank them for sharing their stories and their enthusiasm with me and pray that the reader will be motivated to follow their examples of voluntary service to communities around the world.

Aetna Insurance: Michael G. Bazinet

American Airlines: Heather Bell, Ellen Crane, Jacki Graham

Apple Computer: Elizabeth Armstrong, Jim Armstrong, Donna Mar, Anne McMullin

AT&T: Dolores Riego de Dios

Ave Maria Press: Carolyn L. Sherman

Bank of America: Roger G. Hancock, Katy Jarman, Robin Leidenthal, Pat Lindh

Boeing: Sandy Berglund, Bob Krull, Daniel C. North, Mal Stamper

Boston Children's Hospital: Myra Fox, Joanne Geake, Ann Malone, Nancy Treves

Chase Manhattan: Maria Alvarez, Kerry G. Yeager

Chevron: Grace B. Freasier, Clare B. LeBrun, David W. McMurry

Chrysler: James Kenyon, Denise Marcial, Tony Mason, Dominic Marzicola, Charles Pryor

Cigna: Lauren M. Stern

Continental Airlines: Terri New, Ray Scippa

Ford: Robert C. Reid, Richard P. Siegel

General Electric: Bruce Bunch, Colleen M. Connery, Len Doviak, Cristina M. Harter

GTE: George Boggs, Walter Carleton, David Fay, Rebecca Hudson, Edward L. McGraw

Hayes Street Music/New Hayes Music (ASCAP): Pat Halper

IBM: Kathleen A. Ryan, Zanny Shealey

Independent Sector: John H. Thomas

Merrill Lynch: Bobbie Collins, Stephen Hammerman, Westina Matthews, William A. Schreyer

Opinion Research: Judith R. Greener

Philadelphia Police Department: Al Lewis

Phoenix Home Life Insurance: Jo-Anne Leventhal

The Points of Light Foundation: Patricia Bland, Mary A. Galligan

Rohm and Haas: Toni M. Feeko, Delbert S. Payne, Carol M. Pyle, Ben Lerner

Safeway Stores: Brian Dowling

Texaco: J. David Albrecht, Cynthia Boyd, Charlotte Richmond

United Airlines: Bill Allison, Joe Hopkins

USX: William E. Keslar, Richard B. Jacobs

Walt Disney: Jeff Hoffman, Marlo Lee, Joan McCarthy, Tammy McFeggan, Ross Osterman, Patty Randall, Shannon Ross

Thanks also to the following individuals: Jerry S. Albrecht, Dr. Ken Blanchard, Senator Bill Bradley, Herb Brown, Dr. Tony Campolo, Bob Eskew, Erma Griffin, Maura Jorgensen, Jill Lewis, Christopher Rade Musulin, Don Schlitz of New Don Songs, Richard F. Schubert, Sheila Schwartz, Mother Teresa, and Bernard "Bud" Umbaugh. I wish to express my deep appreciation and love to my wife, Chris, and friends Ruth Cooke, Ralph Giannattasio, and Phil Warren for their guidance and advice; and my heartfelt thanks to my editor, Alan Shrader, for his patience in this neophyte's first attempt at writing professionally.

The Author

David C. Forward was born and educated in England and settled in the United States in 1974, assuming U.S. citizenship in 1981. He is no stranger to volunteerism and humanitarian service. David initiated disaster relief campaigns for victims of the Pennsylvania flood, Colombian volcano, Italian earthquake, and Miami hurricane tragedies. He has traveled around the world on a number of volunteer efforts, frequently conceiving the idea for the project, motivating others to respond, and then providing relief at the point of need. His projects have included building an orphanage in the Dominican Republic; rebuilding a house for the homeless in Camden, New Jersey; delivering toys to injured children in war-torn Beirut; and providing medical supplies to Romania.

A much-requested public speaker and fundraising expert, he acts as a consultant for corporations and nonprofit agencies whom he advises on establishing, recruiting, and improving volunteerism activities. As southern New Jersey district chairman of Rotary's PolioPlus Campaign, he gave over one hundred speeches and media interviews, resulting in the donation of over $1 million to vaccinate children around the world from polio and other crippling diseases. David has been a Rotarian for over sixteen years and has served as club president three times. He also has served on the board of Trevor's Campaign for the Homeless and as president of the International Children's Aid Foundation.

*Heroes
After
Hours*

. . . .

· ·

Introduction

Changing the World One Step at a Time

As a teenager and young adult in my native England, I admired the American "can-do" attitude and yearned to break away from an environment where inactivity seemed part of the status quo, maintained simply because "that's the way it has always been done."

In the twenty years since I moved from England to my adopted homeland, the United States, I have been involved with many organizations that have made volunteer *activity* part of their status quo. Some wanted to provide their employees with a vehicle for performing community service; other groups already engaged in such service wanted to add volunteers or enhance the productivity of their staff. But none of the recognition I received for my work with these groups—no letter, no plaque, no paycheck—has ever brought anything close to the satisfaction I received from actually volunteering for charitable work myself.

Today there is a great deal of interest in volunteerism—and not necessarily because people have more hours to spare or extra resources from which to draw. Americans, for example, are no longer the wealthiest people on earth, and when it comes to available time, they have less than half the annual vacation days most Europeans enjoy. Yet whenever I have volunteered, whether in war-torn Beirut with children made orphans by the fighting,

I

helping to build an orphanage in the Dominican Republic, sending blankets to earthquake survivors in Italy, or, most recently, helping both needy adults and orphans in impoverished Romania, it has always impressed me that most of the people working tirelessly to make the world a little gentler, the suffering a little less harsh, have been Americans.

Why has that been so? Why would an employee with no great financial wealth give up his entire annual vacation and spend his own money to travel on a humanitarian mission? If one discounts the mystique of the travel experience, one can still find citizens of the U.S. responding to needs in their own communities in greater proportion than employees of any other nation. What motivates people to tutor at-risk kids, take food to the homeless, and care for the sick and needy instead of spending their time working on the garden or golf game?

These questions prompted me to write this book. As I traveled the country interviewing the wonderful people whose inspiring stories make up the first sixteen chapters, their answers came almost as one orchestrated response: We receive back far more joy and personal gratification than we give. A similar chorus of affirmation came from senior executives at companies with programs that encourage employee volunteerism. They maintain that the dividends employers receive in increased worker morale and productivity—and in recognition from their customers for being good corporate citizens—far outweigh the minimal costs of such programs.

Heroes After Hours has two goals: to provide examples of employee volunteerism and to inspire readers to get involved. The examples are presented in sixteen chapters divided into three parts, each focusing on a different kind of need. The volunteers in Part One are working with needy children, from kids in a Harlem classroom to those across the country who lack guidance in skills and character building. Part Two highlights volunteers working to improve our cities and to help its needy citizens. Part Three describes global volunteer efforts addressing a range of environmental, humanitarian, and even political needs.

The stories are followed by a section designed to offer

guidance in identifying volunteer opportunities and getting started as an individual volunteer.

Researching and writing this book has been an experience I shall cherish forever. Putting aside the temporary annoyances such as deadlines, hectic travel schedules, and the lonely hours apart from my family, the experience has been inspirational and deeply moving. I visited almost all the volunteers mentioned in the following chapters and sat with them for hours as they told their stories. We met in locations such as Mal Stamper's home, affording a spectacular vista of Puget Sound; in smoky lounges at airports; and over a dozen cups of espresso at San Francisco's St. Francis Hotel. The common denominator was that after just a few minutes, all extraneous noise and distractions seemed to disappear because these people had such wonderful stories to tell. It was so easy to listen to them that at times I would forget I was supposed to be writing it all down.

A number of companies never bothered to respond to my request for employee volunteerism examples, or answered that they have no programs to recognize or encourage such activities. They are missing many opportunities to be good corporate citizens. For the sake of the communities they and their employees call home, I hope they plan to make employee voluntary service part of their mission soon.

I thank the management and employees of the companies featured in this book. They have been very accommodating in providing me with research material and have made my task much easier. The staff members I spoke with ranged from entry-level employees to CEOs and chairmen, and I am convinced that their commitment to volunteerism is far more than just a public relations exercise. These companies really do care about their communities and the needy people who live there.

To the individuals whose activities were described in these pages I wish to express my deepest gratitude, profound respect, and admiration. As I got to know them I felt a change in my own life occurring. They are the reason the title changed to *Heroes After Hours*, because without exception, they felt uncomfortable about being highlighted for their volunteer activities. But employees around the nation who read these pages will undoubtedly be inspired to follow their lead and volunteer for service in their own communities. I hope this is a reward the subjects of this book will cherish.

Working to help the needy not only brings growth to the provider and cheer to the recipient, it also inspires the observer. Although I remember being involved in community service as far back as high school in England, it was when I booked a speaker I'd never heard of, at the suggestion of fellow Rotarian Ernie Bareuther, that my life really changed. I was convention chairman of a large three-day conference in 1984 and needed someone to give the 7:30 A.M. keynote address at a breakfast session. At Ernie's suggestion, I booked Tony Campolo, the dynamic author, professor, Baptist minister, and trainer of missionaries. As he addressed the audience, I literally felt myself being transformed.

From that moment, I have been richly blessed with the life-changing experiences of numerous mission projects and rewarded with a circle of friends who embrace the spirit of voluntary service as a guide for their daily living. People like Frank Ferrell, whose eleven-year-old son Trevor started what became known as Trevor's Campaign for the Homeless. Although the media lavished the boy with extensive coverage, it was his dad who felt the increasing pull of the campaign as a calling from God and who subsequently gave up his business—and the substantial income it produced—to become full-time volunteer administrator of the movement. I look to people like Lee Grossman, who tirelessly volunteer to go out onto the streets on blazing summer days and frigid winter nights taking food, clothing, and friendship to the homeless; Dick and Kay Rickards, who spend every free moment of their time renovating homes, operating the thrift shop they started, and teaching self-development to the desperately poor citizens of squalid Camden, New Jersey; of Steve Martorano, another Rotarian, whose own business almost failed because he could not say no to the parade of requests for help from his own neighborhood and in countries across the globe. I am motivated by people like Susan H. Rhoades, a busy mother, wife, and member of countless extracurricular committees, who, as an employee of Varig Brazilian Airlines, saw the terrible plight of thousands of abandoned street children in São Paulo, Brazil. Sue helped found an orphanage and vocational training school and lined up dozens of American sponsors whose financial and spiritual support shows those children there are people in a faraway land who care for and love them.

But to make a difference you don't have to be the initiator like Sue or have the public speaking skills of Tony. When I made my second humanitarian trip to Romania in 1993, Dave Twombly accompanied me. He was so moved by the suffering he saw both in the orphanages and the peasant villages that he made a few telephone calls to hospitals, clinics, and medical professionals when we returned home. Within ninety days, Dave had touched the hearts of others: an EKG machine and three tractor-trailer loads of medical supplies were donated and, through his contacts, shipped free to Romania in time for our next visit there. So you don't have to come up with new ideas or have a lot of time or money. You simply have to care enough to act.

· · · · · · · · · · · · · · · · · · ·

Saving Our Kids

No person was ever honored for what he received. Honor has been received for what he gave.

—Calvin Coolidge

1

· ·

Chase's Maria Alvarez

From the Boardroom
to Harlem's Classrooms

Maria Alvarez was born in Mexico to working-class parents. They immigrated to the United States when she was a child, seeking a better life for their family. By making enormous personal sacrifices for the sake of their children, Maria's parents put her through private school and on to college, where she worked a full-time job to earn enough to continue her education. She was the first person in her family to go to college, and upon graduation she was accepted into one of the top graduate schools in the country, from which she earned an M.B.A. Today, she is a vice president with one of the premier banks in the world, with an office high above Wall Street at Chase Manhattan's world headquarters.

Maria grew up in El Paso, Texas, and as a child she spent summers and school vacations with her grandparents in Mexico, "so I really felt like I grew up in both countries," she says. "My parents sacrificed everything to put us through private Catholic school, as did many of the other middle- and lower-income families whose kids attended with me." One hundred percent of the children graduating from the school went to college, and it was there that Maria got started in voluntary community service. "I remember how a group of us went out one day and cleaned up a cemetery," she recalls. "Then we decided to take food to a very poor orphanage in Juarez, Mexico, in which the brother of one of my college friends lived. It was out in the middle of nowhere, and as we drove up, the kids ran out and hugged us, they were so happy to see visitors." She tells of finding dozens of bunk beds stacked on dirt floors inside the orphanage and how her father, whom she had cajoled into reluctantly driving her there, was deeply moved by the experience. He had never participated in community service before but became a committed volunteer from that day on. So did Maria, who throughout her college days regularly gave her time to help in such settings as a shelter for battered women in El Paso.

After graduation, Maria was accepted into Columbia University's M.B.A. program, requiring her to move to New York City. Compared to El Paso, the only other big city she had ever seen, Alvarez was shocked by her sudden exposure to the homeless, runaway teens, drug pushers, and the high crime rate of her new home. Interestingly, her primary reaction was not one of repulsion or fear for her personal safety but a feeling of compassion. "I remember thinking, 'What is going on here? I really love this city, but I can't stay here if I can't do something to help,'" she says today. During Columbia's intensive graduate program there were precious few moments for extracurricular activities. In May, 1988, proudly armed with her M.B.A., Maria Alvarez was hired by Chase Manhattan Bank.

Soon after Maria joined Chase, Kerry Yeager was hired to establish and enhance the bank's community service volunteer program. Yeager had previous experience as a volunteerism consultant, and once on board with Chase, she assembled a coordinated philanthropy program. She made a list of different community needs, time commitments, and areas of interest and distributed it to every employee in the company. She then arranged seminars to which employees were invited to attend and hear representatives of some of the major service providers describe their type of work and their specific volunteer needs. Maria attended one of these seminars with several hundred of her colleagues, and it became a life-transforming experience. She remembers being especially moved by the Junior Achievement program, with which Chase has a strong affiliation, and the New York Cares organization. She signed up on the spot as a Junior

Achievement volunteer, agreeing to be a senior advisor at Park West High School in Manhattan's infamous Hell's Kitchen neighborhood.

Motivating Inner-City High School Students

Maria's Park West experience was like none she'd ever had before. "It is one of the tougher high schools in New York," she says. "There are a lot of gun problems there, and we were warned not to wear jewelry or hang out in the hallways because teachers are often assaulted. It was visually terrifying: armed guards patrolling the school, security people at the doors who wouldn't let you in without your photo ID cards. It certainly was a new experience for me!"

Maria became totally committed to being effective in her mentoring role, but one of her initial concerns was her inexperience in relating to African-Americans. "In El Paso, only about 2 percent of the population was black," she says. "I guess as I look back now if I had to give someone advice on how to deal with those kids I'd say just treat them with respect. The result will be mutual respect in return." She tells how many of the students were really bright but behaved as if they assumed they were going to fail their courses. She sensed that she had to cross the "us-them chasm" that they perceived existed between students and faculty. Alvarez told them about her own background, which in many ways was similar to theirs. "I told them how we were dirt poor," she says, "where my parents sacrificed everything for our education, how my dad was a mechanic for Greyhound and worked extra jobs whenever he could. I told them how I remember seeing him struggling to lift an engine out of a car using a chain rigged up around a tree—all so we could get a good education." Her natural skills at interpersonal communication that have helped her career with Wall Street bank executives were clearly just as effective with high school students. "I grew very attached to those kids and I think they felt the same way about me. I don't know how many of them went to college because of me, but there are different types of success." She talks about the horrendous high school dropout rate among Park West's students: "I urged them to stay in school despite their grades," she says, "and I think I had an impact on many of them to remain in high school."

To give her lessons real-life meaning, Maria spent a lot of time with the female students, urging them to set goals for their own careers. She taught the classes how to write résumés, discussed career choices and salaries, and role-played interviewing skills. Responding to the kids who advocated giving up high school, she went along publicly with their hypothesis, listing budget items on the blackboard. "Where would you work, as a high school dropout?" she asked. Almost without exception, the answer came back, "McDonald's." She would then elicit from them the costs of rent, food, entertainment, and clothes, adding the figures to the budget. Long before completing the list of necessities, it was clear to the students that it is impossible to live in New York while earning the menial wages high school dropouts receive. "I tried not to lecture them," she says, "but to teach them that staying in school, doing homework, doing drugs—it's all a matter of options. It's your choice which option you take. Nobody else's." Maria Alvarez worked as a Junior Achievement advisor usually three to four hours per week for two semesters every year for four years.

Making Vacations a Reality for Disadvantaged Youth

As she mingled with other Chase volunteers, she became interested in New York Cares, an umbrella service organization that supports needy causes throughout the city. One of them is a program unique to New York called the Fresh Air Fund, and as soon as she learned about it, Maria volunteered her services. The Fresh Air Fund sends ten thousand poor inner-city children on what is often their first vacation, to stay with families in the country for two weeks in the summer. Since the program started in 1877, over 1.6 million disadvantaged kids have been placed. "It's an amazing project," says Maria. "They work through community organizations who choose the children and then match them up with families, typically in Pennsylvania, West Virginia—even as far away as Canada. Many of the kids stay with Amish families. Sometimes the family will first take a child for two weeks when he or she is six years old and will develop such a bond that they'll invite them to come back for their vacations together forever. I know of one situation which started that way and the 'child,' now seventy, still visits his ninety-year-old host every year." Volunteers are needed to keep the costs of the operation down, and they make tens of thousands of telephone calls and organizational arrangements. They must not only register ten thousand children but also match them precisely with the receiving families. Fleets of buses must be chartered and each child scheduled for a seat on a particular bus.

Maria has been involved in many positions in her four-year stint as a Fresh Air Fund volunteer. Most recently, she has interviewed families to ensure they meet the strict criteria and background checks performed on all hosts. "More than 60 percent of the families ask for the same child to come back the next year," she reports. "Eddie Murphy was a Fresh Air Fund child, as was boxer Riddick Bowe." She tells how she just interviewed one family wishing to host a child and asked them how they had heard of the Fresh Air Fund. "From the sports section of the newspaper," the husband answered. "Riddick Bowe was telling the reporter how much of an impact on his life the Fund had been. So my family read it and said, 'We have to call.'"

Maria tells of the real pleasure of working with the host families: "These people are the most amazing, giving folks," she says. "They have their own children to care for, they often have only two weeks' vacation, and they invite some Harlem kid they've never met before to come spend it with them." But some of the most rewarding moments are when the kids who have lived their whole lives in an inner-city tenement step off the buses after two weeks in the country. Instead of talking about the historic sights or major activity the host family took them to, the first thing they excitedly tell their mom or siblings is, "I went to the beach," or "I saw a cow," or "I touched a frog."

Launching a Saturday Tutoring Program

New York Cares put on another seminar for Chase Manhattan's employees, and Maria Alvarez felt particularly moved by the plight of the young children of homeless people who were housed in New York's infamous welfare hotels. "If you want to do something that will wake you up fast, this is it," she says. "What a sobering experience that was. Families of up to twelve people jammed together in very, very unsanitary conditions. There were crack vials everywhere, and rats, too. I'd have to wait outside or in the lobby for the kids to come down, and you'd see mothers drunk out of their mind at 8 A.M." Maria recalls the morning she picked up a little boy to take him to the zoo for the day. As they were leaving the welfare hotel, she noticed a prostitute on the sidewalk smiling and waving at the little boy. She came over, kissed the boy on the cheek, and then walked back to her curb. Maria suddenly realized it was the little boy's mother. "I felt so bad, so judgmental," she says. "The woman obviously cared about her boy, and maybe she had fallen so far that she was doing the last thing she knew how in order to feed her son."

She found that the children whom she mentored or took on field trips had become street smart at a very young age. "By six years of age they knew the entire New York City subway system," she recalls. "They had to, because they spent so much time fending for themselves. Then I'd come along and take them for a wonderful day out to the park, the zoo, or a museum, and they'd have a great time. But when it was time to go home they'd break down and cry. It was so sad." It became apparent to Maria that most of the children did terribly at school, and as rewarding as her field trips were, she felt they would have been more valuable to the children if their time together had included an academic component. As the weeks went by and she met more and more disadvantaged kids, her conviction became stronger, and she put together the outline of an idea. When she tried it out on her fellow volunteers they endorsed it unanimously.

Maria's idea was to take a group of seriously at-risk children and give them an intensive one-on-one study course on Saturdays. She approached the New York Board of Education for a school to use but ran into a roadblock because the custodians' union forbade them to open classrooms on weekends unless a principal was on duty, and there was no money in the budget for that. Then one day she received a telephone call from Grace

Navarro, a human rights activist and teacher at P.S.115 in the Washington Heights section of Manhattan. "We have some of the worst reading scores in New York, and our kids could really use your program," she told Maria, who was astonished that this woman from the other side of the city had even heard of her idea. The two of them decided they needed a curriculum, and Grace volunteered to put one together.

Then Maria went to see the district superintendent. Grace Navarro's mother was a well-known and respected community activist who also sat on the school board. The superintendent could hardly believe Maria. "Who are you?" he asked, and when she told him, he was even more puzzled. "Why would a successful banker give up her Saturdays to come to Harlem?" "Because I have all these adults that want to work with your kids," she told him. "Well, how much will it cost us?" he questioned. She replied, "Not a penny. The volunteers will pay for everything, even the students' lunches." She won that round—and the match. The superintendent told her that the custodians' rules applied only to the schools, not to the Board of Education offices. He made available the conference room and building facilities whenever she needed them. All of a sudden, her project was a go, but this time there was no New York Cares, Junior Achievement, or Fresh Air Fund office or procedure manuals to refer to; it was her idea, and the proverbial buck stopped at the desk of Maria Alvarez.

The children's neighborhood is one of New York's toughest. Many immigrants from Central America settle there, and when they arrive, their children often speak no English. In the home, the local stores, and with their friends and neighbors, Spanish is spoken almost exclusively, so when the children attend school they understand very few of the lessons, all of which are taught in English. By the time they get to high school, they are so far behind, academically, that many of them drop out, often succumbing to the promises of easy money that drug dealing and crime offer them.

Alvarez points out that it is not just suburbanites who know Washington Heights is a dangerous place. "These immigrant families live with the danger at their doorstep every day," she says, "so they're very protective of their children." It was very common for the kids to have to stay inside their apartment from the time they returned home from school in the afternoon to the time they left the next morning, just for safety.

Maria met with each parent before the program started and described it in detail, in Spanish. All the parents she spoke with signed up their children—who had been picked for her program by their teachers. "I feel very honored that they trust me with their kids," she confesses. "Their kids are like my kids. I'd be devastated if anything bad ever happened to one of them."

Once the program was under way, Maria, her band of volunteers, and the children would all cram into the tiny conference room on Saturday mornings. For the first two and a half hours, the students would be tutored one-on-one according to their individual needs. Each student would have the same tutor every time, so some wonderful relationships were built. The entire class would then play an educational game such as "multiplication bingo." Each volunteer would bring and pay for all the necessary school supplies, and Maria would take care of lunch for everybody after the learning games. Then they would all go on a field trip, usually emphasizing its educational aspects. "We'd take them to museums, an arts and crafts project, or the zoo," Maria says. "Sometimes we'd go to a show, or take them ice skating. They had so much fun, and we often discovered it was their first visit to a museum or a skating rink. The afternoon was a fun reward for their attendance and attention in the morning."

Clearly, the project has meant as much to Maria as to the parents. On the much-publicized Take Your Daughter to Work Day in 1993, she took five girls from the program to spend the day with her at her office in Chase Manhattan's world headquarters. "It was a real culture shock for them," she says. "Even at their young age their Hispanic tradition had trained them to think of a career as a man's domain, while women stay home. The first reaction was to ask, 'Isn't it a bad thing that these women are working?'

"I really feel this is a group of kids we're going to have an impact on," Maria declares. "We've already seen a difference. Their grades have improved—particularly in reading. Math is doing OK. Their writing is much better, and their English has dramatically improved." The rule on Saturdays is that English is spoken exclusively. As if to recognize the ethnic melting pot that is New York, Maria organizes culturally diverse arts and crafts projects. The volunteers have U.S., Chinese, English, Puerto Rican, and African-American heritages, so the children are introduced to their traditions, which helps expand their own horizons.

Grace Navarro keeps in touch with Maria. "One day she called me to say that one of our students got suspended for doing something dumb in school," remembers Maria, "so the next Saturday, I took him aside and told him I wouldn't let him come to our program if he misbehaved in school. He was so embarrassed and apologetic. He straightened up from then on and has never had a problem since." Another of her favorite stories concerns eleven-year-old Louis. "He appeared extremely street smart from the very beginning," Maria recalls. "At first we thought he wouldn't last, because he needed lots of help in literally every subject. He'd get really upset when he consistently came up with wrong answers, and it's such a shame, because he gets no parental pressure at home to study or do homework." Then, to make matters worse, Maria's program was moved to a larger building on 196th Street, much farther away from Louis's home. "But he has never missed a class," glows Maria. "He now walks twenty-two blocks each way in all weather and has perfect attendance. What's even better, we've seen a dramatic improvement in his work—and when he started, he didn't speak a word of English."

Receiving the Recognition

One day in January 1993, Maria received the strangest telephone call in her life. "This is the White House calling," the voice said, just a day or so after Bill Clinton had been inaugurated as president of the United States. "The First Lady is coming to New York next week and wants to see your program in action." Maria's mind raced. Which one of her friends was playing this prank? But it was no joke, and a few days later, Maria Alvarez and Hillary Rodham Clinton each received an award for their contributions to children from the National Child Labor Committee, after which this young banker, who herself had arrived in this country just a few years earlier not speaking a word of English, spent the morning escorting the First Lady of the United States around the classrooms where her program was being taught. "She was warm and attentive and intensely interested," says Maria. "The kids took to her immediately—and she even ran a game of multiplication bingo for them." Although she tries to explain it was not her doing, Maria still gets shopkeepers and residents of Washington Heights coming up to her and thanking her for bringing the First Lady to their neighborhood.

Maria Alvarez has come a long way since she discovered the joys of voluntary service back in El Paso. Her family is still there, and they are immensely proud of her achievements in school, at Chase Manhattan, and in her private hours of community outreach. She received a volunteerism award from the bank in her very first year with Chase. "Sometimes I think, 'Maybe I should be back in El Paso, helping there,'" she muses. "But I really like it here, and I love my job. When I was interviewing with companies, I set a criterion that the firm must be socially responsible. I have to have the company backing me or I couldn't do the things I do. We have so many volunteers working extra long hours on boards, community service projects, the 'Y,' fire companies, et cetera. Chase is extremely supportive of all our volunteerism. It's a value they have."

A contemplative Maria Alvarez declares, "Being an immigrant influences many of the things I have done. I'm aware of how fortunate I am to be here in this country, and I just want to pay something back for the blessings I've received." She rests her cheek on her hand, and her eyes sparkle as she says, "I've only been working in New York five years, and the CEO of one of the largest banks in the world sends me personal notes of commendation, and I'm walking around with the First Lady of the United States—isn't America great!" And thanks to Maria Alvarez and the dedicated volunteers she has inspired, many other immigrant children, homeless kids, and disadvantaged teens have been given *their* opportunity to excel in school so that they may someday spread their wings and fly out of the ghetto to new heights of excellence in any career they choose.

How do you measure the joy a handicapped child feels
when he joins his family on a bicycle ride for the first time?

The wonder an elementary school student senses when she
discovers science is all around her in everyday things?

The feelings of a teenager touched by poetry?

The pride of a mentally-challenged adult who knows
in his heart he has done a job well?

You can't.

What you can do is see that when many people work together
for others about whom they care, there is a tremendous power
to touch lives . . . to change things for the better.

The effects may be immeasurable;
the "cost effectiveness" difficult to compute.

But through this kind of social investment, one thing is clear:
the balance sheet is unquestionably in our favor.

> **—Delbert S. Payne**
> **manager, corporate social investment**
> **Rohm and Haas Company**

2

. . . .

GE's Cristina Harter

Bringing Good Things
to Children's Education

Schenectady, New York, is not likely to be on a tourist's itinerary. It is an old town on the outskirts of the state capital, Albany, and filled with sturdy red brick buildings of a century ago that typify many northeastern industrial cities. Schenectady has many of the problems of those cities of yesteryear, but it still has some strong assets. The General Electric Company was actually founded here after Thomas Edison moved his original Edison Machine Works from New York City in 1886. Today, GE still employs over ten thousand people in a sprawling complex right off Interstate 890.

Schenectady's greatest asset has to be its citizens, however. Stop for just a moment with a puzzled look on a downtown street, and someone will ask you if you need directions; sit at the counter for lunch, and nearby diners will include you in their conversation. It is a place where people seem to care about their town and each other—and they even talk to strangers in the elevators!

Cristina Harter was born and raised in nearby Amsterdam, and twenty years ago, with the ink still wet on her M.B.A., she joined GE as a financial management trainee. She followed a family tradition: both her parents were longtime GE employees. Cris has held many different positions with the company and is currently director of development for the GE Power Funding Corporation. She participates in the arranging of the enormous multi-million-dollar financing syndicates that enable utility companies and governments to buy a GE power station. Her territory covers all of Europe, Africa, and the Middle East. Yet this senior executive who commutes to Europe at least once a month is as likely to be found with her arm around a child, helping him with elementary math, as she is arranging a hundred-million-dollar loan in francs and yen with foreign cabinet ministers.

"I've always been a volunteer," Cris Harter admits. "In high school, in college—I was always doing projects for the community or the needy of one sort or the other." After joining General Electric, she met a co-worker, John, and they were ultimately married. John decided that his real interest was in law, and after their marriage he left GE, went to law school, and is today an attorney with a firm in Albany. "When John was in law school, I found myself with time on my hands," Cris recalls, "so I joined the Junior League." She cautions that unlike the perception many people have of Junior Leagues being primarily tea clubs for wealthy ladies, the Schenectady chapter is truly a working organization. "They do so much for people in need in this community," she says. "I saw how an individual can make a small impact when acting alone, but when acting as a group they can make a really big difference by magnifying their contribution." Her fifteen-year membership has been filled with various activities, but one of the most notable was the Vaudeville Museum in Schenectady's historic Proctor's Theater. It so happens that the town was a major stop on the circuit all the big stars played in the golden days of vaudeville. Cris co-chaired a committee that collected many historic mementos of these old shows and famous artists and established a museum—one of the only vaudeville museums in the country—in Proctor's Theater, which they bought from the city for one dollar. The 1983 grand opening was a gala affair at which the ribbon was cut by Maureen O'Sullivan and Hal Holbrook. "Nobody believed we could do it," she says, "and now there's so much history on display there, it's turned into a very successful thing for Schenectady."

Making Science Fun

Cris has always been fascinated by science and was disturbed at the report that children at Martin Luther King Elementary School were doing so poorly in the subject. She thought that if she could get the students to see the practical applications that made science interesting, they would improve their grades. So she created Inventors' Week. "The school is in an impoverished area of Schenectady and is regarded as a pretty tough place," says Harter. "I remember the first time I met then-principal Skip Aycox, how for the first time in all my meetings with teachers and administrators he kept talking about 'my kids' and 'what's the best for my kids.' I knew right then I was dealing with someone special." Cris explained how fortunate she was that the global headquarters of the GE Research and Development Center, one of the richest sources of scientists in the world, is right in Schenectady. So she picked an inventor for each day of the week and had them go to the school, explain their particular invention, and stress to the kids the importance of a good education if they ever wanted to follow in his or her footsteps.

Cris tells of the day she had arranged to have Dr. Redington, leader of the team which invented GE's MRI (magnetic resonance imager), come to speak. Before he arrived, she noticed Michael, a very bright but bored fourth grader, acting up. The teacher told Cris, "Just ignore him. He's never interested in anything. He's just a troublemaker." Something inside Harter told her not to write him off as his teacher did, so she went over to talk with Michael. "This is *so* boring," he said. "I fell asleep in the first session, and I'll probably do the same in this one, too." Cris realized she had to come up with something better than, Don't you realize this is an incredible, world-famous man who's invented one of modern medicine's greatest miracles? so she looked him directly in the eye and said, "Michael, this man has invented a way of looking into little boys' brains to see what they're thinking, and if you're asleep he might just pick *you*." That got his attention. "It was incredible," she laughs. "Michael sat there, bug-eyed, throughout Dr. Redington's entire talk, just fascinated.

What made it even funnier was that when the scientist showed slides explaining how the MRI works, his subject was a little black boy, just like Michael, with a cross-section of his brain shown." Michael didn't just stay awake; he was excited. When Cris went to the school to start the next day's class, she asked him, "Are you going to be paying attention today?" "Yes, yes," he replied. "Yesterday was wonderful."

Inventors' Week was a great success. The scientists enjoyed their new role. It didn't cost any money to produce, but most importantly, it changed the perceptions of many children who had believed that science was a boring subject to be ignored or, at best, endured. "The kids lined up afterwards to ask each scientist for his autograph," says Cris Harter. "Even the teachers were astounded. They said they'd expect the students to do that for basketball stars, but not for scientists. At the end of Inventors' Week, one child sought out Cris and asked if he could come by her office sometime to see what it is like, because he'd decided to become a scientist and work for GE. That student was none other than Michael.

Cristina Harter has an amazing ability to manage several projects simultaneously. Perhaps that is why employers such as General Electric encourage their staff to volunteer for community service projects: someone who can balance several diverse projects between their work and personal commitments has just demonstrated good management skills. "I know my limitations," advises Cris. "I gear my involvement in volunteerism to the amount of time I have. And I'm not going to be on some board just for show. I've always preferred working on actual projects to sitting on a board of directors, anyway." Nevertheless, when the Elfun Society, an organization of GE leaders devoted to professional and philanthropic causes, decided to nominate Cris Harter as Elfun of the Year, the dossier detailing her community service volunteer work weighed almost one pound. Cris gets very quiet when asked for amplification of her volunteerism. "I don't think anything I do is the best in the world," she says, "but it's the best I can do." She fidgets a little, clearly uneasy now that the conversation is focused on her. "I'm not very comfortable talking about my volunteer work, or having it published. Other people help so much. I coordinate, and I shouldn't be the highlight. Let's talk about something else."

Launching a Corporate Mentoring Program

Let's talk about COMPASS. After the success of Inventors' Week, Cristina realized that there was a serious and urgent need to provide students—particularly poor and minority children—with something extra to get them ahead in the system. She just couldn't put her finger on what the program should be. Then, one day in 1989, GE's chairman, Jack Welch, came to speak at the annual Elfun Society meeting in Fairfield, Connecticut, which Cris was attending as the vice chairperson of the Schenectady chapter. "It really struck me when Mr. Welch said, 'When you do good things for the community, it reflects very well on GE, so it's not only OK for you to do volunteer service, I *want* you to do it.'" As an example, he mentioned a very successful mentoring program that GE employees in Cincinnati had recently launched.

Cris decided to find out if mentoring was something the Schenectady schools might need. "Actually, that's not how I first went about it," says Cris. "In typical GE fashion, I went in with a fancy printed presentation with charts and graphs and all my ideas along with what I'd learned about the Cincinnati program . . . and the school showed me I didn't have the slightest understanding of their needs, because my proposal would be absolutely useless to them. For example, part of the proposed mentoring plan showed GE volunteers working with the students after school, at 5 P.M., meaning that the employee would leave work and meet their student." The school administrators rejected that idea. "If you're going to sit down with the students after school it has to be at 2:30." Well, management will never approve that, thought Cris Harter. She went on with the presentation, demonstrating how many volunteers use their vocational experience to help in their community service work, and vice versa.

"They actually taught me a lesson for my job," she adds. "From that day on I've learned the importance of listening to a person's needs before I open my mouth with a solution." Once back at her office, Cris put together a new proposal requesting some funding, a 2:30 employee work release time, and top management's visible support.

She sent the outline to the top executive of GE Industrial and Power Systems, David C. Genever-Watling. Not only was her entire proposal accepted as submitted but Genever-Watling made speeches to GE employee groups promoting the program, for which he allowed them to spend up to two hours of work time per week mentoring in the schools. Cris had projected using thirty employees in the first year, "but after indoctrination, thirty became sixty, so I had to go to him again for an OK." His response was, "I'm elated—go for it!" she recalls today.

She named the project COMPASS, an acronym for Corporate Mentoring Program at Schenectady Schools, and when they finally got under way in 1990, it began with fifty-five GE mentors in four schools within the Schenectady City School District. "Without the tremendous support of the Elfun Society and the many wonderful mentors, the project would never have happened," says Harter. "They helped make COMPASS a program for the kids in the middle that other plans ignore. This was not designed for the at-risk kids, nor for the exceptionally bright ones." The primary focus in the first year was to develop student proficiency in math, science, and technology in grades K through 12. "It was an ambitious undertaking—and an overwhelming success," says the COMPASS annual report. It goes on to say that the hallmark of the COMPASS program is its flexibility. Some members work four hours at a time, others work one hour per week. Some mentors prefer working one-on-one with students, others with small groups, and yet others as a teacher's assistant with the entire class. Pupils were coached on subjects as diverse as physics, math, chemistry, violin, and creative writing, and one mentor worked with a physically challenged student on wheelchair mobility skills.

The mentors used real-life examples to make the concepts more understandable to their students. The GE Foundation provided a grant that funded field trips to places such as the GE plant in Schenectady, a power station, and the New England Aquarium in Boston. "Students are not the only beneficiaries of COM-

PASS," said Arden Rauch, school coordinator at Linton High School. "Most teachers view the mentor program as a morale boost—evidence that someone cares about schools, about kids. And this caring is not just rhetoric; it is tangible, functional, operational—and it produces results." COMPASS was such a success that even before the first year was over, people were talking about increasing its reach in the 1991–92 school year. "It got so big that there was no way I could devote the time required to administer the entire program," says Cris Harter, "so from the second year, the Schenectady County Chamber of Commerce took over the coordination of COMPASS."

When the chamber took over the administration, they set a goal to involve volunteers from additional companies in the area, thus not only expanding the number of mentors and schools involved but also broadening the focus of the program beyond math, science, and technology. The chamber was able to interest two other organizations in providing mentors in the second year. The Lawrence Group, an insurance firm, supplied employees to mentor in geography and writing skills, and they specifically adopted the Van Corlaer Elementary School, providing every teacher with a Lawrence Group mentor. Union College, Cristina Harter's postgraduate alma mater, had the faculty of their science and math departments, together with a group of their students, adopt Zoller Elementary School. The second year began with an incredible 82 percent of GE's first-year mentors returning, and with the new volunteers, COMPASS had over 220 mentors working with 1,500 students. Cris went back to the GE Foundation and persuaded them to add $15,000 to the original $25,000 grant. By the end of the second program year it was a real badge of distinction to be a mentor for COMPASS.

The chamber's report gives example after example of minor victories and major accomplishments with students previously considered unsalvageable:

• At Linton High School, "the impact of the program was felt everywhere. Most of the students responding to our survey indicated an improvement in grades—particularly in math. At least one student went from an 'F' to an 'A.' Many students were accepted at the college of their choice, in part due to improved grades as a result of COMPASS."

• At Mont Pleasant High School, GE mentor Kader Elgabry was paired with Tamim Noor, a refugee from Afghanistan whose poor English was causing him to have trouble with his grades, especially in biology. Kader helped him not only improve his English language skills dramatically but also understand the American system of college opportunities, college financing, and career choices. When the school year started, Tamim had settled on attending a community college. By the end of the year he had selected a four-year college that will give him a degree in pharmacology, which he had chosen as his profession. To the immense pride of Tamim and his mentor, he received the school's Achievement in Science Award as he completed the year.

• At Oneida Middle School, the seventh and eighth grade math teams were mentor-assisted and placed first in the regional competition of the New York State Odyssey of the Mind contest; of the students earning the highest scores in the seventh grade New York State Math League competition, nearly every one had a mentor; seven out of the eight who scored 90 percent or better on the Regents' exam were mentored students; 77 percent of the students at Oneida were touched in some way by one of the twenty-seven COMPASS mentors in 1990–91. When the students were surveyed for suggestions on how the program could be improved, some said it couldn't be. Others asked that mentors come more often or spend more time with them. Speaking for the mentors, Pete DeCarlo is quoted as saying, simply, "I receive more than I give."

• At Martin Luther King Elementary School, the faculty was particularly positive about the COMPASS program, citing improvement in the students' overall attitude, attendance, and grades.

• At Pleasant Valley Elementary School, children who had been "reluctant readers" blossomed under the one-on-one attention from their mentors. School coordinator Sally Willette reported, "Attendance went up, test scores went up and self-esteem went up" when the students started working with mentors. When asked how the program could be improved, one child wrote, "Get lots more [mentors] so the other kids don't feel so bad they don't have one."

• At Zoller Elementary, the school adopted by Union College, the program had a positive impact on the mentors and their students. In the school district science fair, mentor-assisted pupils from Zoller won ten awards.

• At Van Corlaer Elementary School, adopted by the Lawrence Group, mentors even taught third graders the importance of community service as they visited nursing homes. The academic program went extremely well for students and mentors. At year end, mentor Don Bradley summed up the feelings of his many co-workers as he wrote to the principal thanking her for the mentoring opportunity and noting that on the last day of school his students presented him with a poster, photographs, and forty-eight thank-you letters—one from each student. "It's a good thing I waited until I got home to read all the letters," he wrote, "as I am sure the kids would wonder what made an old man cry."

As the third year began in 1992, the number of mentors more than doubled over the previous year to 450, impacting in excess of four thousand students. "Between David Genever-Watling and the Elfun Society, we've committed ten thousand dollars per year to the program for the next five years," says Cris Harter. "Since there are several other corporations now getting behind COMPASS, that's a great feeling to know it's assured long-term financial stability."

Since 1970, GE has sought nominations from among its employees for an award recognizing extraordinary acts of community service. Named in memory of a former GE chairman, Gerald L. Phillippe, the Phillippe Award is only given every two years and comes with a one-thousand-dollar donation to the charity of the winner's choice. While the recognition is largely unknown outside of the company, to the 230,000 GE employees around the globe it represents a very high honor. In 1992, 260 nominees were submitted to the company, and Cristina Harter was a winner—due in great part to the significant difference she made to so many students' lives because of COMPASS. "Cris Harter epitomizes the spirit of voluntarism I see throughout GE," says John F. Welch, Jr., the company's CEO and chairman.

Providing Support for Grieving Children

Cris Harter loves working with children. While serving as chairperson of community affairs for the Junior League, she received a call from the president of Haven, an organization that provides emotional support to survivors or family members of people who have died, whether by suicide, illness, or accident. "It was originally established in 1977 by Jeanette Neisuler after the prolonged illness and death of her husband," says Cris. "She saw other people also having difficulty dealing with death and dying. The patient has a hospice to tend to their physical needs, but there was nobody to provide for the emotional needs of those people left behind until Haven was started." At the time of the call, the Haven people were getting ready to move from their two rented rooms to two whole floors in a house that had been donated to them. They wanted to know if the Junior League of Schenectady would be interested in helping start a children's grieving program at Haven—a much-needed service that was unavailable anywhere in the area. "My friend who has two teenage children had just lost her husband," Cris recalls, "so I know what a family goes through. How do you, as lay people, help that child understand the loss?"

She put together one of her now-routine dynamic proposals and obtained $3,500 from the GE Foundation for appliances and a $25,000 grant from the Junior League. But more than that, this program lit a spark inside Cris Harter that soon became a raging fire. The rooms designated for the children's grieving center at Haven's new home were in need of total renovation. Cris appealed to both her Junior League colleagues and GE co-workers, and throughout the long, hot summer of 1989 this international financial executive could be found late into the night scraping, sanding, papering, and painting. "I remember finding Cris lying flat on her back in the bathroom, fixing the toilet seat," says Haven's executive director, Patricia Herman. "Cris put her whole heart and soul into this project—she really does what she believes in."

They accepted their first child "clients" that fall. Talking to Cristina for more than a few minutes, one becomes aware of how this program, of all the many projects she has helped in her lifetime, is especially close to her heart. The need was proven, as over two hundred children have received counseling and support so far. From her physical work refurbishing the second floor to provide a happy place for the kids to come to, to the leadership and guidance she has brought Haven as a board member, "This and COMPASS are the two projects I'm most proud of," she says. "They are really significant to me."

Making a Difference, One Step at a Time

There are literally dozens of volunteerism projects that Cris Harter initiated, led, and inspired others to participate in that go untold in this narrative. Perhaps they will be divulged in a full-length *book* on Cristina Harter. But then again, it is doubtful she would ever permit one to be written.

How does one summarize such a person? An international financial executive for what *Forbes* calls "the world's most powerful company"; the woman who goes face-to-face to make mega-dollar deals in countries where that is considered a man's domain, yet a woman whose office is decorated with teddy bears; a woman who doesn't want to talk about herself, yet whose volunteerism is spoken of reverently both by co-workers in the elevator and by diners in a restaurant across town. Why does she do all these volunteer projects? "I guess because it's inspiring to me," she muses. "It's not easy to put one of these programs together—it takes lots of perseverance. But to talk to someone like Michael [the child in her Inventors' Week story], the mentors, the teachers who keep in touch . . . it's so inspiring, so exciting to me. It pays an enormous dividend on the back end." She sits forward in her chair and straightens up a slouching teddy bear. "Let me tell you a story," she continues. "A young man was walking on the beach one morning and saw in the distance something that looked like someone dancing on the sand. As he got closer, he saw an old man picking up something from the beach and running toward the water and throwing it out beyond the breaking waves. This puzzled the young man, and he approached the old man to ask, 'What are you doing?' The old man replied, 'The surf has washed these starfish onto the beach and they will die when the sun rises. So I'm throwing them back into the sea, so they'll live.' The young man said, 'There must be thousands of starfish on this long beach. You can't possibly make a difference.' The old man ignored the young man, stooped down to pick up another starfish, and gently tossed it back into the sea. Then he looked at the young man and said, 'I made a difference to that one.'" "I can't solve all the problems of the world," says Cris, "but I try to make a difference in whatever way I can by giving back some of the love and compassion that people have given to me in my life. The world really can be a better place if we can each just do our little bit to make a difference."

One of the best things that's happened in my business lifetime is a shift in attitudes about corporations and society. Today, it's clear that our stockholders and customers not only want us to be involved with the community, they expect us to be.

—Wayne Hedien
  chairman and chief executive officer
  Allstate Insurance

3

. . . .

Chrysler's Tony Mason

The Spark That Saved the Kids

In 1988, Tony Mason and a fishing buddy, Bob Johnson, were talking about the problems facing poor, inner-city kids today. From teenage pregnancies to children of drug-addicted single mothers to the lack of parental guidance—leading to crime, more drug abuse, and unwanted babies when those children grow up— the two friends agreed something had to be done.

"One of us had just read a newspaper article which asserted that by the time a kid is in high school, it's too late," says Tony. "To really make a difference you have to get to a child in elementary school." They noted that the incidence of single-female–headed families was reaching epidemic proportions. "Kids desperately need role models," says Mason. "Yet most young black boys today don't have a positive black male role model until it's too late. Think about it. They often don't live with their father; almost all inner-city black elementary and middle school teachers are female, and the first time they actually have a positive African-American male role model is the football coach when they reach high school. By then it's all over, because they've been influenced by the drug dealer with the fast cars, gold jewelry, and beautiful women."

Experts in childhood development confirm their beliefs. In the June 28, 1993, cover story of *Time*, author Nancy Gibbs writes: "More children will go to sleep tonight in a fatherless home than ever in the nation's history. Talk to the experts in crime, drug abuse, depression, school failure, and they can point to some study somewhere blaming those problems on the disappearance of fathers from the American family." Her article goes on to report that "more than 40% of all children born between 1970 and 1984 are likely to spend much of their childhood living in single parent homes. In 1990, 25% were living with only their mothers, compared with 5% in 1960." Gibbs points to "studies of young criminals [which] have found that more than 70% of all juveniles in state reform institutions come from fatherless homes."

Tony and Bob ended their discussion with a pact: that when one of them rose in his career to be able to do something about these kids, they would do whatever they could to be a part of the solution. As time passed and their own careers and families grew, they never forgot their pledge.

Recognizing the Need

In June 1986, Tony Mason was promoted to production manager of Chrysler's massive Detroit Axle plant in Detroit, Michigan. This enormous facility—encompassing over 1.1 million square feet—employs around one thousand workers to make axles for Jeeps and other Chrysler vehicles. Inside the factory, the visitor notes how quiet and modern it is: computers everywhere, floors so clean they literally shine, and motivational quality control messages in every direction. It is outside the plant that one senses danger and despair. The neighborhood shows signs of once-proud stores and homes, many of which have been demolished, leaving vacant weed- and trash-infested lots. Other buildings remain as burned-out shells. Many of the homes that appear occupied are in dire need of repair. Drug dealers are in evidence on street corners.

In December 1991, Tony decided to drive around the deteriorating neighborhood near his plant to see for himself what it was like. Just four blocks from his office, Mason found Lynch Elementary School, an imposing structure built in 1917—

coincidentally, the same year the Detroit Axle plant was started. Lynch accommodates almost four hundred children from pre-primary through fifth grade. At first glance it was not a very appealing place. The fence around the school yard was broken down, and the playground itself was overgrown with weeds, trash, and broken equipment. The doors to the school were kept permanently locked—not to keep the students in, but to keep the bad people out. Tony Mason remembered the conversation long ago when he and his friend pledged to "do something" when the first man had the power to act. He suddenly recalled the admonition, "but to have any effect on the kids you have to start when they're in elementary school." Tony Mason decided the time had arrived.

Making a Commitment to Act

He immediately made an appointment to meet Lynch's principal, Erma Griffin, and her staff coordinator, Sharon Lawson. Mason listened intently as the two devoted educators painted a word picture of the children and the special needs at their school. One hundred percent of the kids qualified for the free lunch program. Almost one in three students were from families so poor that they received free breakfast at school. "In fact," they pointed out, "when school is closed, such as in a bad snowstorm, many of these kids just don't eat breakfast or lunch." Mason listened as he heard stories of children living in leaky, abandoned homes and whose mothers or fathers were drug addicts. He realized that the newspaper article that started him and Bob Johnson talking years ago still had validity. Here was a school full of young children with very little chance of ever making it out of the neighborhood to college and a secure, prosperous, positive life experience. He made a unilateral decision. "The Detroit Axle plant will adopt your school," he told a surprised but elated Principal Griffin.

Did Mason not worry about how the plant's workers—most of them union members—would react to his commitment, made without their knowledge? "I figured, I've been at the plant five years," he says. "I came up through the ranks myself. We've got a thousand people in that factory, and I know every one of them by their first name. Besides, I knew that if we'd held a plant meeting to ask their opinions first there would be a lot of vacillating. So I just decided to go ahead and do it." Tony had guessed right when he anticipated their approval. "The response from the employees was tremendous," he recalls.

Developing a Plan of Action

With the general concept agreed upon, it was time to prepare a detailed plan of action showing what needed to be accomplished, how they would do it, and the costs, priorities, staffing requirements, and so on. Tony Mason also met with the Lynch PTA group, and they officially welcomed his revolutionary idea. One cold Saturday in January 1992, twenty-five Detroit Axle employees and five Lynch representatives came together for an organizational meeting at the plant. They broke down the tasks and assigned them to eighteen committees named after their areas of responsibility, including Computer Program, Field Trips, Library Assistants, Mentoring, Playground, Scholarship Fund, and Upgrade Facilities. They decided to call the project the Save the Kids Committee. "You'd think we were talking about needing big bucks to achieve the goals of eighteen committees," said Mason. "But out of all the needs the committee identified, only one involved the outlay of money. What was really needed was for people to just get involved and put their arm around a child."

Shortly after their first meeting, Tony Mason discovered that thirty-six children were from such poverty-stricken families they didn't even own a winter coat. They had applied to the Detroit Board of Education for coats, but with the recent funding cutbacks their requests had been denied. Thus thirty-six little children had to brave the bitterly cold Detroit winter without such basic protection as an overcoat. When Tony brought this sad tale back to the factory, the employees' response was generous and immediate. Within forty-eight hours, they had contributed enough of their own money to buy every needy child a new coat, along with food baskets for their families.

Mason realized that to be successful, the Save the Kids project must interest more than just a few key employees; it had to excite the entire plant. First, he took his four area managers over to Lynch Elementary. They joined in his excitement and vision of the opportunity to really affect kids' lives. The next step was to bring the union officials on board. They, too, endorsed the idea and even offered the local union hall for activities. What followed was a tribute to the work force of the plant. One thousand employees, mostly UAW members, stood side-by-side with supervisors and management to make the project work. They adopted the following mission statement: "The Mission of the Detroit Axle Plant Committee to 'Save the Kids' is to support the efforts of Lynch Elementary School staff, student body and parents for the sole purpose of helping the children to develop a positive self-image and rise to his/her fullest academic potential."

By early February 1992, the school advised Tony that of the eighteen committees his team had suggested, there should be a priority placed on five: Mentoring; Playground; Computer; Library; and Activities: Parents and Children. To explain the mentoring program and recruit volunteers, an article was printed in the next edition of the plant's monthly newsletter. Mentors were sought from each department, and screening was done to ensure the right people were accepted. Meanwhile, at Lynch Elementary, their own selection criteria were designed to identify the students who would benefit from mentoring. Parents were then contacted and their support and approval obtained. Finally, with the auto workers and children matched, the committee held an ice cream social for children, parents, teachers, and Chrysler mentors to meet each other.

Putting the Plan into Action

The program was soon under way. Each mentor bought the school textbook that his or her assigned child was studying and they met at lunchtimes, after school, or at other mutually convenient times to work through the book together. "It was so impressive," recalls Tony Mason, "seeing this big, burly assembly line worker walking over to Lynch on his lunch break to sit with some little tyke in a quiet corner to practice her reading lesson." Sometimes they thought about "their" child long after work and

school were over. "They'd call up from home and read a chapter—right over the telephone," he says, laughing. "I'm telling
you, these people were *committed!*"

The playground at Lynch had long been too dangerous to
play in. Broken glass, busted fences, and inoperable equipment
were evidence that vandals had taken their toll. Weeds were waist
high, and graffiti was everywhere. The Playground Committee
organized a cleanup day and spread the word. On the scheduled
Saturday, two hundred employees, parents, students, and teachers showed up to volunteer. Even the Detroit Axle plant manager,
Phil Bray, went along with his wife. They scrubbed, weeded,
painted, and repaired. Then, when the day was over, two hundred
tired, aching people surveyed with pride the cleanest, safest, perhaps prettiest playground in Detroit. From that day to this, the
playground has been meticulously maintained, and the 370 children of Lynch Elementary School have a place once more to have
fun between classes.

The Activities: Parents and Children Committee was based
on the premise that it is mutually beneficial for parents and their
children to do things together. The Lynch teaching staff had
pointed out that it was rare for inner-city families in extremely
poor circumstances to have access to many of the excursions suburban families take for granted. The first activity was planned for
March—just three months after the Chrysler-Lynch partnership
was launched. Detroit Axle's employees chartered a fleet of buses
and took the entire school—370 children, their parents, and
many plant employees—to the circus. "It was a wonderful outing, for all of us, adults and kids," recalls Charles Pryor, the production chief steward at the plant. "I've been here twenty-six
years, and I've never seen anything like it. The guys really do love
those kids."

Not all activities had to be as distant or so logistically complex as the circus outing. In April, employees staged an Easter egg
hunt. Trips to the Ice Capades, a basketball game, and a rodeo—
always accompanied by hot dogs, soda, and ice cream—were
arranged in the months ahead. Then, just before the school year
ended, the Activities Committee planned an awards banquet for

all the students, parents, and teachers of Lynch School. When the big day arrived, Principal Griffin closed the school early, and the children all marched four blocks to the UAW Local 961 union hall. "Everyone was so excited," says Tony Mason. "The little girls looked so pretty in their Sunday best dresses, patent leather shoes, and hair ribbons. The little boys looked squeaky clean with fresh haircuts, suits, and sharp creases in their pants." Three hundred and fifty children, sixty school staff, and scores of parents and plant employees all joined in the parade, with the two children in front holding a banner proclaiming, "Detroit Axle–Lynch." "As we marched along Van Dyke Street, people honked their horns in approval, and merchants came out of the shops to greet us and helped block off intersections," Tony says. A spaghetti luncheon was prepared and served by more Detroit Axle volunteers, and then the awards ceremony began. Many children were presented with perfect-attendance trophies. Seven teachers were recognized for their participation in the Save the Kids project, as were several Chrysler employees. In between the presentations, students entertained the audience with a song recital. After an afternoon filled with fun and food, singing and clapping, ice cream and balloons, the Lynch choir sang "Love Power," a song written for and dedicated to the Chrysler Detroit Axle employees. When the kids came to the third verse, they sang,

> I used to think that nobody cared,
> Then a blessing came out of the blue.
> Detroit Axle said, "We're on your side,"
> Now I know what I must do.
> Keep reachin' for the sky,
> Trouble will pass me by,
> Oh so great am I,
> I've got the power of love.

Parents, teachers, and auto workers were fighting back tears. Today, a proud Tony Mason admits, "It was regretful that this perfect day had to end."

Inspiring Action in Others

Clearly, Mason's idea was one that touched the hearts of many people, adults and children alike. "We got a lot of help from people in the shadows who didn't want recognition. They just chipped in where necessary," says Dominic Marzicola, chief steward—skilled trades, a twenty-nine-year Chrysler veteran. "I remember when we were cleaning up the playground, neighbors came to help. They'd lived by that school their whole life and never did a thing for it until they saw the Detroit Axle workers out there." Adds Charles Pryor, "The kids nowadays have to have computer skills to get along in the world, but they couldn't afford them at Lynch. So Chrysler donated computers to the school, and then we had several of our computer people act as mentors, teaching the kids how to use them."

Not every employee had the interest or ability to commit the amount of time that volunteers such as the mentors gave. So the committee initiated the Birthday Club. A list was distributed to all one thousand employees showing the birthdays of Lynch's children. Each employee was then invited to select a student whose birthday corresponded with his or her own or that of a loved one. The employee would then send a card and do something special on the child's birthday. "Here are people who really *want* to help and who never ask for anything in return," says Principal Griffin.

According to Tony Mason, about 850 of the plant's employees—an incredible 85 percent—support the project in some way. Roughly 600 are passive supporters who don't have time to continually volunteer, but they do participate when able, and they each contribute twelve dollars annually to the Save the Kids fund. The other 250 are active supporters serving on one or more committees, acting as mentors or chaperones, or helping in other ways.

Before long, word of the Save the Kids project and the impressive results it was generating—reflected in the students' grades and attendance—spread beyond the neighborhood. Tony Mason, Erma Griffin, and a coterie of volunteers were on hand in city hall when the Detroit City Council awarded them a testimonial resolution "Commending Chrysler Detroit Axle employees for making an extra effort to give back to the community which has been its home for seventy-five years." On September 29, 1992, television Channel Two in Detroit aired a one-hour documentary on the project entitled, "It takes a whole village to raise a single child." The program was distributed so widely that it caused an avalanche of complimentary mail and calls, including some from Chrysler senior executives who had hitherto been unaware of the project. A. C. Liebler, Chrysler's vice president–communications, wrote, "To say that I was moved and touched by the Channel Two broadcast on your accomplishments at Lynch Elementary School would be an understatement. I wish more people had the same dedication and vision." Chrysler's ebullient chairman, Lee Iacocca, wrote, "I am proud of your leadership . . . you and your fellow Detroit Axle employees are an inspiration to us all. Thank you for making this fine example of community outreach. You have made a significant contribution to the betterment of our future. Giving children a chance to succeed is the important key. Sincerely, Lee." Other Chrysler plants called to get advice on how they could establish similar projects in their communities. On Christmas Eve, 1992, the "ABC World News Tonight" nationwide broadcast featured Tony Mason's Save the Kids project as the lengthy subject of Peter Jennings's "American Agenda" segment.

Tony Mason is clearly uncomfortable in the role as star of a national television program. Talk to him about "stars" and he'll tell you about the plant employees who attended planning meetings on their own time for months on end. Or those who took days off without pay to chaperone the kids on field trips. Or the teachers at Lynch who have given hundreds of hours of their time, without pay, to ensure the program's success. How does he feel after all the meetings and phone calls and letters he has to fit into an already burdensome schedule? "I feel great!" he exclaims. "I've seen employees almost fight over children they want to 'adopt.' It's a great feeling, because we are now seeing the kids get better grades, have improved attendance—and we've had really positive feedback from the parents. The school lost its librarian to budget cutbacks a long time ago. So now we have plant employees who volunteer as librarians. The mentoring program is going so well that sometimes if a mentor is a little late getting out of here, his kid is waiting for him at the plant gate."

Denise Marcial, a secretary at Detroit Axle, says, "We are very proud of what we've accomplished with our kids. It is important that you understand what we are doing. No one has dictated that we get involved in our community; no one is getting paid or promoted for this. Our volunteers have nothing to gain but a personal satisfaction that they are making a difference in this neighborhood and the lives of its young people. We all work very hard, and we all have outside responsibilities; we just give what time we can. Nothing formal—no glitz or glimmer—just some time to spend in the neighborhood and letting our kids know someone cares." It seems strange to see two steadfast union chief stewards so enamored with a management-inspired project that involves volunteer service. But they concur with Denise. "This is a great idea," Charlie Pryor nods. "Really something great."

Mother Teresa once wrote, "I never look at the masses as my responsibility, I look at the individual. I deal with individuals as I find them one by one." And so it is with the Save the Kids project. Talk with any of the volunteers and you notice their conversation doesn't dwell on the 370 children they're helping; it focuses in on 370 individual friendships and truly special bonds that have been forged: real children with real fears and real needs that these employees are helping to meet. Children like Tykesha, who has brain cancer and misses lots of school due to the multiple operations she has endured in the past two years; or DeAngelo, a seven-year-old autistic boy in Lynch's special education program who can instantly name the capitals of all fifty states and several foreign countries; or the desperately poor family with four school-aged children, all of whom are on the honor roll; or the little girl with such bad eyesight she couldn't see to read or study. When the Save the Kids Committee paid for her to get an eye exam and glasses, her first words, squealed in excitement, were, "Mama, I can see!"

"Our employees are working together better because of Lynch," declares Tony Mason. "We've got foremen and shop stewards working closely with each other. This isn't the end—it's the beginning. Even my boss is motivated." So what comes next? Mason talks enthusiastically about the latest development in the project. "We are constantly being invited out to lunch meetings by the numerous vendors who supply the plant with everything from office supplies to steel," he says, "so management has asked them to skip the lunch and put the money they would have spent into the Lynch Scholarship Fund. We've even put some of the vendors on the Fund's board of directors." They project being able to say to the elementary school students that if they maintain good grades and attendance through four years of high school, the Save the Kids Committee will provide a full four-year college scholarship.

Erma Griffin believes in Tony Mason's dreams nowadays. An educator for twenty-three years, she has seen the power of volunteerism transform a playground, a school, and children's attitudes. Perhaps dreams are the one thing an overburdened budget office cannot take away. "I've seen such a difference in these kids' personalities, as well as in their work," she says. In her tiny office, where policy manuals and administrative paperwork cover every inch of work space, there is a framed copy of Dr. Martin Luther King's famous "I Have a Dream" speech. Do inner-city kids from broken homes—kids with crack-addicted parents or who live in abandoned houses—do they have dreams? she is asked. With just a moment's pause, Erma Griffin replies, "Yes, they have a dream. And that's why I'm here: to keep the dreams alive for them by encouraging them to work their way out of those circumstances through a good education." She tells how she has already seen four of her former students die violent deaths this year—and it is still only May. "You know some are going to make it, but you don't know who, so you have to touch them all. That's why we're all here." Dream on, Erma Griffin, Tony Mason, employees of Chrysler Detroit Axle. Your dreams have already touched the lives of more people than you will ever know.

The worst sin toward our fellow creatures is not to hate them,
but to be indifferent to them: that's the essence of inhumanity.

—George Bernard Shaw

4

. . . .

GTE's George Boggs

Taking a Byte out of Loneliness

George Boggs and David Fay met on the job and became close friends almost immediately. They are both research psychologists at GTE Laboratories in Waltham, Massachusetts, a suburb of Boston. They not only shared a lot of personal interests but are also both considered experts in a technical specialty called "human factors," the interaction of humans with computers.

It was because of his expertise in that field that George received a telephone call in 1986 from a concerned friend. He told Boggs that his son, Ben, had leukemia and was being sent to Boston Children's Hospital for a bone marrow transplant. This was a frightening prospect for the eleven-year-old, since he would be required to be in a sterile room on the isolation ward for anything from six weeks to three months. "How can we use a computer to relieve the boredom of Ben and the other pediatric patients on that ward?" asked the friend. George Boggs started working on a solution, then realized that many minds were better than one, so he asked his co-workers for help. Almost immediately, more than sixty colleagues volunteered their talents, and they dubbed themselves the KidBits Committee.

The first idea was to link the patients' rooms with an electronic mail network so that the children could send notes back and forth to each other. After designing the software and pre-

45

senting the concept to Boston Children's Hospital, the largest pediatric health care institution in the United States, George was disappointed. The hospital turned the idea down flat because they were "very sensitive to confidentiality, and didn't want the children's names released," according to Boggs. The administrative staff was unreceptive because many of them were unfamiliar with computers, but the employees with direct patient contact thought it was a great idea and wanted to proceed.

Building a Volunteer Partnership

Myra Fox directs the Child Life Department at Children's Hospital and clearly remembers the day when Dr. Samuel Lux, the hospital's chief of oncology, approached her about George Boggs's request. Ultimately, because of the enormity of his proposed project, a meeting was called with senior staff in the medical and administrative fields to fully discuss KidBits. "We probably acted slower than George and the GTE people were expecting," she says, "but there were so many issues that had to be resolved: privacy, safety, cost—to name just a few."

When the GTE technicians told the hospital they needed access to the telephone system, the administration really lost their sense of humor. "We can't afford to have someone mess up our entire telephone network," they told Boggs. "Beside which, where are you going to lay all those computer connection cables? And how can we be sure the computer equipment you're putting in each room is sterile? What about infection control, and electromagnetic radiation?" It was back to the drawing board for GTE's intrepid engineers. "It was a frustrating time for us all," recalls George, "but I soon realized that they weren't being difficult just for the sake of it; they were hesitant because they were so concerned about the health, well-being, and privacy of their patients." David Fay concurs. "It was a very rocky road at the beginning," he adds. "In hindsight, they wanted to know what our motives were and be 100 percent certain nothing would detract from the general well-being of the kids. It was love at first sight for our team, whereas the hospital wanted a long courtship."

The hospital certainly got its long courtship: it was three

and a half years before the first computer was installed in the bone marrow transplant unit at Boston Children's Hospital. "It was very difficult to hold the enthusiasm of our volunteers during three and a half years while nothing much was happening," says George Boggs. During the time George and the hospital staff were negotiating, the other GTE Labs employee volunteers spent hundreds of hours of their own time in small group sessions and alone, planning the configuration of the KidBits program.

"We have many people contributing things to Children's Hospital," says Myra Fox, "from money to games to teddy bears. But most donors feel so uncomfortable about spending much time here. The big difference with KidBits is that the GTE volunteers have not only spent hundreds of hours of their own time preparing things on the outside, but they have then shared their time, caring and mixing with our sick children here. It's been such a gift."

Of the 750 employees at GTE Laboratories at the time the project was started, approximately one hundred volunteered for KidBits at one time or another. They formed subgroups to work on specific solutions in areas such as networking, games, hardware, graphics, word processing, education, and security. One group was formed to focus on the physical problems of their intended setting: how could they fit relatively bulky computer equipment into small hospital rooms already filled with lots of large medical equipment? "There were so many times when I thought it would never be a go," remembers George. "Oh sure, I often thought it might never get off the ground," adds David Fay, "but I never thought for one moment that *I'd* give up. I knew that if there was any way to do it, we would." If George ever felt his enthusiasm for the project waning, all he had to do was wander over to Children's Hospital and see the seriously ill kids. "They'd turn on the TV in the afternoon and find nothing but soap operas," he says. "And many of them would wake up in the middle of the night when there's nothing on TV and nothing else for them to do. The doctors' focus was medicine—making the child healthy. We wanted to focus on making them happy."

The first program was called "Kids Connection," a computer-controlled interactive network of prerecorded messages which the young patients could access right from their bedside telephone. So any time of the day or night when they were lonely, scared, or bored, they simply dialed a number and would hear a friendly voice say, "If you want to hear some riddles, dial one. For a fairy tale, press two. To hear some jokes, press three." The messages were changed every few days, which kept the jokes committee on their toes as they searched far and wide for appropriate material for their tough young audience.

The only problem they encountered was the fifty-cent charge the hospital levied for each outside telephone call, so after a while the administration agreed with Boggs that the Kids Connection should be set up as an internal, free, call. Greg Wester and Lori Eggert of GTE Labs designed the program. They loaded trivia questions, riddles, and other entertaining software into a computer's memory and then connected it to the hospital's internal telephone system. Ultimately, the hospital staff took over the responsibility of updating the recorded messages.

Expanding the Project Parameters

As the KidBits Committee finished designing their next project, which required computers to operate, volunteers noticed the company had a number of surplus Apple computers on hand, and they convinced GTE to donate them to the hospital for their patients. Another GTE Labs employee, Chris Spencer, contacted the Boston Computer Society, of which he was a member, and persuaded them to donate their entire library of public domain software—over one hundred programs—to the KidBits project. These programs were then loaded into every computer.

The members of the steering committee realized from their meetings with hospital staff that many people, adults as well as children, had serious doubts about their computer aptitude. So Rebecca Hudson suggested they hold a computer fair, right in the hospital's entertainment center. Ambulatory patients and staff from the Child Life Department spent hours there, going from computer to computer as GTE volunteers showed them how to operate the different software programs.

The computer fair was a great success—so much so that the hospital asked if it could be repeated again in the future. It has been held every three months ever since, often attracting more than sixty young patients. New attractions or enhancements are always being added, such as balloons, cookies, and personalized certificates of proficiency. At Halloween, the GTE volunteers come dressed in costume, and a standard attraction at all fairs now are the T-shirts the volunteers buy with their own money for each young attendee. The shirts are plain except for a silk-screened KidBits logo, and a local company donates Puffy Paints, which the children use to decorate their own shirts while waiting for a turn on the computers. "People had so much fun at the quarterly computer fairs, they'd still be talking about them weeks later," recalls Rebecca. "We would teach the kids valuable skills on the computers, but we'd have fun playing games on the screens, too. And while they were waiting to get a turn on the computer, they'd have such a good time decorating the T-shirts with the donated Puffy Paints. That afternoon of fun and learning and cookies, balloons, and T-shirts would be a three-hour transformation from needles, medications, doctors, and chemotherapy."

While many children today are quite conversant with computers, many adults are not. So George's co-workers established a formal computer education program to teach the Child Life Specialists—the staff who are concerned with the happiness and general well-being of the patients—how to operate and have fun with the KidBits computers. These well-attended workshops were held at the GTE Labs facility and included lunch for all participants. Many hospital employees who had felt intimidated by computers before found out how easy and fun they can be through their tutoring sessions with the GTE volunteers.

Nancy Treves has been a Child Life Specialist at Boston Children's Hospital for ten years, with the last five spent on the bone marrow transplant unit, where the kids are in sterile isolation rooms. "It's a challenging population," she says. "These children are kept in a hospital isolation room for up to three months, cut off from their friends, so having diversionary activities such as games is very important." From the dedication shown by people like Nancy, it is easy to see why the GTE volunteers felt so committed to their project. "These are very, very sick children," says Nancy. "Most of them have cancer—usually leukemia—and when they come here, they're using their last option to eradicate their disease. Working with them is so rewarding, but of course we have some situations which are terribly sad."

Nancy remembers when the staff would arrange "intercom bingo" with her at the nurse's station, and the children in each room would play via their intercom. "It was one of the rare opportunities to have everybody doing something together," she says. But with every room on the isolation ward usually occupied now, they can no longer play the game. She was delighted when George introduced KidBits to her patients. "I think KidBits is wonderful!" she exclaims. "Children need peer support, and on the outside they receive it from their siblings and friends. But once here in a sterile room there was very little opportunity to interact with other kids."

There are now computers, brand-new Apple Macintosh SEs bought for KidBits by GTE, in seven of the thirteen rooms on the bone marrow transplant unit, and there is another computer and printer in the playroom. Dozens of other computers—all Apples—are on other wards throughout Children's Hospital, set up on mobile carts to facilitate easy movement between rooms for sharing by all the children. The software, some custom-designed by GTE volunteers and some donated by the Boston Computer Society, allows kids to write letters to each other and play interactive multi-person games throughout their stay. "Computers are such a part of kids' lives nowadays," says Joanne Geake, nurse manager of the hospital's bone marrow transplant unit. "It's pretty clear KidBits was a great idea, because the children use those computers a lot. They consider the computer their friend, and it has had a real positive impact on them."

The computer whiz-kids at GTE Labs have more than games in mind as they plan the next phase of the KidBits project. One idea is to design a complete hospital orientation program for new patients when they are first admitted. Another is an exciting concept where the computer would help the patients follow their own medical progress. Other plans on the drawing board include establishing computer links between wards in the hospital so more children can interact with each other, and setting up a system for linking a child's in-room computer with his school so that he may receive homework assignments and study aids to keep up with his class. Two high school–age patients recently participated in a pilot program that networked them with their schools using a modem, although Nancy Treves says, "I think they spent most of the connection time communicating with their friends that weren't able to visit them rather than doing homework assignments." Clearly, however, the time they spend on the computer is time their attention is diverted from their loneliness, pain, and uncertain future. "One program allows them to make cards, banners, and letters on the computer," says Nancy, "and many of our patients have been so weakened by their illness that the computer allows them to do this with less effort than if they had to make them up by hand."

The KidBits program has become so popular that the word has gone out to children far and wide, and now, when they visit Children's Hospital for a familiarization tour prior to their actual admission, the very first question many of them ask is, "Will I be getting a room with a computer in it?" No wonder: "Kids are becoming so computer literate nowadays, I've seen four-year-olds who know their way around a keyboard," Nancy adds. She considers the electronic mail program George Boggs and his co-workers installed to be "outstanding" and notes that the kids actually prefer to send messages by computer to the chilren in other rooms rather than call them on the telephone. She says that the other child is frequently not feeling well at the time and won't be communicative by telephone, whereas the electronic mail message is automatically stored on their screen and may be answered when they feel up to it. Some people type into the computer without actually sending the message to anyone, more as a way of expressing their feelings. Nancy recalls going into one room just after the child had been discharged after months in isolation. "WOULD SOMEONE PLEASE GET ME OUT OF HERE?" pleaded the message still on the screen.

Reflecting on the Volunteer Experience

One thing is certain: although the relationship between Boston Children's Hospital and the GTE Labs volunteers got off to a very slow and cautious start, it has today evolved into unreserved mutual respect and admiration. "What I find so extraordinary with the GTE volunteers is that they've given so much of their personal time, and have hung in there for the long run," says Myra Fox. "They've demonstrated their commitment in both financial and physical presence. They spent at least fifteen thousand dollars on just the hardware for the bone marrow transplant unit, and David Fay must have spent a thousand hours of his own time to get those units on line." Walter Carleton, GTE's director of public affairs, insists the credit for KidBits goes to the employees, not the company. "Unlike most corporate volunteer programs, the GTE Labs/KidBits project has been a true grass-roots effort: conceived, planned, organized, motivated, and implemented not by management but by the employees themselves," he says. Rank was less important than the simple desire to help the children with KidBits, a point that impressed many people at the hospital, where letters after one's name often play the most important role in determining the pecking order. "Everyone at GTE Labs was involved," says Myra Fox, somewhat in awe, "from the president and chief financial officer to secretaries."

David Fay agrees: "Even during the early days, there were some people at Children's Hospital, like David Adler, who were visionaries. They were enthusiastic about KidBits from the very beginning. But now, every one at the hospital is 100 percent committed to this project. They will do everything in their power to support it." Open the KidBits storybook even a little bit and one hears those words over and over: "commitment," "hung in there," and "enthusiasm." Ann Malone, the hospital's director of public affairs, uses them again: "Many times people come up with ideas to help us or our patients," she says, "but then they lose steam and fall off as time goes by. The GTE Labs folks have just been wonderful. They've hung in there from the beginning and demonstrated a real commitment to this project."

George Boggs somehow does not seem surprised at the

success of KidBits. "We all understood from the outset that the project would not succeed by simply giving money and equipment to the hospital," he says. "That's why we spent months interviewing the kids, their parents, and the hospital staff in order to truly comprehend the situation and what was needed." In 1991, the KidBits project was nominated for the President's Volunteer Action Award. Out of thirty-five hundred entries, it was selected as the only award winner in the Special Project category.

George subsequently left GTE Labs and moved to Chicago to accept a position as a senior member of the technical staff in the research and development department of Ameritech, a regional "Baby Bell" company. He has already set his sights on starting a "new and improved KidBits" program at Chicago's Children's Hospital.

Being a KidBits volunteer can be a very emotional experience. After George left GTE, Rebecca Hudson took over the chair of the KidBits steering committee, a position she held for four exciting years. Then, in 1993, Rebecca was asked to accept a promotion to become employee communications manager at GTE's corporate headquarters in Stamford, Connecticut. Most people would have jumped at such a prized opportunity, but Rebecca found she was really struggling with it. "It was one of my hardest decisions, leaving KidBits," she sighs. "It was one of life's great equalizing events, watching brave kids struggling to live. Every child just grabbed at my heart. Most companies would have just given money to a needy cause and moved on. But we gave more than money. We gave people. I learned a lot about life, and inner strength, from the people at Children's Hospital." Asked for an example, Rebecca pauses thoughtfully for a moment, as if in a quandary over which of the many anecdotes she should recount. "There was a young boy, a lad about nine years old," she recalls, "and he was in the hospital for a long time, seriously injured from when a car jumped the curb, ran him over, and then sped off. This poor guy's body was so broken up, he had pins sticking out of every part of his little body. And I said to him, 'Aren't you angry?' 'Why should I be angry?' he asked me. 'Well, because the person who did all this to you was a hit-and-run driver,' I said. 'Don't you wish you could get hold of him right now and tell him what he's done to you?' The little boy looked at me quizzically. 'Why should I be angry?' he asked. 'What's the point?' What a lesson I learned that day."

After Rebecca left Waltham, David Fay, the friend to whom George Boggs confided his original KidBits idea thousands of volunteer hours ago, took over as chairperson of the steering committee. "I've always been involved in volunteerism," he says. "In high school I tutored kids at an inner-city school in Boston. In college I started a program to visit patients in a mental hospital and provide them with friendship and emotional support. One of the reasons I got so excited about George's idea was that I wasn't involved in volunteerism at the time and now had professional skills to offer. People now find things to do with our KidBits system that we never dreamed of." David still averages four to five hours each week on the project. "That's a lot of time on top of your full-time job." Why does he do it, especially since he has his own young family? "I was offended by the attitudes of the eighties," he says, emotion rising in his voice. "The personal answer is: it makes me feel good to help people who are in a bad way. The kids I deal with at Children's Hospital are scared to death. It just breaks my heart how they've drawn a short straw in life. Anything I can do for those kids, I'm happy to do. I don't think we can do a whole lot to help, but whatever we can do, we should do."

Myra Fox and her staff are most closely involved in the minute-to-minute happiness of Boston Children's young patients. She was there at the first dawning of the KidBits idea and has participated in countless staff meetings as the pros and cons of the project were debated. She has seen the results of over twenty thousand hours of GTE Labs' employee volunteer time and watched the leadership pass from George to Rebecca to David—all with perfect continuity. "Not long ago, we had a wonderful party," she says, "and the volunteers brought a huge cake, so beautifully decorated, and right on the cake they had the GTE and Children's Hospital names and the KidBits logo. I remember thinking that now you knew we're together as one.

"I think our association with GTE Labs makes Children's Hospital a better place today," she adds. "It was—and is—a wonderful association."

America built the Panama Canal, split the atom, developed the polio vaccine, explored outer space. And yet, our kids aren't learning to read and write.

—Lee Iaccoca
chairman
Chrysler Corporation

5

. . . .

Boeing's Mal Stamper

A Retired Executive Brings Learning
and Love to America's Classrooms

Talk about a worldwide reputation: sometimes it seems as if the man is so well known that if an executive of a foreign airline only knows two or three words of English they are likely to be, "Malcolm Stamper, Boeing." Mal joined the Boeing Company from General Motors in 1962, and his career literally took off. He is known in aviation circles around the world as the guy who headed the revolutionary Boeing 747 program from its inception. The project was on such a large scale that the company's sales of these wide-body jets actually influence the entire nation's trade figures when a large order is won.

In 1972, Mal was promoted to president of the Boeing Company, and he became vice chairman from 1985 until his retirement in 1990. But talk to people in the Peach Tree State and they will remember Mal Stamper as the Orange Bowl football player and perennial supporter of his alma mater, Georgia Tech. Around Seattle, people will say, "Mal Stamper? Oh sure, he is chairman of the Seattle Art Museum, and he headed up the entire King County United Way campaign a few years back, setting standards by which all subsequent campaigns have been measured." One other common denominator is that regardless of whether people know him as Mal the airplane builder, football star, or philanthropic giant, everyone thinks of him as "Mal the superachiever at whatever he focuses on."

Although at sixty-nine Mal Stamper still has the towering presence of a football player, one only has to hear him talk for a short while to realize that for all his fame and fortune, he is a gentle, caring man. His children and even his grandchildren have inherited these attributes, too, and nowhere was that more evident than the day his son, Jamie, then nineteen, found a baby raccoon cowering in the woods near the Stamper home. The tiny, frightened animal, just two and a half inches long, had been abandoned by its mother, and after taking it back to the house, Jamie drove to the local veterinarian to give the raccoon a checkup. As soon as he examined her, the vet explained to Jamie the reason the young animal had been abandoned: she was almost totally blind from cataracts. Realizing that to release her back in the woods was a sentence of certain death, Jamie decided to keep her.

When he went back to college, Jamie took the raccoon but realized he faced a potential problem: no landlord would ever rent to a college student and his pet raccoon. So, not wanting to have to lie about not having any animals, Jamie named his raccoon Kitty. Then as he checked out apartments and the landlords asked if he had any pets, Jamie would quite truthfully answer, "It's just me and my Kitty," and he never had a problem. For years, the entire Stamper family laughed at Kitty's playfulness and antics when she and Jamie came home. The boy even wrote a book, *Kitty the Raccoon*, that tells the moving, true story of the relationship between this most unlikely animal companion and her human partner.

After Mal retired from Boeing, Jamie called with a proposition: Jane Weinberger, wife of former defense secretary Casper Weinberger, had published *Kitty the Raccoon*, but it was not selling very well on the West Coast. He thought maybe dad could use some of his accumulated Boeing marketing expertise to promote the book in the northwestern United States. But wait—he was not asking his dad for a freebie; he would pay him a dollar a year for his work.

Mal Stamper was proud of his son's compassion for animals

and of the attention he had paid to his schoolwork. But the more Mal read the newspaper headlines, the more he was concerned for the very future of the commercial enterprises that made America great. Stories abounded of students dropping out of school in increasing numbers, of functional illiteracy among many of those who manage to graduate high school, and of the crime rate among teenagers and even preteens that has reached epidemic proportions. "Simply put, our future as a nation can be no brighter than our children," says Mal. "This year, as in every year, one million four hundred thousand students will drop out before graduating high school, most of them functionally illiterate. If we can't do something to stop that trend, by the time today's kindergarten students graduate from high school, over *eighteen million* more young people will have joined the growing army of underachievers in America." And many of these young adults, unable to compete in the job market if they lack the literacy to complete a basic employment application form, will drift toward what sociologists call "psychosocial morbidity," a life dependent on crime, drugs, gangs, and other forms of antisocial behavior, according to Stamper.

Telling Stories to Teach Values

Mal Stamper came to recognize that many of the ideas taught in the simply told story of the relationship between Kitty the Raccoon and Jamie, such as the value of tenderness, the importance of respect for differing backgrounds, and the primacy of love for all living things, could easily be applied to interpersonal relationships. Since all children enjoy animal stories, why not use *Kitty*, and other books like it, to improve a child's reading skills while teaching them positive values?

Based on this idea, Mal started Storytellers Ink, a unique publishing company that still operates from the family home overlooking beautiful rose gardens and the tranquil waters of Puget Sound. Stamper decided to build a series of books under the banner "*Light Up the Mind of a Child*," and soon manuscripts were pouring in to his office. Each book had to feature animals, and whenever possible, he wanted manuscripts that told a true story. The target audience was identified as kindergarten through sixth grade, and Stamper cautioned prospective authors that he wanted more than just a cute or exciting story: the narrative must contain a subliminal message that reinforces for young readers the notions of compassion, justice, responsibility, and the love of all living things.

Storytellers Ink is the model of a family business: Mal is the unpaid publisher; his wife, Mari, is the volunteer editor in chief. "She was an editor when we first fell in love fifty years ago, so she has the fancy title. But around here she's known as 'slash and burn,'" deadpans Mal. "Then our daughter, Mary, is president. I call her 'clip and singe,' because she's still learning from her mother." There are currently fourteen books in the *Light Up the Mind of a Child* series. Three other series of books are planned for the future, including *Different Cultures of the World*, *Role Models*, and *All About Health*, for a total of forty titles by the end of 1994.

As new titles were being considered, Stamper also discovered that the classic tale *Black Beauty* was now in the public domain, which allowed anyone to rewrite or publish it. Mari agreed to rewrite the story, making it exciting and easy to read, and including messages that demonstrate to the readers the folly of drugs, smoking, ignorance, stealing, and laziness. As Mari Stamper was finishing *Black Beauty* (she used the pen name Quinn Currie), the groundwork for an amazing coincidence was being laid six thousand miles away in London.

Judy Golden is the executive director of AHES, the American Humane Education Society. Over one hundred years ago, the AHES founder, George Angell, bought the U.S. rights to *Black Beauty* from England and then published and distributed millions of copies free of charge to any child who asked for a copy. He considered the story of Black Beauty's abuse so gripping that any child who read the tale would be inspired to never treat any animal badly. The promotion was so well received that George Angell sought a canine version of *Black Beauty* for a follow-up free offer, and he soon found it in the emotional tale of an abused dog called *Beautiful Joe*.

In 1990, with the one hundredth anniversary of Angell's

magnanimous act approaching, Judy Golden obtained the Society's approval to offer readers of *Animals* magazine a free copy of the centennial edition of *Beauty* called *The Annotated Black Beauty*, which she had found in London.

In the meantime, back in Seattle, Storytellers Ink now had an impressive little collection of books in the *Light Up the Mind of a Child* series, and Mal Stamper had an outrageous suggestion: instead of trying to sell the books, why not get corporate support and give them away free to entire schools? "They say that publishers lose money on 80 percent of the books they put out, that half the books are not sold and half of those that are, are not read," says Mal. "So we bought back the rights to Jamie's book from Jane Weinberger and published it ourselves. We were impressed by the work the Humane Society was doing to combat the growing problem of animal abuse by teenagers, so we gave out eleven thousand free copies to AHES members and to anyone who asked for it and simply said that if people felt like making a donation, we'd give all the money to the Humane Society. We were swamped with donations and suggestions for other books. One of the often-repeated suggestions was that we rewrite and publish *Beautiful Joe*. As soon as Mari finished *Black Beauty*, which was given away free, she rewrote the classic story of Beautiful Joe and gave that out free, too."

"I finally realized that if you want to help the world, why not give away books which the kids can use to learn to read while at the same time they're learning about important lessons such as honesty, kindness, and tolerance," said Mal.

Reaching Out to Children Nationwide

At about the same time as the Stampers' successful book giveaway was in progress, he received a direct mail advertisement from AHES that offered *The Annotated Black Beauty* free to their subscribers. Mal called Judy Golden, and they agreed to meet in the future. Shortly thereafter, Mal flew to Boston for a rendezvous with Golden that would change the course of his retirement years. Golden was deeply moved by the energy and attention this supposedly retired man was devoting to improving the literacy and ethical standards of the nation's children. Both of them were simply stunned at the coincidence of Stamper's free book give-away of the very same two books George Angell had given out one hundred years earlier. From that meeting came the coopera-tive venture known as Operation Outreach–USA.

This unique program, now a tax-exempt, nonprofit orga-nization, reaches into elementary schools without costing the school district a dime or causing any change in policy. It addresses two of education's most formidable problems: illiteracy and char-acter formation. Starting in kindergarten, every child receives two books each year to read and keep, so by the sixth grade each will have a complete set of the *Light Up the Mind of a Child* library. Meanwhile, the teachers receive special training in the Operation Outreach goals and objectives, along with thematic lesson plans, books, magazines, posters, slides, videos, and a haiku poetry kit to use in their classrooms. All of this is free to the students, teach-ers, and school districts. The actual annual cost is ten dollars per student and teacher, and corporate, foundation, and individual sponsors are sought to underwrite the program for a student, a grade, or an entire school. It has already become a phenomenal success, with over thirty-five hundred teachers trained and books given to more than one hundred thousand children in just the first two years.

"Corporate sponsors are so enthused about Operation Outreach–USA because it is not just a charity—it's an invest-ment for their own good," claims Stamper. "For example, let's say you're CEO of a large discount store chain and you have out-lets in downtown Detroit. You want clerks that can add, employ-ees that can read; you want to hire people that you can groom for future promotions from within the company. So by funding a program that instills literacy and character traits such as honesty, integrity, and loyalty in every child going through the local school system, you've just made an investment in their—and your—fu-ture. And you can sponsor our program in that entire school for around $3,700—that's less than your local advertising budget for just one weekend."

Stamper seems to have picked a timely subject. In one July 1993 week, both *Time* and *Newsweek* featured cover stories on teenage violence, with the former pointing out that this is no longer a big-city phenomenon: they based their article on the problem in Omaha, Nebraska. Stamper states that one survey showed there are more teenagers with guns today—this "army of despair," he calls it—than there are soldiers in the U.S. Army. He points to headlines so repulsive that one can hardly bear reading beyond the eye-catching large type:

> "Children in Camden, New Jersey, blind dogs after school to see what they will do."
> "Eighth grader from Washington, D.C., shoots a school guard in the stomach for trying to break up a gang fight."
> "Live cat is cooked in a microwave at a school graduation party in Milwaukee."

"If we want to reduce violence among children and keep guns out of schools and knives out of book bags, we're going to have to start putting humane literature into the elementary school classrooms," Mal asserts. Over a century ago, critics of AHES founder George Angell asked him why he worked so hard defending animals when there was so much cruelty in the world against people. "I'm working at the roots," he replied. "If you teach the children to be kind to the animals, they'll be kind to other children." Angell's words from one hundred years ago provide an appropriate endorsement for Operation Outreach's goals today.

The program is successful wherever it has been initiated—which happens to have been in some of the country's toughest school districts. Boston, New York, Philadelphia, Baltimore, Detroit, Los Angeles, and Washington D.C., have books sponsored by Operation Outreach in at least some of their schools, and the network is expanding rapidly. Reviews from parents, teachers, sociologists—and the children—have been universally positive. Barbara Samson, a fifth-grade teacher at P.S. 640 in New York City, wrote, "The children loved *Black Beauty* . . . the most macho and very hard to reach boys were deeply touched by the story. Most of the children have never had any contact with horses, but through the book they seemed to be so sensitive and feeling . . . *Black Beauty* is written in a universal language and most deeply touched my class's heart."

Sheila Schwartz agrees. As the coordinator for the United Federation of Teachers' Humane Education Department in the New York City School District, Dr. Schwartz leads teacher training programs that include the *Light Up the Mind of a Child* book series. "The books are just wonderful," she says. "They are all literature based and promote literacy skills while at the same time improving children's knowledge of the need for treating animals humanely. We teach the series from pre-kindergarten to the sixth grade, and, especially in poor neighborhoods, the fact that the child gets to keep the books after they've read them makes each one a real treasure."

Mal Stamper has been equally successful in garnering support from some of America's top corporations, including K-Mart, Woolworth's, Michigan Bell, BellSouth, Black & Decker, Chrysler, Seafirst Bank, Northrop, and, of course, Boeing. One of the very first sponsors was Japan Airlines, who also supplied a free haiku writing kit for every teacher in the program to use in their classrooms. Jill Lewis, an American who is fluent in both verbal and written Japanese, met Stamper while he was in Tokyo as the guest of the Japanese government and volunteered to try to enlist Japanese financial support for the main U.S. project while also attempting to persuade the schools in Japan to introduce the books into their own curriculum. She was successful in both goals, and about half the books in the series have now been translated into Japanese and published in that country, while Mal Stamper is working on a plan to put the books into rural schools in Japan on a trial run. Jill created so much media coverage for Operation Outreach that they received financial support as diverse as the NHK Corporation's funding for a thousand students to a young boy who sent in a letter saying, "This is so some American boy can learn to read the same as me." A five-hundred-yen coin was attached to his letter. "The way the children respect this program is the real mark of success," Jill says. "If the children didn't enjoy the books, they wouldn't read them. But because they love each book in the series the kids are keeping the program alive and kicking."

Half a world away from Japan, Bob Eskew was just beginning to see the light at the end of the tunnel. He was serving as district governor of Rotary International's District 6900, the voluntary, unpaid leader responsible for visiting all sixty-one Rotary Clubs in a large geographic area of Georgia and motivating their forty-seven hundred members to perform volunteer community service themselves. From about one-quarter of the way through any district governor's term, he can tell you instantly, without thinking, how many weeks, days, hours, and minutes he has left in his term, following which most governors want a period of about two years with nothing more energetic to do than hold a fishing pole. Bob Eskew would have liked that, but halfway through his term he was approached by friends who told him about the "Georgia Challenge." Mal Stamper had visited Atlanta and attended a football game at his alma mater. During a social event afterwards, he excitedly told his friends and former classmates about his literacy project. They became so motivated by its potential to help the children in their state that one couple, George and Jane Matthews, committed to funding the entire overhead for the Georgia Challenge: the plan that every elementary school child in the state—some six hundred thousand children—would be reading Operation Outreach books by the time the Olympic Games go to Atlanta in 1996.

"They want the world to come and see their people as well as their stadiums and skyscrapers," says Mal Stamper. They needed somebody enthusiastic, motivated—and free—to coordinate such a massive undertaking, and when they asked Bob Eskew he knew he could not say no. So the very day after he became a *former* district governor, he picked up the challenge and is well on the way to meeting the exciting goal. "Teachers from six schools were trained in 1992," he says, "and we project we'll have the sponsors for all of Atlanta's schools by the end of the '93–94 school year. We *will* have the entire state covered by 1996." Eskew, who sees numerous volunteers in his extensive Rotary travels, speaks of Mal Stamper with enthusiasm and admiration.

"He's a great volunteer," he says, "a man of tremendous vision, compassion, and drive. He's an inspiration."

Mal Stamper will have none of that. "I'm not the person who should get the credit," he protests. "It makes me upset when the media run a story like, '747 executive now publishes children's books.' The real story is, How in the world could we get ourselves in the position where *we* became the endangered species? And how people like Judy Golden, Jill Lewis, and Sheila Schwartz have turned the tide of childhood education. That's who should get the credit." And with that, he has a plane—preferably a Boeing—to catch. "I'm seeing a potential corporate sponsor in Hartford, Connecticut, on the way to Washington, D.C.," he says. "Then tomorrow we meet people in Philadelphia about increasing the number of schools we're in there, then Los Angeles for a similar meeting tomorrow night and Chicago the next day."

How fortunate for sixty-nine-year-old Mal Stamper that he retired to get away from the rat race. But how much more fortunate for the over one hundred thousand elementary school children of this nation that read, and owned, his books during 1993 alone. Of course, if one talks to Mal Stamper about the rat race, he is likely to publish a cute book about a loveable little rat with impeccable manners who went through life learning that even though people called him nasty names, he should still love them anyway.

. . . .

Brightening the
Urban Landscape

If you do good, people will accuse you of selfish, ulterior motives. Do good anyway.

If you are successful, you will win false friends and true enemies. Try to be successful, anyway.

The good you do today will be forgotten tomorrow. Do it anyway.

Honesty and frankness make you vulnerable. Be honest and frank anyway.

People favor underdogs, but I notice they follow top dogs. Fight for some underdogs, anyway.

What you spend years building may be destroyed overnight. Build, anyway.

People really need help, but they may attack you if you help them. Try to help people, anyway.

Give the world the best you have, and you'll get kicked in the teeth. Give the world the best you have, anyway.

**—Author unknown
adapted by Karl A. Menninger, M.D., 1893–1990**

6

. . . .

Police Captain Al Lewis

Building Bridges of Friendship to Philadelphia's Inner-City Neighborhoods

Philadelphia's Twenty-second Police District is the smallest district in geographic terms, yet it encompasses two square miles of the most dangerous city streets in America. Located in the heart of poverty-stricken north Philadelphia, the district's five public housing projects contribute to a population of ninety thousand residents—more than three times the average city density of thirteen thousand people per square mile. Despite its small area, the Twenty-second District—Philadelphia's infamous Double Deuce—has always been one of the busiest and most dangerous police districts in the city. A significant percentage of the population is either senior citizens or children, the latter being primarily raised by female-headed single-parent families.

Despite the burgeoning population, there are no banks, no libraries, no hospital, and no supermarkets in the district. Tensions have often reached the breaking point, particularly in the three high-rise public housing projects, and in the early eighties the Twenty-second's police officers had a reputation for abuse. It was in this very neighborhood that the last riots in Philadelphia occurred when residents, angry because the police shot an alleged car thief, surrounded the Twenty-second District police station for several nights, pelting it with rocks and bottles before the siege finally broke up.

In June 1987, Captain Al Lewis was appointed com-
mander of the Double Deuce and transferred there. "It was a social shock to me when I was first appointed," says Al Lewis today.
"It had one of the worst reputations for police attitudes in the city
and was certainly not considered an attractive command." In fact
Lewis's selection may have seemed odd, for the unique strains
and stresses that accompanied command of the Twenty-second
District demanded special abilities. Lewis's predecessor was Willie
Williams, who went on to become the Philadelphia police commissioner and was then selected, after a nationwide search, to
head the Los Angeles Police Department after the riots that followed the first Rodney King trial. "Most commanders would ask
for another posting if they were given the Twenty-second," says
one veteran officer. Indeed, the *Philadelphia Inquirer*'s Acel
Moore referred to it as "a district known as much for its police
abuse of citizens as for fighting crime." What made Lewis's appointment so unusual was that it was his first line command in a
twenty-three-year police career. He had served in the press office
and the juvenile aid division and had been a drill instructor at the
police academy. Lewis had even commanded Philadelphia's gang
control unit and headed the bomb squad. But he had never commanded a precinct.

Al Lewis accepted the post with his typical positive attitude. "I don't use the word 'can't,'" he says. "I saw my mission
as building bridges with the community, putting an emphasis on
crime prevention as my priority. I believe the police should be
tough on crime but yet have compassion for the community they
serve." And could he apply those theories to the tough streets of
the Double Deuce? "I'm a positive thinker," he asserts. "The district was ripe for a person who could make a difference, and there
was no doubt in my mind it would be a different place when I
left." Gallant goals indeed, but a visit to the district was a sobering experience even for an optimist. The station house was de-
pressing: its ancient structure showed peeling paint, inoperative
toilet facilities, and an unkempt appearance. Demands on the officers often detracted from their primary mission. For instance,
with no public ambulance service and with taxis refusing to enter
the neighborhood, people would call the police for rides to the

hospital. In the Twenty-second District alone, this involved removing officers and patrol cars from their normal duties to transport an average of five hundred residents a week to the hospital, year-round.

Captain Lewis had some programs in mind for improving relations with the community, but he realized that he could not put them in place without first building a foundation of personal confidence and mutual trust with the local residents. "I started reaching out to them," he recalls. "Before you launch a boat, you must find out how deep the water is." So Al Lewis began attending community meetings after his shifts, sometimes visiting three to five gatherings a night, to find out what the people were most concerned with. His first "bridge to the community" was the introduction of monthly workshops. He made note of such problems as noise from local taverns, the high incidence of cancer and heart disease, and security in the schools. Then Lewis scheduled officials from the liquor control board, Cancer Society, Heart Association, and school board to answer questions from the residents at the workshops. These meetings were very popular, growing from the initial five to ten attendees to standing-room-only crowds a few months later. "It was very positive two-way communication," recalls Lewis today.

He then visited every one of the twenty-two public schools in the district and talked with the students about the importance of being responsible citizens and of getting a good education. Lewis shared the concern expressed by many parents of getting the young children safely to and from school by safely crossing many busy city streets. So he enlisted the help of the local AAA agency, Keystone Automobile Club, to put together a safety patrol training program that was taught in each of the eleven elementary schools in the district. Each safety patrol had an average of thirty children who were carefully selected volunteers. It became a real badge of honor for the kids to wear their bright orange regalia, and they responded positively to the important lessons on such topics as punctuality, responsibility, and the need to follow instructions.

Meanwhile, Captain Lewis had discovered the Wagner Institute of Science, a wonderful, but underutilized museum nearby. He initiated a program to reward his corps of four hundred "safeties" with trips to the institute. Police officers volunteered their time as escorts, and the children took personal pride in being pulled out of their school class and transported in police patrol cars and paddy wagons. "The three-to-four-hour tour including over a hundred thousand scientific specimens fascinated them, but I think they were equally excited about their ride in the police vans," says Lewis. They interacted so well with the police officers that Lewis planned other field trips for the safeties, each centered around formal scientific lesson plans. When summer arrived, the captain and his volunteer officers held a six-week education program at no charge to the students. Children with perfect attendance were rewarded with a small cash stipend, averaging ten to twelve dollars per student, which came from Al Lewis's pocket. The project was so successful that Lewis then went beyond the safeties and offered the science curriculum to entire grade classes. "I've been here forty years and never knew what it was!" exclaimed one parent after her child excitedly recounted his visit to the science institute.

From these interactions with students, parents, and teachers, Captain Lewis realized the problem of illiteracy was rampant, yet stood the best chance of being eliminated when addressed at the grade school level. So he initiated a remedial reading program for two hours each week, held right at the police station. Officer Jeanette Barnes, a former schoolteacher, and Roslyn Gunter, the district's community relations officer, headed up the course, and the curriculum was checked by the Philadelphia Community College and the Board of Education. Each Wednesday evening for twelve weeks, police officer volunteers would teach reading comprehension, critical thinking, crossword puzzles, and brainteasers. The course objective was to go beyond pure academics to demonstrate the importance of literacy in everyday life. The youths were given sample job application forms to complete and were told how difficult it would be to obtain a good career if they were unable to fill them out. The officers pointed out a particular question on every employer's application form: "Have you ever been arrested or convicted of a crime?" "Now how are you ever going to get that good job that will enable you to live beyond these streets if you get yourself into trouble for doing something dumb as a teen?" Al Lewis would ask. The participants were tested before and after they took the course, and the results showed impressive improvements.

It was during the Wednesday tutoring sessions that Al Lewis discovered that none of the students had a dictionary or encyclopedia at home, and there was not a single public or school library in the area. Once again, it was time for Lewis to build a bridge of friendship. He put the word out to his police officers, and almost immediately they brought in one thousand dictionaries, encyclopedias, and reference books. Each child in the safety patrol and remedial reading programs was given a set of books. But Lewis dreamed of larger projects. Why not *build a library*, right in the 535-family James Johnson housing project? As Lewis wrestled with the idea, he was notified that he had won the George Fencl Award, an honor bestowed on police officers for outstanding community service. The news was even more warmly received when he discovered the award came with a one-thousand-dollar check. Lewis donated part of that money to help build the library and established three one-hundred-dollar scholarships for high school students in his district.

By now the officers of the Twenty-second District were motivated to do community service work, and many of them volunteered to help establish the library. Ed Hood, a forty-five-year-old with twenty-three years as a police officer in the Twenty-second District, used his days off to build bookshelves. "We take things for granted," he said. "How could I not volunteer a few days of my time when that might give a kid an opportunity to read—perhaps to develop an interest in medicine that helps him become a doctor when he grows up?" Other officers drove all over the city picking up donated books. One officer brought in fifty books his own son had collected. Others volunteered many hours of personal time undertaking the painstaking job of organizing and cataloging the thousands of books and developing a card file system. Several officers volunteered their free time once the library opened to tutor the children in reading skills.

On August 17, 1989, the library opened to the enthusiastic cheers of residents, children, and proud police volunteers. His bridge of friendship built, Captain Lewis declared, "We want to interest children in books, to make them read, to force them to stay in school and show them that education is a way out." As his words rang out, a dozen or so children sat oblivious to the speeches, already engrossed in reading books inside the library.

A few months later, Lewis opened an even larger library with over four thousand volumes at the Perkins-Morris Shelter, a facility that housed 530 homeless men, women, and children. Within two years, Al Lewis and the officers of the Twenty-second Police District had established five libraries, each fully stocked with books, and were running self-improvement courses for children and adults in all of them. In the shelter alone, Lewis established an after-school homework program for over 250 homeless children.

At Christmas the officers would collect toys for delivery to homeless or impoverished families at sponsored Christmas parties. Officer Larry O'Neill's eight-year-old son Michael overheard his father discussing the plight of many fatherless families that just could not afford to make ends meet. "But if those kids don't have a daddy how do they get their toys? How can they even have a Christmas?" he asked. When his Dad explained that is why the police officers were heeding Captain Lewis's request to collect toys, Michael, who walks with braces and crutches since being stricken with spina bifida, said, "I have too much," and donated many of his own favorite playthings. Captain Lewis was so moved when he heard the story that he sent for Michael, dressed him in a Santa's helper costume, and had him ride in the police car when they delivered the toys.

Al Lewis's mind is constantly set in a problem-solving mode. "I try to get across to people that for everything we do in the community this is *their* community. We're just passing through," he says. That may be true, but after Al Lewis had passed through, the Twenty-second District had a chess club, an art class, and volunteer clothing and food drives. It had a weekly class dealing with parenting techniques in which Evelyn Rogers, a Philadelphia Board of Education counselor, talks about family guidance and the tools and skills needed in good parenting. It had a rumor hotline and a Black-Korean Task Force that Captain Lewis formed and chaired during the racial tensions between African-Americans and Korean-Americans in 1990. The task force was so successful at calming interracial concerns and promoting mutual restraint that Philadelphia's Human Relations Commission honored Lewis with its Human Rights Award in 1991.

Lewis is a strong proponent of the value of a good education to poor inner-city children. "They just need a chance," he says. "I constantly ask myself how they can get that chance." Al called Temple University's dean of admissions and arranged to take the fourth and fifth grade students to Temple for a college education orientation class. "Don't talk to them about Barney the Dinosaur or Sesame Street," warned Lewis. "They're practically teenagers. Motivate them. Tell them what career fields are open. Let them know they've got something to hope for."

As Captain Williams volunteered his time for the good of the community, so other police officers in the Twenty-second District became more involved in relating to the kids and the families in the area. "Whenever a new guy comes in there's a lot of skepticism," admits Officer O'Neill. "But Captain Lewis was a really special person. The way he demonstrated caring for people in need has been a great influence on me and many other officers."

Many officers donated their free time to help neighborhood children with remedial reading and other self-improvement classes. The Twenty-second assembled a group of 288 clergy from which volunteers would ride with officers on weekend night patrols when family disturbances are at a peak. The high population density of the public housing projects, often combined with alcohol, drugs, and the easy availability of firearms, can lead a simple family argument to a deadly conclusion. A police officer responding to such a call in the Double Deuce would often inflame tempers on both sides of the disturbance. But Lewis realized that people trusted and respected pastors. He was right: having a volunteer minister on the conflict resolution team led to a dramatic increase in the number of fights that were settled amicably. "When a minister says something, people believe it," says Lewis. "The pastors saw how our officers were treated and how *they* handled the public. The next time someone pulls out that old 'police brutality' line, the minister could say, 'Now wait a minute! I've ridden all over the district with many different cops and I've never seen any such thing.' "

As the police-clergy bonds grew stronger, Al Lewis entered the Raymond Rosen housing project—tagged by some as the worst, most dangerous housing project in the country—and he started a Sunday-school program. Lewis convinced police clergyman Reverend William Mouzon to lead the services, and every Sunday morning more and more children would attend, many for their first exposure to a religious service. After Sunday school, the kids were taken to the community room where Al and his bridge-building cops were waiting to serve them breakfast, courtesy of McDonald's and the officers' personal contributions. The Reverend Leon Sullivan donated almost five hundred dollars to provide the required study materials for each Sunday-school attendee.

Captain Lewis clearly took a proactive stance toward building bridges of friendship between the police department and the community. But all of his initiatives, the twenty to thirty hours he spent *every week* on volunteerism, would have meant nothing if he had been an ineffective police officer. His supervisors had posted him to command the Twenty-second—and they expected results. Al Lewis was, first and foremost, *Captain* Al Lewis. His ramrod six-foot-one-inch frame, tight features, and drill sergeant appearance command respect. This is a man who takes his responsibilities seriously. He attacked the drug pushers' sites with a vengeance. Vacant homes that were used as crack houses were bricked up. Abandoned cars, frequented by prostitutes and drug dealers, were removed. In less than three years, while crime in Philadelphia reached an all-time high, the crime rate in the Twenty-second District actually dropped—while operating with a forced 20 percent personnel reduction. And still the officers shuttled five hundred people a week to and from the hospital!

Al Lewis was promoted to inspector, responsible for three police districts. Not surprisingly, he cleaned up those districts, too, volunteering much of his own time for the neighborhood. Lewis's next assignment was to command the narcotics field unit, and in January 1991, Al Lewis became deputy police commissioner of Philadelphia.

Al tells of a telephone call he received one busy June day

in 1990. "They say they're the White House calling for you," his secretary reported. "Oh come on, who is this?" asked Lewis, convinced one of his friends was playing a practical joke. It was no joke. The White House needed to run a background check on Lewis, because he had been nominated to receive the Points of Light Award from then-president George Bush. Two weeks later, he received the formal invitation to lunch with the president at the White House. "It is clear that you understand that the true measure of an individual is love, responsibility, and charity. You are a bright point of light," Bush commended Lewis. A few weeks later, Lewis and his wife were invited by President Bush and Disney president Michael Eisner to an all-expenses-paid, three-day visit to Walt Disney World in celebration of the theme park's twentieth anniversary. Of all the VIPs, captains of industry, and political leaders present, Al Lewis was invited to the president's table for lunch. "It's a humbling experience when the president of the United States puts his arm around you and tells you that you're doing a great job," Lewis told reporters afterwards.

Why did he bother going the extra mile? Didn't Lewis risk derision from the officers in his command with his extracurricular community outreach programs? "You are what you are," he says. "You carry those values you had instilled in you in the past. Those things surface when you get in an environment where you have the opportunity to use them." Lewis looks away, his expression pensive. The walls of his office are devoid of the usual plaques and trophies a person who has received so many awards would normally display. His attention returns, focused benignly on the press photograph of a Captain Lewis bending over almost in half to help a three-year-old girl read after dedicating a new library at her housing project. "It was simply the right thing to do," he asserts. "If you're fair, perceptive, honest, those traits will prevail and will help you pass them on to others."

Volunteers make a difference and they're very special people. They care about others and fill unmet needs.

—Richard L. Gunderson
   president and chief executive officer
   Aid Association for Lutherans

7

· ·

AT&T's Dolores Riego de Dios

Pioneer for the Homeless

Dolores Riego de Dios is a very busy person. So busy, in fact, that she has the perfect excuse not to volunteer for any needy causes that seek her help. The mother of six children and eight grand-children, Dolores is a full-time, twenty-eight-year veteran of AT&T in Norfolk, Virginia, where she is employed as a senior operations clerk. She has demonstrated a lifetime of commitment to the Telephone Pioneers of America, the nationwide service organization of telephone company workers and retirees. A prolific participant in many local benevolent projects, she is also a member of the Virginia Opera Chorus and music minister at her church, Holy Trinity Roman Catholic Church in Norfolk's Ocean View neighborhood. It was natural, therefore, for Dolores to sit in on the end of a meeting her pastor was holding after her choir practice ended one night in November 1988.

The discussion centered on homelessness in Norfolk, and Reverend Joe Slattery, then-pastor of Holy Trinity, knew about this problem. It had bothered him for so long that in 1988 he called a meeting and invited interested church members to discuss how they could help provide a solution. "Father Joe decided it was time to do something after finding homeless people sleeping in cardboard boxes literally on our own church property," Dolores recalls. "We were all surprised, because everybody

79

thought of homelessness as something you found in New York City, not in our own churchyard in Norfolk, Virginia." Those attending the meeting agreed that what Norfolk really needed was not a shelter per se, with two or three nights' lodging, but transitional housing, providing longer-term residency and counseling. With such a facility, social workers suggested, homeless people could restore some of their dignity and hope, get themselves cleaned up, and use the address for any benefits to which they were entitled, such as welfare or military pensions. With help from the counselors they could learn job interviewing skills, promote their abilities, and get a job.

The meeting seemed to go on interminably, with tangential conversations dragging on and seemingly minor objections blown out of proportion. Dolores rose to speak. "I just thought it was time to inject some common sense into the meeting," she says today. "I certainly wasn't looking for a job." But her straightforward solution-centered philosophy made sense to many present, and before long they elected her president of the committee.

An abandoned three-story building at 131 D View Avenue was soon found. The good news was that it was close by, in the Ocean View neighborhood. The bad news was the condition of the house. "It was deplorable," recalls Dolores. The property had been repossessed by the U.S. Department of Housing and Urban Development (HUD) and had remained abandoned and for sale for three years. Dolores theorized that its dilapidated condition and the worthiness of her cause would make HUD drastically reduce the price below their current listing of $109,000. She was wrong. The bureaucrat responsible for disposing of such properties refused to move on the price, even though their own appraiser quoted a substantially lower actual value. Dolores went to the employee's supervisor and got the same answer. "I was determined to get *somebody* to give us a fair break," she says. "So every time I got the same response I'd say, 'I don't accept your answer. Who is your boss?' and then I'd talk to him."

Finally, Dolores got to an official high up the HUD ladder in Washington, D.C., who agreed that her proposed use of the building and its structural condition deserved special consideration, and they reached a mutual decision to buy the building for

$72,000. Her battle with HUD had lasted well over a year, and now she had only two problems left: to renovate the dangerously deteriorated structure, and to come up with the money to do so. In fact, having negotiated the purchase price down to $72,000, Dolores had no idea where a single penny of that figure would come from. She went back to the HUD officer and arranged to lease the property for one dollar per year while fundraising and renovation activities progressed. Now she could start the rebuilding effort, just as soon as the zoning change to permit multiple families in the home was approved.

Once again, the entire project was almost derailed when city planners refused to supply the necessary permits. Then Dolores discovered that the city was holding back thousands of dollars of their grant money because the project was not tax exempt at the time they settled on the property—even though the lack of tax-exempt status was because the city had lost their paperwork. Dolores took some time off work one morning and drove to city hall. "I don't have an appointment, but I'm madder than heck at the mayor," she told his secretary. "I'll wait here as long as it takes to see him." Riego de Dios got her audience with Norfolk's chief executive and explained the needs she was planning to meet. She showed him the statistics that Norfolk had 2,545 more requests for emergency shelter than it could provide, and that the extensive renovations planned for the property would eliminate a neighborhood eyesore that had been vacant for five years. Dolores got her permits. Now all she had to do was raise the money and undertake the massive restoration.

Mrs. Riego de Dios had no experience in grant writing or extensive fundraising, but she is a quick learner. She went to her co-workers at the Region Ten Telephone Pioneers of America, and they pledged both their financial and physical support. She enlisted her own church and then made presentations that garnered assistance from several other area churches. She would talk to anybody who would listen and in doing so spread her enthusiasm and vision to groups and individuals throughout the Tidewater area. Two of the people who gave the most of themselves were Frank "Pete" Craig, Jr., and Richard "Mike" Abbott.

Mike, a former C & P Telephone Company executive, was

an active volunteer in his Pioneers chapter and had extensive construction experience. He was so moved by the project's potential for improving peoples' lives that he took a one-year unpaid leave of absence from his job as superintendent of Bayside Building Corporation to head up the entire renovation effort. Pete Craig, a retired civil service engineering technician, offered both construction knowledge and bookkeeping abilities: when he wasn't up to his knees in building debris he was keeping meticulous records as the treasurer.

"We had such dedicated people," Dolores recalls. "I never would have made it without them. Once we took possession of the building and started tearing walls down, we found its condition to be far worse than we had expected." Three stories of seventy-five-year-old wood had to be removed and replaced. The entire building had to have new electrical wiring installed. The roof was no good. The furnace had to be replaced. "It was a nightmare," says Dolores. "We would have a meeting scheduled after work at this awful cold, dark, dilapidated building, and only four people would show up. We'd hear the latest discovery of something wrong, and I actually remember saying to God, 'Why me, Lord? Take this project away from me.' "

It was time to give the project a name, and after much discussion by the core group, they went with the executive director's suggestion: the Haven Family Assistance Center. "Haven" connotes safety, a refuge from the dangerous, unhealthy doorways, bushes, and cardboard boxes the homeless sleep in; and "Family Assistance Center" sets it apart from the typical overnight shelter, stressing the many support services that the staff planned to offer its future residents.

As if Dolores needed another volunteer commitment, just as she was in the midst of the reconstruction project the Hampton Roads chapter of the Telephone Pioneers selected her as their council president, a duty that involved considerable travel and numerous meetings to attend. She visibly glows with appreciation when she tells of the times she'd stop at the property at 8 A.M. or noon or late into the night, sometimes in 100 degree heat, other times as bitter sub-zero winds whipped off the Chesapeake Bay, and there, always, were Mike Abbott, Pete Craig, and often a crew of other volunteers. "I watched them, literally, tear the guts out of that building with their bare hands," she recalls. As word spread across the city, newspaper and television reports started appearing, and this wonderful free publicity brought new offers of volunteer help and material contributions. One company supplied the kitchen and bath cabinets and equipment, another donated a copy machine, and others brought food and furniture—or themselves—to 131 D View Avenue.

It became painfully obvious that the problem of homelessness was not a distant concern; it was, literally, at their front door. Mike and Pete found evidence that a homeless person was showing up after they went home each night and was sleeping in the portable toilet unit in the yard. Other people slept on the open front porch, and yet another person slept in the newly delivered bathtub, using the cardboard box it came in as a mattress. Nearby residents observed a homeless woman and her two young children sleeping at night in the tiny garden shed in the property's backyard. Volunteers found an old mattress that the lady would use, having her children sleep on half of it while propping up the other half against the dilapidated shed's walls to keep out the wind.

Six Pioneers worked at the house on an ongoing basis, and they never had to look far to find new problems that needed rectifying. The health department determined that the house was covered with lead-based paint. Beneath it they found walls, floors, and supporting columns riddled with rot, and every window in the house had to be replaced for the same reason. The previous residents had heated the home with space heaters in the fireplaces, but this was ruled dangerous; the fireplaces had seriously decayed and had to be removed. Thus an entirely new, unanticipated expense was incurred when they had to install a central heating plant. The roof was so rotten it was dangerous to work on, so it, too, was replaced, as was the complete plumbing system.

After the interminable bureaucratic negotiations to acquire the property, followed by the almost total destruction of the building, it seemed at times to Dolores that the project would follow her to the grave. But it was finally finished. One glorious day in November 1991 saw the dedication ceremony of the sparkling blue and white home at 131 D View Avenue. In fact, so impressive is this home that the City of Norfolk presented it with an award for Best Aesthetic Improvement for a Neighborhood Project. But the real point of this house is not its aesthetic appearance; it is what happens *inside*. The Haven can accommodate up to eleven formerly homeless families—about thirty-five people—in an environment of safety and self-respect. It offers counseling and skills development to help the adults get a job and get back on their feet. There are already many success stories of single-parent mothers using the Haven to find a job, getting stabilized, and then moving to an apartment; of families that are now contributing taxpayers where just months earlier they were unemployable and homeless. It had taken three years from that first church meeting to this day when proud, exhausted, tearful volunteers celebrated its completion.

Region Ten of the Telephone Pioneers of America bestowed their top award on the project and dedicated a room in the name of Dolores Riego de Dios for her leadership and volunteerism. Pete Craig and Mike Abbott were given citations by the City of Norfolk, but this time not for building code violations: they were noted in a proclamation by the mayor and city council for their "many hours of volunteer labor...[that have] contributed to the betterment of our community." It concludes they "are to be commended for their dedication to the renovation of the [Haven home] and for their untiring efforts on behalf of homeless families." A paid staff of five is in place, and Haven Family Assistance Center has an operating budget of almost $200,000 per year.

Dolores continues her hectic pace of volunteer activities as president of the Haven's board of trustees, speaking to churches and business groups, Rotary and retiree meetings—in fact, to anyone who might help keep her dream alive. She has a way of motivating others to voluntary service: "A group of thirty marines showed up last week," she glows. "They scrubbed and polished floors, cleaned windows, woodwork, and carpets—the entire structure! They're returning in a couple of weeks to help install a playground." In her spare time, Dolores continues to be music minister in her church and to sing with the Virginia Opera Chorus.

In May 1993, she organized an all-star opera concert in Norfolk featuring not only the Virginia Opera and Virginia Ballet but guest stars such as Tyne Daly and David Garrison from the Metropolitan Opera in New York. Over fifteen hundred people attended the concert, which she convinced her employer, AT&T, to sponsor, and they raised over sixty thousand dollars for the benefit of not only the Haven Center but all shelters in the Tidewater area. The Met stars were so happy with her planning role and the effect she had of motivating so many volunteers that they asked her to help plan a six-city tour that will benefit AIDS research.

"Oh, guess what!" she bubbles excitedly. "Life Savings Bank just called and told me they're having trouble selling a twelve-unit apartment building they had repossessed, and so they're donating it to us."

Why did she do it? Why would a devoted wife, mother, and grandmother put herself through all that frustration, stress, and time-consuming volunteerism just at the point in her life when she can start to anticipate the joys of retirement? The quizzical look on her benevolent brow changes instantly. "Because I care," she responds. "Somebody has to care. The poor and the home- less don't have a voice—so I'll be their voice." With Dolores Riego de Dios as their voice, the homeless of Norfolk, Virginia, can finally have something to hope for.

Helping to feed people in a homeless shelter or teaching a child to read is tangible. You can see it, you can touch it, but more important, you can feel it. I believe that when they volunteer, employees feel personal fulfillment. They feel good about themselves—and that often translates to feeling good about the company. I know for a fact that if we were to eliminate the volunteer programs that UTC employees are involved in, there would be a mutiny.

—Robert Daniell
chairman and chief executive officer
United Technologies

8

· ·

Bank of America's
Robin Leidenthal

These Bankers Give More than
a Mortgage: They Rebuild Homes

Robin Leidenthal could be described as a three-career woman. By day she is an upwardly mobile banker with Bank of America in the San Francisco area. Her second full-time occupation is as the wife and mother to husband Steve and three young children: a six-year-old and a pair of five-year-old twins. Robin's third career, occupying many hours every week, is as a volunteer. "I've always been very interested in volunteerism," she says. "Even in high school I remember giving a lot of my time to help out in a senior citizens' center. I even went to Mexico with a team from my church, and we helped build a dormitory for children in an orphanage there."

Robin joined the Bank of America in 1978 as a clerk in the note department of her local branch. She worked hard and steadily earned praise and promotions up the corporate ladder to her current position as vice president in operations support services, responsible for automation projects. In 1989, her performance review was generally very positive except for a notation she had never seen before. It noted the intensity with which Robin handled her business responsibilities and recommended that she "get out and be more active with other employees." At first, she didn't know what she could do to comply with her supervisor's suggestion. It was not her style to go out drinking after

87

work with her co-workers, and with three young children she hardly had time to go bowling with the office staff. Then an opportunity presented itself: they needed a coordinator for her department for the annual United Way campaign, and she volunteered to take it on.

"Every year we dreaded the United Way appeal time," she says, shuddering at the thought of pressuring her friends and co-workers for money. Once appointed, Robin decided to change the focus of the campaign. "I wanted to make it more fun," she recalls, "and then to alter it from emphasizing fundraising to being more involved with the problems around us." Robin realized that the two hundred people in her department needed more than just solicitation stuffers in their pay envelopes: they needed motivating. She scheduled speakers from local needy causes for the 8 A.M. staff meeting. "At eight o'clock in the morning this will either go over great... or I'll get lynched," she remembers thinking. The first week's speaker was a priest from the AIDS Foundation. "He was a great speaker," a relieved Leidenthal recalls. "He went over really well."

Two weeks later, Robin decided it was time for a field trip, so she took the staff to visit Bayview Hunters Point School. They were shocked to see the conditions and hear the plight of the families whose children attended it. State funding cutbacks had even restricted the number of books the school received, making a comprehensive curriculum for every child virtually impossible. Robin told her colleagues that if they were not going to contribute money to the United Way campaign, they at least could give a book to the school. Ideas like this field trip and scheduling motivational speakers helped Robin lead her department to a record in contributions that year.

When the 1990 campaign came along, it was automatically given to Robin to "volunteer" to run it. She followed a similar strategy as that of the previous year, but the more she got involved, the less enthusiastic she felt about the emphasis on giving money. She felt a growing urge to participate in hands-on projects. Her colleagues shared her interest, and after the campaign was over, they joined together in a group called Take Part and started looking for a needy cause.

It didn't take long. One day, Robin received a call from Katy Jarman, Bank of America's vice president in charge of their volunteer network. Jarman told her she had received a call for help from the Christmas in April campaign and asked if she would be interested. "Interested?" responded Leidenthal. "This is just what we've been looking for. It's a great idea." It was time for Robin to motivate again. She called a meeting and explained to her colleagues that Christmas in April is a nationwide organization, started over twenty years ago in Texas, that matches volunteers with people whose homes are in disrepair. Those people are often elderly, sometimes handicapped, but are always too poor to afford to pay for the reconstruction themselves. The organization estimates that nationwide, some sixty-two thousand volunteers now work on over twenty-five hundred homes each year.

Robin's motivation worked, and about twenty-five co-workers and their spouses volunteered to help. "The project was attractive to the employees because it's a one-day job, and they could bring their spouses," says Robin. The bank provided baseball caps for each volunteer, and the Take Part team set off to find their own version of "This Old House." Christmas in April establishes strict guidelines for houses to be included in their program. It primarily serves people on fixed incomes, and the work needed must be to provide warmth or safety.

The lady's home to which Robin's team was assigned had significant structural defects and was in generally poor condition throughout. Nevertheless, Robin was surprised to find sufficient skills and resources within her work group to accomplish the renovations. They even had a professional roofer on their team. After a long, hard day, they had achieved all their goals, and the elderly homeowner was thrilled. "It was so nice to be helping someone who really needed assistance," Robin says. "But it was also a good opportunity for the employees to get to know each other and their spouses. And the role reversals worked out great: managers, vice presidents, or secretaries—nobody has a title on these work teams." The project was deemed a great success by all concerned, and a complimentary article was written in the bank's employee newspaper. Her colleagues had only one question: "What's next?"

They did not have to wait long to find out. That summer, Robin found out that an Episcopal sanctuary served evening meals to between 150 and 200 homeless people every night. They needed help from volunteer staff who could come in on a regular basis. After clearing the project with Lorraine Stimmel, a bank senior vice president, she presented it to her co-workers. Once again, they volunteered immediately, and for the rest of the summer Robin and her department showed up every other Tuesday night to serve a hot meal to an enormous crowd of homeless people and then clean up and wash all the pots and dishes so that some other volunteer group could do it again the next night. In working with these clients, Robin noticed many of them asking if she had any clothes to give away, and a number of them had clothing reduced to shreds by the elements. So Robin started a clothing drive, collecting appropriate clothes from colleagues, friends, and her fellow church members and giving them to her homeless friends. "This project showed our employees that the homeless are not like their perception of stereotypical street people," she asserts. "In addition to clothing, many employees brought in personal hygiene items." Her department had two hundred people traveling all over the United States during Bank of America's merger with Security Pacific Bank, so they collected hundreds of unused soaps and shampoos from hotel rooms. "The project is still operating," says Robin. "We have the same core group that were with us when we started in 1990, plus others who have joined the team since then."

By the spring of 1992, Robin Leidenthal had a large contingent of employees committed to hands-on voluntary service. Christmas in April asked if they could handle two houses that year, and Robin immediately agreed. The first was the home of a lady in San Francisco who had herself performed many acts of kindness for the needy in her younger days, even earning San Francisco's Volunteer of the Year Award. When Robin's team arrived, they found her home in serious disrepair. The roof had a hole in it that the volunteers repaired, and they completely replaced a wall and the floor. The second home was in Oakland, and again the Bank of America employees restored it to habitable condition at no cost to the elderly homeowner. "The employees would work very hard all day long," says Robin, "but they all were so happy to do it, and were really grateful to me for arranging things." They also were pleased that the bank supported their volunteerism work. Participants received T-shirts identifying them as Bank of America Take Part team members, and they wore them with pride throughout the year. As motivated as they all were during a project, people started asking why they had to wait a year before the next one. That was Robin Leidenthal's cue.

Her next idea was to "adopt" a poor family for Christmas by providing all the food their family would need over the holiday, together with some gifts. After she revealed her plan to the other employees in her department, many of them embraced it and also wanted to sponsor families. Just before Christmas, a holiday spirit–filled delegation delivered bounteous food baskets and gifts—carefully matched to each home—to twenty-three impoverished families. "There were a lot of smiles and a lot of tears that Christmas," Robin recalls, "and the tears were tears of joy—from both the recipients and the donors." The food baskets were not bare-bones necessities, either. Each family actually received several boxes of groceries, worth an average of $150 per household. When they were picking out gifts, they followed Robin's suggestion of choosing one practical, useful item and one fun gift.

As employees talked with colleagues in other departments of the bank, they shared the feelings of personal gratification that had come from participating in the community service projects. In turn, many of those colleagues contacted Robin to ask how they might establish voluntary service programs to help people in need. The Bank of America is an enormous institution with branches throughout the western United States as well as in every major city in the country from Alaska to Florida to Hawaii, so there were plenty of opportunities to launch community service outreach projects.

Robin Leidenthal has a way of inspiring people, not only with words but by her deeds. So many co-workers were touched by her Adopt a Family project that the next year her department served almost twice as many people, buying and delivering food and gift baskets to forty-three families. Meanwhile, colleagues in other departments of the bank who followed her lead delivered baskets to 519 families that Christmas. "It was so successful that in Contra Costa County, for example, we ran out of needy families," says one participant.

Robin's success with the Christmas in April project was being talked about enthusiastically throughout the bank. The volunteer network teamed up with the Christmas in April organization to identify homes in need of repair that could be matched with local Bank of America locations that were putting together volunteer teams. Robin told the bank's executives that there were often financial needs for each property, that homeowners who qualified for the Christmas in April program could not afford the cost of materials needed to repair their homes. Bank of America was so impressed by the enthusiasm of its staff and the results of their home improvement work that they agreed to fund the cost of materials needed to repair each house—an average of two thousand dollars apiece. In 1992, the volunteer bankers repaired eleven homes in California, Oregon, and Nevada. Approximately two thousand employees participated in the Adopt a Family program. "In 1993," said Katy Jarman, "we committed to renovating a home in every community where Christmas in April has a chapter. We succeeded except for one location in southern California."

Nineteen ninety-two saw some of the biggest changes in Bank of America's history. In one of the largest mergers ever in the banking industry, Security Pacific and Bank of America agreed to become one financial services behemoth, retaining the Bank of America name. The commitment to encourage community service through employee volunteerism was actually strengthened by the merger. Roger Hancock, the dynamic young vice president of Security Pacific's Community Affairs Department, assumed a similar position at Bank of America, where he was charged with the responsibility of coordinating all employee volunteerism and community outreach programs. Hancock has a track record that befits his position, having served in numerous hands-on projects and on the boards of many needy causes. Because of his community service, he was named Citizen of the Year in Glendale,

California, in 1985—just four years out of high school and five months after graduating from college.

He entered his new position with excitement and anticipation. "My first priority with the merged company," he says, "was to establish an identifiable vehicle through which employees would be encouraged to volunteer, and a data base to get a handle on the opportunities available to them." Each employee is invited to fill out a simple questionnaire detailing current voluntary service and indicating areas of interest for possible future service. All volunteerism is now coordinated under the name TeamAmerica, and its logo appears on T-shirts, stationery, recruitment flyers, and anything else connected with Bank of America's volunteerism program.

"We put absolutely no pressure on employees to participate in the projects," vows Roger. "Management funds the TeamAmerica department to provide the assistance to employees who *want* to volunteer. In many ways it's like a clearinghouse which matches needy causes we've checked out for authenticity and employees who are eager to give their time and talents. The employees choose what they want to do, and they then have ownership of their chosen project." Does an employee who performs a lot of community service volunteer work have an advantage in a promotion opportunity over one who doesn't? "I believe it shows better management skills," he replies. "It gives the volunteer employee bonus points that make them a better individual. Frankly, I believe the person who gives something back to their community *is* a better employee."

Robin Leidenthal is clearly one of those "better employees" Roger Hancock referred to. Her job responsibilities keep her work days rushing by at a frenetic pace, with continual meetings, travel to different branches, and unanticipated emergencies to handle. "I'm a workaholic," she admits, "and both at work and at home with three small children I'm as busy as anyone else. But I wanted to make a positive contribution to the community." Her husband, Steve, works alongside her on most volunteer projects, as have her children. "I think it's important to bring home these situations to the kids and show them the needs, but also the upside of volunteer service," she says. For example, they help her shop, wrap, and deliver the Christmas food and gift baskets. "It gives them an appreciation for what they have," she adds.

One thing is certain: Robin Leidenthal has certainly followed the suggestion of the supervisor who wrote on her 1989 performance appraisal that she needed to "get out and be more active with other employees." In 1993, Bank of America's employees will perform two hundred thousand hours of volunteer work in their communities across the length and breadth of the United States, and many of those hours will be helping people on projects inspired by Robin Leidenthal. When asked what motivates her, she replies, "I don't do it because I have to; I do it because I want to. On a professional level I'm rewarded by being recognized as a leader. That's a big motivator. On the personal side I must tell you that to shop for another family for Christmas gave me the warmest feeling I've ever had. I thought of them as my family as I tried to pick out the perfect items for them. Then to drop it off to them gave me the greatest thrill, it just filled me with the Christmas spirit." Robin talks about the things that her co-workers enjoy the most about their voluntary service projects. "It is really meaningful for employees to see senior management getting their hands dirty and working side-by-side with them," she says. "And the managers often say, 'I don't want to be a manager today, I just want to be a helper.'"

She suddenly realizes that she has not answered the original question. "What motivates me to continue?" she repeats. "I do it because I truly believe we have the responsibility to positively influence our community. I do it because I've found it doesn't take a whole lot to mean so much to people in need. I do it...because it's the *right* thing to do."

We all have something to give. If you know how to read, find someone who can't. If you've got a hammer, find a nail. If you're not hungry, not lonely, not in trouble—seek out someone who is. Join the community of conscience. Do the hard work of freedom. That will define the state of our union.

—Former President George Bush

9

. . . .

IBM's Zanny Shealey

Role Model for Atlanta's Troubled Youth

Zanny Shealey is perhaps the personification of the new "IBM look." The old, stereotypical image of the classic IBMer was the tall, clean-cut, conservative Wasp in a dark suit, white shirt, and that ever-so-confident attitude that the world consisted of only two types of people: those that were lucky enough to be IBM clients and those that wished they were. Zanny Shealey does wear the white shirt and a conservative suit, but he has the build that reveals his college football accomplishments. He speaks with a pleasant Georgia drawl and is one of the most perpetually positive people one will ever meet. His happy disposition shines through on every subject he talks about, from his job, church, and family to his volunteer work—a great attribute during these troubled times at Big Blue.

He was born in 1956 in the town of LaGrange, Georgia, a community of twenty-two thousand people just seventy-five miles south of Atlanta. Zanny Shealey remembers even then how he was different from most of his friends. "Almost all of them were from families headed by a single mother," he recalls, "and with me being in the middle of my family of three brothers and one sister, my mom was always sending one of us over to help this lady or that lady." Even in those days, he noted with sadness how many young people, even in rural LaGrange, had nothing to do

96

with their spare time and so got involved in drugs and violence. His parents, whom he still sees every other week when he drives his family seventy-five miles each way to the church in which they are so active, instilled faith, honesty, and charity in him at an early age. "I think that's how I got so interested in volunteerism," he says. "Even as a child, my mom and dad would make us share our clothes and food with kids who didn't have any. It was very rewarding to be a part of that community."

Zanny did well in high school and left the textile mill town to attend Morehouse College in Atlanta on a football scholarship. One day, he experienced a life-changing event. Dr. Benjamin E. Mays, the famous educator who was president emeritus of Morehouse, delivered a speech that challenged the students: "When you leave the halls of this college you may have all the knowledge in the world, but all that will be in vain if you don't devote some of your time helping someone who's less fortunate than you." Shealey's focus changed. Instead of aiming for the NFL and an uncertain future, he would set his sights on a more academic concentration in college and a career in the business world. He graduated from Morehouse and joined Eastern Airlines in Atlanta until a strike resulted in many layoffs, including that of young Zanny, with his low seniority. For a while, he joined the Atlanta school system as a substitute teacher—a job he enjoyed so much that most of his volunteer work ever since has included teaching children.

On March 15, 1982, Zanny Shealey arrived at another watershed: he became an IBM employee. It was not exactly an event reported in the *Wall Street Journal*, although one day it might be told there. Zanny went to work for the company's Atlanta office as a mail clerk. "I figured, this was a big company with great benefits and room for advancement if I gave them my best efforts, so how could I lose?" he says. Indeed, after about nine months he was promoted, then promoted again, and then again . . . finally arriving at his present position as a staff financial analyst in IBM's internal assets department. Along the way he continued his academic studies at Atlanta University, where he is working on a master's degree in public administration.

IBM has a reputation for being a stellar corporate citizen.

It is based on a management philosophy that dates back more than fifty years to when Thomas J. Watson, Sr., IBM's founder, advised employees, "Take time out from your IBM duties to do a good job in your community." Zanny Shealey was not at the company very long before he realized that his own voluntary spirit and his employer's community service policies were in perfect harmony with each other. In fact, he remembers "my very first manager's sitting me down and stressing to me how the company prides itself on their volunteerism emphasis and had numerous programs to encourage voluntary service in every area."

His first active participation came during the Christmas season, when the IBM branch manager "adopted" an entire housing project in a very poor neighborhood in southwest Atlanta. The children of these families would not have received any Christmas gifts had it not been for the IBM employees, who each volunteered to provide for one family. A number of organizations arrange similar benevolent toy drives and drop the collected gifts off at a central point without ever having much personal interaction with the recipients. The IBM project was different. It required that the employee deliver the toys directly to the family and then spend time with them.

Zanny Shealey spent several hours with a mother and her young children, taking a particular liking to her son, Anthony. "I guess he was about ten years old," he recalls, "and I felt he was right at that age when he needed guidance in his life as he prepared to enter the critical early teen years." Zanny was especially concerned about the bad influence of Anthony's older brother, who was into drugs in a big way. "I know I probably shouldn't have done it," he says, "but I gave [Anthony] my home and office telephone numbers and had him come over to my house several times, almost as a member of my own family. Sometimes he'd be having a bad day at school and he'd call me at the office, and we'd meet after school so I could take him to McDonald's and just talk things over."

Anthony's friendship with Zanny and his respect for him as a role model rewarded them both, and Zanny is proud to point out that Anthony stayed drug-free and maintained good grades throughout middle and high school. "He's an absolutely wonderful artist," says Shealey. "He's now graduated from high school and in his second year at Atlanta Art Institute. He is just a great kid, and I felt a real attachment to him."

Zanny was so moved by the power he had to positively influence a person's life by investing just a small amount of time that he has volunteered for virtually every community project adopted by his office since then, although his favorite projects are those that help children or the elderly. It became a running joke at home as Zanny's wife, Mary, would ask, "And what good cause will you be volunteering for *this* Saturday?" He was so touched by the plight of battered women and the homeless that he continues to work regularly for the two Atlanta shelters that offer a refuge to victims of both those problems. "Then in August of 1989, Junior Achievement of Metro Atlanta asked for volunteers for a different type of project," he says.

Teaching in a Center for Troubled Youth

Atlanta's Lorenzo Benn Youth Development Center sounds a lot nicer than "prison for teenage criminals," yet that is what it effectively is. Approximately 220 kids between the ages of twelve and seventeen who have been convicted of crimes as diverse as petty theft to felony murder are incarcerated there. Because of their age, the state still has an obligation to provide them with an education, and a number of experimental teaching methods have been implemented to try to maintain the kids' interest. One of the center's instructors felt the youths needed to learn economics as it applied to the real world and asked Junior Achievement to place a teacher from the private sector at the Lorenzo Benn Center. By the time Junior Achievement asked IBM, they were desperate. Company after normally reliable company had refused to let their employees go into the correctional institution. "Even IBM was real hesitant," says Shealey. "They were quite worried about safety, and apparently so were the employees: the first three men who were asked turned down the assignment." Then the IBM community service coordinator approached Zanny. "You know I'll do it," he assured her. This perennial volunteer never says no to a project, but what IBM didn't know was that Zanny had a special reason for wanting to help these troubled teenagers. "My own younger brother, who was then twenty-six, was incarcerated at the time," he says, his soft voice filled with compassion for his sibling. "He was one of those troubled kids like the ones over in Lorenzo Benn, and I've always said that if I could spend time with young people like these, maybe someone will do the same for my brother one day."

The economics class at the youth correctional center was arranged, and Zanny Shealey drove over for a security briefing from the administrative staff. "I wasn't concerned about safety at all," he says. "In fact, the only part of their instructions that I remember was, 'we've had a rash of escape attempts recently, so don't ever leave your keys in your car.'"

When Shealey started, he introduced himself to his class and told them he would be showing them how economics as taught in textbooks affects every one of them every day. He then led the class of twenty-five students for three to four hours twice a week. After a very short time, Shealey noticed that their attention span, classwork, and grades had really improved, and they seemed to be enjoying—and learning from—his presence. One young man, Jermaine Collins, really stood out. "He was bright, articulate, and a real leader," says Zanny. "He was in for felony murder and was serving a life sentence. He had just turned sixteen and would stay at Lorenzo Benn until he reached eighteen, at which time he would be transferred to the state prison for adults for the rest of his sentence." Time and again, Zanny noticed this young man who, had he been in a normal school, would probably be in an honors class. After he finished teaching one day, Shealey asked one of the administrators why Jermaine was incarcerated. "It was a classic case of him falling in with the wrong crew and then being in the wrong place at the wrong time," he says. "It's such a shame to see a life so full of promise be wasted away in a prison." Jermaine would soon show more of that promise.

Shealey brought to the prison a program called MESE (Management Economics Simulation Exercise) that is used in junior and senior high school classes throughout Georgia. It is a business simulation game that takes several weeks to play.

Participating teams each start a company and enter all the relevant details into a computer. (Ironically, Lorenzo Benn did not even own a computer for student use at the time: Zanny had to borrow one from IBM.) The teams make all their own decisions on their business, as if they are running a corporation in the real world: they elect officers, figure the cost of raw materials and the selling price of finished products, and handle salaries, union problems and other issues. In the meantime, the computer throws them such unexpected challenges as a cash flow crisis, a recession, labor disputes, and production problems. The game is also a contest: each team competes with other MESE groups in high schools statewide for the highest net profit attained by the end of the contest period. The Benn team voted Jermaine as their captain, and according to Shealey, he demonstrated all the attributes needed to successfully guide a real company: leadership, motivation, and a clear, decisive mind. When the contest ended, all seventy participating high schools waited nervously for the results, and when they were announced, the Lorenzo Benn Center team learned it was second in the entire state, separated from the first place team by just fifty-five dollars in profit. "Just imagine that," chortles the immensely proud Zanny. "Our team was comprised of what some people call 'criminals with no future.' We competed against the best schools in Georgia, including some very exclusive private schools, and we beat all of them but one." Each member of the Benn team was awarded a fifty-dollar savings bond as a prize.

One day, Zanny was contacted by one of the teachers who had also noted the academic ability and positive attitude of Jermaine Collins. He had spoken with Jermaine's attorney, and the two of them had decided to apply to the pardons and parole board for an educational reprieve, to allow him to leave the detention center to attend college in Florida. The proposal was considered an extreme long shot, as the board had never before in history consented to such a request, but the teacher wondered if Zanny would join them in the petition and testify on Jermaine's behalf. Zanny enthusiastically agreed. "Most kids sort of coast, academically, while they're at Benn, but not Jermaine. He worked *so* hard," he says.

With his class euphoric at their success in the MESE contest, Shealey brought them information on the Mock Trial Competition. This called for a totally different set of abilities than MESE; knowledge of the law and legal precedents, a good memory, and persuasive verbal skills. The students all voted to participate, and they voted Jermaine Collins to be the lead attorney. The kids studied and practiced intensely, for the subject matter was completely alien to them. At the end of the contest, the results shocked high schools across the state of Georgia: the Lorenzo Benn Detention Center had come in first.

Another opportunity soon presented itself. Georgia Power, the utility company, sent all high schools details of their public speaking contest. Jermaine Collins, who had never given a speech in his life, decided to enter, potentially pitting himself against every high school senior in the state. The detention center granted him special permission to leave the facility to attend the competition finals in Atlanta. When his eloquent address won first prize in the contest, Jermaine returned to the center a stockholder in Georgia Power, proudly showing the ten shares of the utility's stock that they gave out as first prize. "You could just see the other kids look to him as a leader," says Zanny. "He was so good with people, too. A real peacemaker. I *still* have kids say, 'I want to be like Jermaine.'"

The big day came, and Zanny Shealey appeared before the pardons and parole board and testified about Jermaine's positive character traits and academic potential. To the astonishment of many, the board voted to grant Jermaine his request for an educational reprieve to attend college in Florida. "When I heard the news I was ecstatic," remembers Shealey. The trust they all placed in him for a second chance was apparently well founded, as he has maintained good grades and a spotless criminal record ever since.

The kids at the center looked to Zanny for help as they struggled with their feelings about everyday teenage concerns and news items from the outside that troubled them. "These were very intelligent kids," he asserts. "What got them into trouble was their decision-making ability, so I felt duty-bound to discuss their concerns openly together." Many of the youths were disturbed about the Anita Hill–Clarence Thomas debacle. "Even if he did that stuff, why would a black woman say those things that hurt a black man's chances for the Supreme Court?" they wanted to know. The much-publicized trial of boxer Mike Tyson—a hero to most of the students at the detention center—also caused great debate. Zanny Shealey listened patiently to all their arguments and then talked to them about why a woman's right to say no to sex is sacrosanct, regardless of the time of day, the room she says it in, or the reasons she gives. Another topic frequently discussed was AIDS and why the youths did not feel they should have to wear condoms. Again, Zanny used his quiet, persuasive logic to show them that there was another point of view that deserved consideration. "You made a bad decision once and ended up incarcerated," he told them. "Make a bad decision on a matter like unprotected sex and you can end up dead."

Starting a Real-World Company

In 1992, Junior Achievement gave permission for Zanny's economics class to start an actual student company. It was to be a grass-roots effort, with all the decisions made by the students. They called their company First Step Enterprises, because "this is the first step we're taking in getting out of here." The youths elected the officers of the company, and the first board meeting occurred a week later. As they were debating what type of business First Step Enterprises should be, the center director suggested they do something with the supply of T-shirts that had been gathering dust in the basement. "Instead of making your mother pay twelve dollars at the mall for a shirt with somebody else's message on it, take these shirts and put your own message on them," he said. So First Step Enterprises went into the silk-screened T-shirt business. They selected four different designs for the shirts but needed capital to purchase the silk-screening equipment and supplies. As in real life, they learned that you have to borrow money to make money, so the board put together a pro forma financial statement and business plan, showing what their competition was doing on the outside and projecting their own costs, revenues, and profits. The teachers at Lorenzo Benn were so impressed they personally lent the students the money. Then the marketing staff went looking for business. Actually, they had a major competitive disadvantage since they could not "go" anywhere, of course. All vendor negotiations, marketing, prospecting, and research had to be done by telephone—and the center's rules permitted them to use the telephones for only one hour each day.

They picked up their first order, for 215 shirts, from the Morehouse Business Association, but they had to order more blank shirts since there were not enough in the basement. "It was incredible," laughs Zanny. "They called up a shirt supplier to place an order, and there they were, a new business, with no money, no credit history, just kids—in the prison system—and they wanted the shirts on credit terms. I give a lot of respect to Marvin Sales for having faith in our guys." The shirts were picked up by a teacher, silk-screened, and delivered to the customer on time and on budget.

That first year, after paying all their bills, including repayment of the teachers' loan, First Step Enterprises finished in the black, with over $7,000 in revenues and $700 in net profit. "Just think about it," says their proud IBM mentor. "One day these kids are going to be released into the community. They now have a trade; they have a proven track record in the areas that make them excellent employees: intelligence, productivity, dependability, and decision making." Shealey credits the center's teachers for instilling these attributes into the youths. "Some of those people go far beyond their normal duties to make the kids feel special and to give them a second chance," he adds.

But the administrators at Lorenzo Benn insist that it is Shealey who deserves the credit for instilling values into the character of its students. "Zanny was a great role model for the boys," states Brad Wideman, the center's principal. "He didn't preach to them but showed the students that he, too, came from a poor background and his choices of staying clean, studying well, and working hard landed him a career with a really great company— IBM. He brings real-life experience to our students. They really love Zanny." Elizabeth Ackman, a teacher at Lorenzo Benn for over twenty years, agrees. "Zanny showed the students who are in here for dealing drugs that there is a legal way to make money out there," she says. "Yet he is always so quick to defer accolades to others. He was the first person in my twenty years to recognize what I do is important. I could call him at any time of the day or night if there was trouble, and he would be right over." Ackman tells of the ceremony initiated by her grateful students to award a plaque to Shealey. "Our Success Was Your Achievement," it said, simply. "He's meant so much to so many kids. There are former students now in Arkansas, Florida, around the country, that owe their success to him for what he taught them here," she says. "I can tell you, there were some pretty tough boys here who couldn't even speak at the presentation for the tears in their eyes. Zanny's ten feet tall to them."

Volunteering as a Way of Life

Zanny Shealey is now the father of three young children, aged nine, six, and three. On some volunteer events he even takes his family along to help out. One such occasion is the Georgia Special Olympics, a mirror image of the Olympic Games, but for handicapped children. IBM is a corporate sponsor of the event and erects a large tent which houses many computers loaded with game software. After the contestants have completed their athletic activities, they go into the tent, where volunteers like Zanny are waiting to show them how the computers work. "That's a really fun job," he declares, "not only to work one-on-one with the kids on the computers, but watching the intensity with which they compete in the athletic events. My whole family loves to cheer them on. The contestants include paraplegics and kids with all sorts of other physical challenges, but many of them compete on the field with more drive than most people walking around today. They're unbelievable."

Zanny also gives his time to the IBM student pennant race program. He'll visit with sixth and seventh graders and talk with them about the importance of getting a good education. Then they are challenged to a contest in which they are competing not with other students but with themselves and their own bad habits. IBM rewards them if they improve their grades, maintain perfect attendance, and demonstrate good attitudes toward school and each other. At the end of the contest period, Zanny and his co-workers take all the winners out for a meal at the Coliseum then move on to the stadium to see an Atlanta Braves baseball game, during which the students are allowed onto the field to meet the players.

In another project involving kids, Zanny volunteered to visit numerous elementary and middle schools for the so-called 32 and 8 program. Started in 1990 by local storyteller Warren Holyfield, the program featured him and Zanny telling fairy tales to the young children gathered at school assemblies. But these famous stories were told with a twist, a moral that reinforced safety rules for today's children. For example, "Little Red Riding Hood" would be told as the kids knew it, until the wolf jumped out at her and offered Little Red Riding Hood a cigarette. Then Zanny would jump out and say, "But we *all* know never to take anything from strangers, don't we, boys and girls?" After a chorus of agreement from the audience, he would continue, "And we all know that cigarettes are bad for you, so nobody here would do something dumb like smoke a cigarette, right, boys and girls?" Similar lessons about telling the truth, talking to strangers, playing with matches, and doing their schoolwork made these events very popular, and the Atlanta Board of Education has now granted the program the funds to continue it at schools throughout the city.

Zanny Shealey is clearly one of a kind, and the streets of Atlanta must seem a little less harsh to hundreds of people—especially kids—because of the indomitable spirit of caring, understanding, and benevolence that he has shared with so many. But as much as he gives back to his adopted community, Shealey has never forgotten his roots. He continues to drive the 150-mile round trip to LaGrange every other Sunday, where he has followed in his father's footsteps to serve as a deacon at Central Baptist Church. In May of 1992, the citizens of LaGrange stunned him when he arrived at what he thought was a volunteerism event at Gardner Newman Middle School, which he once attended. The community decreed it Zanny Shealey Day, complete with marching bands, balloons, and speeches from people in lofty positions. Hailed as "a real hero, a model student and a model for our students to follow" by Associate Superintendent of Schools Dave Nichols, Shealey was praised by others for being "a man of character who respected his teachers" and "a real motivator on the field."

Luckily for many people, those attributes have never left him. Today, instead of motivating teammates on the athletic field, he motivates at-risk students in the classrooms where he spends so many of his volunteer hours. Why does he spend so much time on these activities? "Because I enjoy it," he responds, simply. "God has blessed me and my family with so much, this is a very small price for me to pay to repay Him for what He has given me. I'm simply sharing some of His blessings. When I have an opportunity to make a positive impact on someone else's life, that's what keeps me going. We so often get hung up on ourselves: wanting that new dress, fancier car, bigger house. It makes me feel really good inside to know that I'm able to do things to help people by just showing them that you love them, regardless of what they are or what they've done in the past."

At the packed auditorium in LaGrange after the mayor and other notable citizens had finished praising Zanny Shealey, the clearly embarrassed young man arose to say a few words. He first thanked God "for all He's blessed me with" and then his parents for instilling their values in him. Then, seeing the entire student body present, he addressed his closing thoughts to his favorite type of audience. "You don't have to step on people to climb the ladder," he said. "If you're willing to work, you can be the president of the United States, the principal of this school, or the doctor who discovers the cure for AIDS. Maybe you won't get a lot of monetary rewards for what you do, but if you will spend just a little time helping others in their time of need, God will surely bless you." And so He has, Zanny Shealey, as He has blessed all of us who have met you along the pathway of life.

I can't buy the idea that people are too busy. I can program my time to do this. And I run a major corporation. At the same time, I have eight children. And there's nothing unusual about me. The reason I do it, I feel it's a part of my job. One of the qualifications for being a chief executive officer is to be involved in the community.

—James Renier
   former chairman and chief executive officer
   Honeywell Inc.

10

$\cdots\cdots\cdots\cdots\cdots\cdots\cdots\cdots\cdots\cdots\cdots\cdots\cdots$

United Airlines' Bill Allison

Matching Homeless People
with People Who Need Them

"In this country we have the very, very rich, who can afford to pay for the best of everything, and the very poor, who are taken care of by government programs. The real problems are those who are stuck in the middle." Bill Allison doesn't strike one as the type who would rant on about anything. He appears a quiet, gentle man with an air of concern about him. Were he to sit across from you on the subway, you might speculate that he was a pastor, or a social worker. In fact, Bill Allison is creative services manager for United Airlines at their corporate headquarters near Chicago's O'Hare Airport.

For most of his twenty-four years with United, Bill has had a joyous life. He and his wife, Irene, live in the pleasant suburb of Lemont and have raised three children, all of whom now have their own families. Bill has had a successful career with United, and he and Irene have been fortunate enough to use his free travel privileges to fly around the world together as they explored exotic destinations most people visit only in their dreams. Then fifteen years ago, their world was shattered: Irene was diagnosed with multiple sclerosis, a progressive disease that leads to paralysis and for which there is no cure.

In the first few years after her diagnosis, Irene was able to carry on with her life as normal, but by the late eighties it was obvious that she needed help. "When the doctors first told us that she had MS, we took comfort in the fact that the disease is not life-threatening," says Bill. "But we were not prepared for how drastically the progressing illness would change our family's lives. Within a few years, she could no longer take care of herself. She needed assistance with everything—even the daily routine tasks most of us take for granted." The Allisons didn't worry initially. After all, Bill's long tenure with United Airlines carried with it an impressive package of benefits, including a very comprehensive medical insurance program. But upon investigation, they found that no health insurance policy covered the cost of providing the full-time, long-term, in-home nursing care she needed. "Our loved ones *need* care," says Allison, "but they can't be taken care of *solely* by loved ones, particularly when we have jobs we have to attend." Bill searched for someone to stay with his wife and perform basic household duties while he was at work. "There are some very good organizations out there," he asserts, "but who can afford to pay them fifteen dollars an hour for forty-five or fifty hours every week?

Then Bill Allison had an idea. The Allisons had discovered through networking with other MS victims that there were many other families in a similar predicament. In fact, Access Living, a nonprofit group that facilitates independence for the disabled, estimates that as many as one million disabled Americans could live at home instead of in nursing homes if they could just afford caregivers. Bill also remembered reading that tens of thousands of foreigners were trying to come into the United States to work as au pairs, living with families here while taking care of the children or domestic duties. So in 1987, Bill Allison started the Need Foundation with the intention of serving other needy families by acting as an intermediary between the foreign nationals and Chicago-area disabled shut-ins. For over two years, Bill battled with the Internal Revenue Service, who put numerous bureaucratic roadblocks in the way, preventing him from securing the tax-exempt organization status he needed for the foundation. "Without the IRS' approval of our tax-exempt condition we would have been dead," he says, "because people making donations could not have taken a tax deduction." His patience gone, he finally asked for help from Senator Al Dixon and Congressman Philip Crane, and in two weeks the Need Foundation had their IRS tax-exempt approval.

Irene's condition had worsened considerably in recent months, and when her doctors told her to use a wheelchair, Bill knew it was time to find her a caregiver while he was at work all day. As he was thinking through the logistics, a terrifying incident brought the urgency of that need to the Allisons vividly: one day, after Bill left for the office, Irene went downstairs, as usual, on the inclinator—a chair that carries a person up and down stairs electrically on a smooth track. As she reached the bottom of the stairs, Irene's bathrobe got caught in the mechanism, and she fell. The multiple sclerosis had so weakened her body that she was unable to stand or to dislodge her robe from the inclinator, despite numerous attempts. Time after time she valiantly tried to free herself, but to no avail. So she lay on the floor in the very spot where she had fallen until Bill returned from work twelve hours later.

As much as he realized that it was important to act quickly, something in the back of his mind had kept Bill from bringing foreign nationals—about whom nothing was known and no background checks could be run—into trusting, sensitive positions in peoples' homes. He just could not figure whom to use as caregivers in their place. Then on Thanksgiving Day, 1989, he found his answer. Bill and Irene were watching a television program where Joan Lunden was showing the plight of many less-fortunate Americans on that day of sumptuous eating and family togetherness. "Joan Lunden started showing homeless people living on the streets," Bill recalls, "and she talked about the common misconceptions people have: that the homeless are a bunch of shifty, untrustworthy drug addicts and alcoholics. She quoted statistics and interviewed some of them, demonstrating the fallacy of those labels we've all put on them." The Allisons learned that many of the street people are intelligent, drug- and alcohol-free folks with no criminal records; normal people who had experienced tough luck and ended up on the streets. Once they had slept under the bushes or on park benches for a few nights, their appearance was so offensive they were unemployable. "That's it!" exclaimed Bill. "We don't need to bring people in from Russia and the Philippines—we have all the people we need right on the streets of Chicago."

Helping the Needy Meet Others' Needs

According to John Donahue, executive director of Chicago's Coalition of the Homeless, "There are at least sixty thousand homeless people in Chicago alone, and another three million elsewhere in the United States. . . . They are ordinary people who have fallen on hard times and for whom there was no safety net when they fell." Bill's plan was to recruit people off the streets and match them with people like Irene whose disabilities prevented them from performing even the most basic household duties. Nevertheless, he realized that the liability his Need Foundation faced by placing homeless recruits into a disabled person's house required that he establish a rigorous interview, a background check, and rules of conduct, which he immediately set about writing. Drug use and alcoholism became instant disqualifiers, as was a criminal record. He was looking for people who wanted to use the position of resident caregiver as their way out of the trap of homelessness, a way to start a new chapter in their lives. A local detective agency was so impressed with what he was attempting to do that they agreed to run criminal background checks on every applicant at a fraction of their normal fee. He then approached several potential care receivers, people with MS, Alzheimer's disease, blindness, strokes, or other disabling illnesses and discussed the outline of his plan. Many of them made suggestions on how to refine or improve it, but they were unanimous in welcoming the idea. It was time to run it up the flagpole and see if anyone saluted. The next week, a small classified ad appeared in *Streetwise*, a Chicago-area free newspaper published for the homeless:

> WANTED: Homeless people who want to change their lives. Stipend $100 a week plus room and board. Immediate placement. Future career potential.

"From the very start, I never had any doubts that this would work," says Bill today, "and to demonstrate that, Irene and I decided that we should be the guinea pigs to try the program out by taking the first caregiver." When Bill told his own adult children of his idea, they were less than enthused, voicing the concerns so many people have about the character of homeless people. "She may be your wife," one of them told Bill, "but she's *our* mother."

From the respondents to his advertisement, Bill and Irene selected a woman named Jessie Harris and her ten-year-old daughter. The Allisons' lives soon started to improve. "I'd walk out of my house in the morning and know that Irene was going to be taken care of," he says. Caregiving wasn't a particularly hard job, and Jessie had no problem with the chores such as shopping, cleaning, and preparing Irene's meals. In return for her five-day work week (Bill would take care of things on weekends), the Allisons paid Jessie one hundred dollars per week and provided her and her daughter with free room and board. Since she had virtually no expenses, Jessie was able to save almost every penny of her earnings each week. Bill also arranged for the daughter to enter the excellent local school system. Unfortunately, one small problem did occur. Jessie had managed to conceal her alcoholism from the Allisons during the interview process. Once in their home she found it difficult to abstain, and one day they found her in an inebriated state. A strict warning was given, telling her that any further incidence would result in her immediate dismissal. Things went fine for a while, but then they found her drunk again. Sadly, she was terminated two and a half months later and replaced with another caregiver. "We hated to do it, but we have to show that the rules will be enforced," says Bill. "Jessie was great, too. That's one thing I've found during this process: a person may be an alcoholic, but they can still be a really nice person."

People started hearing about the Need Foundation, and Bill realized he needed help coordinating caregiver and care-needer applications, publicity, and fundraising activities. He first turned to his colleagues at United Airlines and found tremendous support from both the corporation and his fellow employees.

Paul Tinebra, United's director of consumer affairs; Pat Bayliss, coordinator of the medical clinic; Brian McGuire, vice president of audit and security, and John Grember all agreed to serve on the Foundation's board of directors. Word spread—and support was received—from far beyond United's Chicago base. For example, some of the most dependable and enthusiastic help came from Randy Ko, United's regional reservations manager in Honolulu, Hawaii, over 4,200 miles away. Allison then made an appointment to see United's chairman, Stephen Wolf. Bill told him about Irene and the thousands of people like her and how the foundation, so aptly named, was filling a double need by providing affordable caregivers while helping homeless people work their way off the streets and regain their pride and dignity. According to Allison, it took only a few minutes of his story for Wolf to make a decision. "He pledged United's financial support on the spot that day," he says, "and he's been there for us ever since. I've been around for a while, and I tell you, there are darned few companies with a CEO as committed to making good things happen to people in need as our chairman."

Wolf is asked why a company that has been hemorrhaging money—United suffered a staggering $417 million loss in 1992—would want to support employee volunteerism projects like the Need Foundation. He replies, "We must focus most of our resources on returning United to consistent profitability, which is in the long-term interest of our employees, shareholders, customers and suppliers. But when Bill approached me and explained the logic underlying the Need Foundation and its potential benefits, I found it a refreshingly creative solution to not one, but two problems facing our society. I firmly believe that this company should do all it can to assist worthy organizations to help people. I would like to think that United's resolve to assist the less fortunate in our society, as epitomized by our modest contributions to further the work of Bill's Need Foundation, is deep and continuous and not something that starts and stops with the alternating phases of the business cycle."

Although Bill Allison is not the type one would expect to see mingling with movie stars, he and Irene have been longtime friends with Arte Johnson, star of the hit television series "Rowan

& Martin's Laugh-In." Bill and Arte share a passion for golf, so it was natural to hold a celebrity golf outing as a fundraiser. Dubbed the "Arte Golf Party," it attracted an array of famous sports, television, and movie stars and was a social, and fiscal, success. The United Airlines Foundation was a sponsor, and the outing became an annual event, held each July at a suburban Chicago golf course.

The board of the Need Foundation changed their recruiting policy slightly, and instead of running advertisements for caregivers they approached the staff of Chicago's shelters and asked them to refer any homeless patrons whom they felt would be good candidates. By the end of the first year, the Need Foundation had matched fourteen formerly homeless caregivers with elderly or disabled hosts. One year later, the total was fifty placements. By mid 1993, the Need Foundation had matched "several hundred" caregivers and care-needers, and it continued to add to those successes, currently at the rate of "about one hundred per year," according to Bill Allison. "And nobody's stolen the silverware yet!" he adds, with a jab at the early nay-sayers.

Assessing the Impact

The program has drawn rave reviews from all sides: the social service agencies, the caregivers, and the people they are helping. "I think the Need Foundation is wonderful," says John Donahue of the Coalition of the Homeless. "It's not only solving part of the homelessness problem, it is also helping the disabled. It moves toward the shared housing concept that we've talked about for years. The type of volunteerism that Bill Allison is doing helps people look at the homeless as a 'we' instead of a 'they.' What he has accomplished is not so much an act of charity as an act of justice." "I've seen the proof myself," says Bill. "My wife and every other person receiving care is getting as good, or better, help from our caregivers as they were getting from any of the expensive private services agencies."

One Chicago newspaper ran a story on thirty-seven-year-old Mark Andrews, who is wheelchair-dependent due to multiple sclerosis, and his Need Foundation caregiver, James Dingle. "A mutual need is what brought Mark and James together," the story begins, "but friendship is what keeps them together." The forty-three-year-old Dingle explains his life before the Andrews gave him another chance: "I was raised in the projects; my mother died when I was 12. I had a bad marriage, which culminated in divorce, and I found myself on the streets. I was homeless all of a sudden." Then, while at the shelter, he found out about the Need Foundation and applied to be a caregiver. The pairing of James with Andrews, his wife, Terri, and their two-year-old son, Carey, has been wonderful. "This is the first Thanksgiving I've had with a family," Dingle told the reporter, Deborah Snow. One day, Mark suffered an adverse reaction to his medication, and James, alone in the house with him at the time, gave him mouth-to-mouth resuscitation until the ambulance arrived, saving his life in the process. "He's a good man," James said of Mark later. "I love him very much."

The success stories are the real paycheck for Bill Allison, who took early retirement from United Airlines in 1993 and devotes most of his day to his position of unpaid chairman of the Need Foundation. Luckily, there are many such stories. Like that of Verdel, a bright, attractive young woman who, because of a series of unlucky circumstances, found herself homeless and near despair over the dangerous conditions that await homeless women on the streets. Verdel jumped at the chance when she heard the Need Foundation was looking for caregivers. She was a model of trustworthiness and saved almost every penny she earned. After one and a half years as a caregiver, with money in the bank and her self-esteem renewed, she moved to Ohio to care for her aging mother.

Letters from caregivers and the patients they serve arrive constantly, bringing joy to Bill and the dedicated volunteers who run the program: "Thank you for all you have done for me," says one. "So far, I love what I am doing and have been very happy in both placements. Every night I pray for Sophie, and for Laverne. I thank God for the Need Foundation. I hope your program will never end. With the help of the Need Foundation...I have regained my sense of humor, my ability to be caring, and my sense of self-worth. You have given it all back to me. Thank you."

"Just a note to say thank you for helping me turn my life around," says another. "This placement has worked out very well for both of us. I have a lovely home to live in and I don't have to fear being homeless any more. If it weren't for the Need Foundation, Fran would still be warehoused in a nursing home, her dog would have been put to sleep, my dogs would have been placed for adoption, and I would have wound up in a shelter. Your organization has successfully benefitted two individuals who had hit the lowest points in their lives. The world is a better place because of you."

The son of a deceased care recipient wrote, "I want to let you know how wonderful Nancy O'Neil was in taking care of my mom. As you know, my mom had a crippling disease known as ALS. Nancy took care of my mom 24 hours a day, seven days a week for six months until her death on April 3, 1993. Nancy went beyond being a care giver. My mom grew to love her as if she were her only daughter. Thank you for introducing Nancy to my mom on October 14, 1992. I don't know what I would have done without her."

Deborah Simkins, who cares for thirty-three-year-old MS victim Kim Santiago and her three-year-old son, says simply, "I feel the Need Foundation more or less saved my life."

Clearly, Bill Allison has solved a need with the Need Foundation, but one had better not say that to him. "It's not Bill Allison," he objects. "It's all these wonderful employees at United Airlines, and the Baxter Foundation, and the volunteers that appear as if from nowhere and help put this whole operation together. *That's* who the credit should go to." What does he feel most proud of so far? "The fact that we're changing people's perspectives of the homeless," he says, thoughtfully. "We're demonstrating that all homeless people are not just bums lying in the street sucking on a wine bottle. If you strip away the poverty and abuse, homeless people are the same as you and me. They think the same as you and I think; they bleed the same red blood; they cry the same as you and I cry."

Bill talks about the future with the same excitement as a college graduate starting his career, rather than a man who has just retired from one. "I've been working on the dream of having a formal job training program for our caregivers once they've completed a placement," he says. "And we've just heard the good news that Marion Joy rehabilitation hospital in Wheaton, Illinois, has received a ninety-thousand-dollar grant to train our people as professional aides." He also talks about wanting to share the wealth of experience the foundation staff has had with organizations considering a similar program in other cities. Thanks to a grant from the Baxter pharmaceutical company, a 150-page manual is being prepared and will be supplied free to any such interested provider.

"I also have a dream of seeing this program nationwide before I die," says Bill Allison. Actually, the second city to see a Need Foundation project may very well be Louisville, Kentucky, in the very near future. Bill and Irene are planning to move there, where their son and his family live, and the milder climate might be gentler to Irene. It is easy to understand why one would go to extraordinary lengths to help one's own spouse, but why did Bill Allison go to all the time, trouble, and personal expense to help other people's families? He reflects on the question momentarily. "I think at my age I felt I owed something for what I've been given," he says. "I realize that sounds a little melodramatic, but there's no turning back. I've always felt that most problems can be solved by people, not governments. We—all people—*can* change things for the better. I don't want to get maudlin here, but I guess the answer to your question is that I really believe what Jesus taught us: to take care of the human race. He told us that each of us has a purpose on this earth. I believe *this* is my purpose."

. . . .

Helping People and
the Environment
Around the World

Helping others can be surprisingly easy, since there is so much to be done. The hard part comes in choosing what to do and getting started, making the first effort at something different. Once the initiative is taken we often find that we can do things we never thought we could.

—Jimmy and Rosalynn Carter

11

Continental Airlines' Terri New

Voices of Freedom Take Wing
with Project Booklift

Even with all the geopolitical history that has been made in the twentieth century, there have been few years that saw as much change as 1989. Wars in Central America and Afghanistan were winding down, the first glimmer of hope for an end to apartheid appeared in South Africa, and political leaders in the U.S. and the Soviet Union were talking more of friendly cooperation than nuclear annihilation. But nowhere were things beginning to change more than in Eastern Europe.

Terri New had a personal interest in these events, particularly the changes that might bring democracy to Czechoslovakia, her great-grandparents' homeland before they fled to avoid Hitler's advancing invasion in 1939. Terri New is a flight attendant with Continental Airlines, based in Los Angeles. She *looks* like a flight attendant, with long, blonde hair; dancing brown eyes; and an effervescent personality that seems to genuinely want to help people. It is almost a comedic caricature to portray people from the Hollywood area as saying, "I'm really an actor; I'm just doing this job while waiting for my agent to call." In Terri New's case, she doesn't have to wait for anyone to call: she makes things happen. Her talents extend to acting, singing, and writing poetry and full-length plays. In October 1989, partly for a vacation, partly to discover her great-grandparents' homeland, Terri flew to Prague, capital of Czechoslovakia.

Czechoslovakia is a country with a rich cultural heritage and a rather sad political history. This landlocked country in the very heart of Europe saw the founding of Central Europe's first university, Charles University. Built in 1348, it still operates today. The baroque capital, Prague, is one of the world's most beautiful cities, with cobbled streets, medieval buildings—many dating back to the thirteenth century—and bohemian cafés and coffee houses. In the years between the world wars, Czechoslovakia enjoyed the freedom of democracy. In fact, President Woodrow Wilson invited Thomas Masaryk, the first leader of a democratic Czechoslovakia, to the United States as his guest. While in Washington, Masaryk became particularly fascinated with the history of Thomas Jefferson and the role he played in the formation of a democratic United States of America. In reading Jefferson's history, Masaryk was inspired to write the Czech Declaration of Independence while on his American trip. Since becoming a nation under the iron thumb of the Soviet Union, Czechs have never stopped yearning for the rights and freedoms to which Masaryk—and Jefferson—subscribed.

Terri New's visit to Prague in 1989 was not very pleasant. "I met two East German students who had escaped from their country," she recalls. "I knew something was going on there, and I wanted to witness it." When she arrived, the atmosphere was extremely tense. Czechoslovakia's location, with its long borders with Western countries Germany and Austria, made it a natural transit corridor for disillusioned East Europeans planning to escape from their repressive Communist governments. The wave of discontent among freedom-seeking citizens in Poland, East Germany, the Baltic states, and Hungary had put additional pressure on Czech authorities. "It was really dismal," she says, "especially for the young people I met. They had no hope for the future. They simply didn't believe the Communist government would ever leave." Given the bloodbath that ensued during the democratic uprising in Czechoslovakia in 1968, it was easy to understand their disbelief that any substantive changes would occur in 1989.

For this gentle, soft-spoken Californian to see tanks and battle-ready troops ringing the city was an experience like none she had ever had. As each train left Prague heading to the West, police with high-power fire hoses were at the ready to knock off anybody they saw hiding above or beneath it as it passed by. On November 17, 1989, students who were in a silent march to urge peaceful change were brutalized by the militia. Despite the cruelty the attackers used, the students refused to fight back. One western newspaper report told how young people who had their right arms broken by the soldiers would then continue their march, holding their protest signs with their left hands.

As events in both the Soviet Union and other Eastern Bloc countries moved the entire axis toward democratic reform, so the Czechs began to finally believe they might see their dreams come true. Terri tells of the watershed event one night when the populist leader Vaclav Havel, a playwright like her, met with the country's Communist rulers. As Havel negotiated for hours to bring a fast, peaceful transition to democracy, people started to gather outside the building in the magnificent Wenceslas Square. As the talks dragged on, the crowd—and the tension—increased. The army tanks were ready to move in as soon as the word came from the military chiefs in the government building. By evening the crowd had grown to three hundred thousand people, all standing in complete silence. Suddenly, one person took out his keys, symbolic of unlocking a door to freedom, and started jingling them. His neighbor followed suit, then another, and another, until the sound of three hundred thousand sets of keys reverberated through the square and into the government conference room. The ringing continued for hours. There was total silence except for what later became known as the Last Ringing. The crowd outside and Havel's strategies inside finally made their point, and the Communist leaders agreed to relinquish power without a shot being fired. Rita Klimova, the Czechoslovak ambassador to the United States, herself a dissident, called it the Velvet Revolution, a moniker that has since gained worldwide recognition.

Moving from Inspiration to Action

Terri New realized that her life had been changed by the experiences she had witnessed on her trip to Czechoslovakia. Although she had to return to California, she immediately started making plans for her next visit. That was to be just a few months later, in February 1990. "I've written plays extolling the transformational qualities of human beings for twenty years," she says, "and to witness these gentle people and their peaceful revolution was just incredible. I knew I had to write about it." New decided to write a play entitled *Voices of the Velvet Revolution*. The "voices" were to be the actual words of the many subjects she interviewed during her trip in February. While there, she was taken to Prague's Civic Forum to meet and interview the sister and brother-in-law of Vaclav—now President—Havel. It was obvious to New that the new country needed everything: telecommunications, pollution control, teaching aids, medical equipment—everything was either in desperately short supply or very outdated. "What is it that you need the most?" Terri asked. She assumed they would say they needed billions of dollars of foreign aid, or modern military armaments, or multi-million-dollar plants and equipment. She was astonished at the reply: "Books," they said, simply.

The official went on to explain that the decades of Nazi and then Communist rule had decimated the country's inventory of books. As she moved about Prague interviewing citizens from all walks of life, she repeated the question, but always the reply was the same: "books." "The people were literally starved for literature," says New. "Under Communist rule, even the classics were banned. Shakespeare, Rousseau, were considered Western propaganda. Even books such as Adam Smith's theories on economics and those on modern management practices were outlawed; if they caught you with the writings of Freud or books on Zen Buddhism or Jungian philosophy you would be jailed for eight years."

The Czechs are voracious readers and typically speak three or four languages. "Just about everyone under age thirty speaks English, so they can read anything we take over from the U.S.," she adds. Indeed, while back at home after her first visit, Terri had collected a montage of reports on the Czech revolution from various U.S. newspapers and magazines. The Czechs were fascinated by it, often learning things that had happened right there in their own city for the first time by reading her American newspaper articles. Terri New had gone back to Prague to interview people for her play, but she remembers throughout the long flight home her mind being consumed by the idea of supplying her newfound friends with that which they'd been denied for a generation. "Books?" she recalls thinking, "I can do books!"

Over the next few months, Terri New's life became a blur. When she wasn't flying across the country for Continental, she was writing *Voices of the Velvet Revolution* and trying to establish her book donation idea. Coming up with the name Project Booklift was the easy part. Getting the books to Prague was not. Continental does not fly there, so New figured on having them fly the shipments to London or Paris. She contacted CSA, the Czech state airline, and they agreed to carry the books to Prague free from London or Paris.

Then came the shocker. Continental's public relations department refused to fly the books to Europe for free. New was desperately disappointed, even angry. Talk to Terri New for more than a couple of minutes and the pride she has in "her" airline is very evident. And now they were turning down her request to bring classical literature and modern business techniques to an entire country. So determined was she to make Project Booklift a reality that she wrote a letter to Continental's then-chairman, Frank Lorenzo. This time it worked. Lorenzo gave the project his blessing, and Continental Airlines agreed to fly the donated books to London or Paris at no charge. They even put several middle-level managers around the U.S. in touch with Terri to offer their assistance.

Continental's current CEO was a little slower to embrace the idea. "I became aware of Project Booklift in 1990 while a senior vice president for the airline," says Bob Ferguson. "To be honest, my perspective at the time was not very different from that of many employees, which was essentially: why are we getting involved in an effort for a country that was not even on our route map?" But by the time Ferguson had become Continental's CEO in 1991, his opinion had changed. "I started to more fully understand the importance of Terry New's initiative and the critical role of the corporation in encouraging and supporting employee volunteerism," he adds. "Our airline supports employee volunteer efforts every day, but this particular project had obvious historical magnitude. I saw just how proud [it] made people feel. It lifted people out of the day-to-day reality of their work and made them feel better about themselves, their jobs, and the world in general."

By midsummer, her play was completed. Its premiere was on August 27, 1990, at the Wilshire Ebell Theater in Los Angeles, attended by eight hundred people. Terri asked each person attending *Voices of the Velvet Revolution* to bring a book to the play, which would launch Project Booklift. As word of this unusual "admission charge," and of the play itself, spread, newspaper reporters started calling Terri for interviews. As these articles were published, Terri's project came to be noticed by the local National Public Radio station, and they did a lengthy news story on her that was picked up by the network and broadcast on NPR stations nationwide.

The word was out. Terri's telephone started ringing day and night with people wanting to donate books to her cause. The son of a deceased attorney called, saying he had been waiting to do something special with his father's extensive library of classic literature and having heard of Project Booklift could think of no better cause. Ten bookstores in southern California embraced Project Booklift, not only as donors but also as local drop-off points for individuals with books to give.

Her much-welcomed but unanticipated barrage of donations caused a problem: how could she cost-effectively get them all to Los Angeles? Once again, her employer came to the rescue, and soon she could tell people across the U.S. to drop off their books to the local Continental Airlines office and they would periodically fly them free to a central consolidation point. Ladislav Brank, general manager of Boston's swank Bostonian Hotel, called. He is of Czech heritage and was so moved by Terri's project that he offered the hotel as a collection center for those in the Boston area. Federal Express also offered to fly books free of charge from those cities where Continental did not have a presence.

By this time, the management at Continental's Houston headquarters were both supportive and enthusiastic. Ray Scippa, the airline's employee communications director, wrote an article on Terri and Project Booklift for the flight attendants' magazine that drew a tremendous response from her colleagues around the country—and beyond: Continental's station manager in Montego Bay, Jamaica, called with books the local staff had collected. "All told, we probably had sixty to one hundred employees actively involved in gathering books in their communities," says Scippa.

Pursuing a Labor of Love

Collecting and coordinating the book donations were taking almost every waking hour of Terri New's life. "But I didn't think of it as 'giving' on my part," she says. "I really felt it was a labor of love." An apt description considering the many heartwarming personal inscriptions that donors wrote in their books. Terri tells of two particularly poignant messages: One was by the noted author Edward Albee, who sent one of his own works inscribed, "To my friends in Czechoslovakia. Brave, Persistent, Stubborn, Ingenious—and altogether spendid. Signed with deep affection." Continental Airlines' then-president, Hollis Harris, sent a leather-bound edition of *Thomas Jefferson and the New Nation* with the personal inscription, "To the people of Czechoslovakia, in honor of your great courage, commitment and love of freedom, we at Continental Airlines are proud to have played a role in Project Booklift." It was presented to President Vaclav Havel personally.

By the time Terri was ready to make her third trip to Czechoslovakia—her first for Project Booklift—an incredible forty thousand books had been donated and were ready for delivery. In making the first shipment, Terri was accompanied by some of the flight attendants and managers who had been most supportive of the program. After the exhausting flight from Los Angeles to London, followed by a long wait in transit and then the CSA flight to Prague, the team was ready to crawl into bed and sleep for twenty-four hours. "As I walked off the airplane, I noticed this large crowd of about 150 people who suddenly started moving toward me," recalls Terri. "I suddenly realized,

'Oh my God, they're here for me!' I was shocked." The Continental volunteers were ushered into a reception room for an official welcoming ceremony by the large group of Czech dignitaries. President Havel sent his personal representative, and the chancellor of Charles University also attended. A sampling of about three hundred books were displayed on the tables in the reception room, and when the Czech delegation saw the quantity and titles of the books that had been brought, many of them broke into tears. "I couldn't believe how much they cherished those books," says Ray Scippa. "They were oblivious to what else was happening in the room as they pored over them, examining each page as if it were the most valuable thing they'd ever seen." Czechoslovakia's foreign minister, Jiri Dientsbier, told Terri's team, "This is the first concrete evidence that the world cares about us."

Just seven days after Terri New arrived in Prague with forty thousand books, President George Bush arrived to help commemorate the first anniversary of the Velvet Revolution. After writing the Czech Declaration of Independence while in Washington, Thomas Masaryk had never brought it home. During the Communists' rule, U.S. authorities considered it safer to hold on to the original document; but now, more than seventy years after its creation, George Bush—the first American president to set foot on Czechoslovakian soil—presented President Vaclav Havel with the original copy of the Declaration, along with a replica of the Liberty Bell.

Terri New was overjoyed at the value her new Czech friends put on the books she brought. "So many of these were probably laying unread and unappreciated on bookshelves and garage floors across America," she says, "and it took so little to do something that means so much to these people." As she returned from Prague, Terri was more convinced than ever that this trip was not the culmination of Project Booklift—it was just the beginning. Her co-workers agreed. "Without exception, every person who went on that trip commented on what a wonderful thing it was for us to be involved in," recalls Ray Scippa.

As news reports of their trip created even greater interest in Project Booklift, the task became an all-consuming interest for

Terri. She was putting in sixteen-hour days answering calls and letters, arranging transportation, establishing collection drops, conducting media interviews, and driving around to pick up donated books personally. In the midst of this, she moved to Santa Barbara—which meant all the donated books in her garage had to go, too. "I moved forty-five thousand books by myself," the diminutive Terri groans. "Never again!" Finally, in the summer of 1991, she asked Continental for help. Ray Scippa agreed to take care of much of the shipping coordination and public relations work, removing an enormous burden from Terri. "Ray Scippa is one of the heartbeats of Continental's humanitarianism," she declares.

As the fall of 1991 approached, New merged Project Booklift with the Prague Spring Foundation, a Santa Barbara–based nonprofit organization. Not only would their experience help Terri's one-person operation, but as a nonprofit, tax-exempt foundation they could help her with grant applications. In November 1991, Terri New flew back to Prague with sixty thousand books. Once again she was received with deep gratitude and affection by Czech dignitaries. "It was amazing how much things had changed in just two years," she says. "The people now are joyous. The coffee houses that are such a part of Prague's bohemian culture are full, and people have vision and hope and a real belief in the future."

Project Booklift was becoming too successful. Getting sixty thousand books across the Atlantic on Continental's big Boeing 747s might have to be spread over two or three days. But from London and Paris, CSA flew only short-range, narrow-body aircraft with minimal cargo capacity. What little freight space they had was usually taken by revenue-producing cargo shipments, meaning it might take weeks to complete the transfer of sixty thousand books from their European gateway to Prague. Terri started planning her next shipment for June 1992, and she realized she must now find a better way to transport the books on their final leg. The most cost-effective method was by truck, and New applied for—and received—a grant from the United States Information Agency for the cost to truck future shipments from Paris to Czechoslovakia.

Books continued to pour in from numerous sources around the country: Friends of the Library from Ventura County, California; overstocked bookstores in Pittsburgh and Seattle; and her motivated co-workers at Continental's stations across the U.S. "Just as I think I have a count on the current number of books," Terri laughs, "I'll get calls from Continental employees saying, 'We've got 6,000 in Newark, 5,500 in Houston, and 4,000 in Denver.'" Richard Lisser, the airline's vice president in charge of Continental's huge Newark, New Jersey, hub, says, "Project Booklift has touched the hearts and minds of our local employees. The response extends from the lunchroom to the departure gates. Our local staff have truly rallied around this cause." In June 1992, Terri headed back to Czechoslovakia with an incredible shipment: one hundred thousand books. This time she also took her concert with her, performing the stories and songs from *Voices of the Velvet Revolution* to the very audiences who were her inspiration for the play back in 1989. Joining her in the cast was James Ragan, an American poet of Slovak descent who has been nominated for a Nobel Prize for his poetry.

She has asked that the books be distributed fairly throughout the country, and she was invited to the town of Pizek during the trip to witness the opening of the first English-language library. When she arrived in Pizek, Terri found the citizens waiting in the streets to greet her as if she were a foreign dignitary. She soon found out why they were so excited about her visit: to the people of Pizek, Terri New had done more for them than any visitor their village had ever known, and they had written a play in her honor. So that she would understand it, the performance was in English; they had worked on it for two years. As the children spoke the lines in perfect English it was Terri's turn to fight back tears. "It was such a beautiful evening of shared artistry," she says.

On January 1, 1993, Czechoslovakia ceased to exist, being replaced by two independent countries: the Czech Republic and the Republic of Slovakia. The transformation to democratic rule and free-market economies is going well, and outsiders credit the indomitable spirit of the citizenry for the progress. At the same time, Project Booklift continues. Its books are in the libraries of tiny rural villages such as Pizek and in big-city centers of academia like Prague's Charles University. They are distributed to all corners of the nation: to Masaryk University of Moldavia in Brno and Comenius University in the Slovak capital, Bratislava. The numbers alone are impressive: Terri New has so far delivered over a quarter of a million books. But instead of just imagining her idea as a huge pile of books, consider the following: There are now attorneys practicing law in Czechoslovakia who read their first book on democratic justice from a Project Booklift shipment. Thriving businesses are making profits thanks to the owners who read management and accounting books never before available in that country until Terri's books arrived. Students are studying the classics, drama classes are performing their first Shakespearean plays, and political science students are reading Solzhenitsyn's *Gulag Archipelago* and facts about their own country's history—all for the first time, using books from Project Booklift. "Milan Kundera is a Czech writer whose work was banned under the Communists," says Terri. "We've taken many of his books over so that his countrymen will be able to read his works for the very first time, although they'll have to read them in English until a Czech translation is printed."

Terri continues to champion Project Booklift, and she recently won a Golden Mike award for a documentary program she produced while in Czechoslovakia. She has created a weekly television alternative to violent cartoons for children to watch on Saturday mornings: "Our House," produced by her own Insight Productions, will be an interactive children's television show, "sort of a cross between 'The Waltons' and 'Little Rascals,'" she explains. After all the sixteen-hour days and the telephone bills and the missed social life while putting Project Booklift together, would she do it again? "Absolutely!" Terri affirms. "Just seeing those wonderful people who had suffered under such oppression put together a peaceful revolution where not a single shot was fired, not a life was taken—they gave the world a gift with that lesson in peaceful change. I just wanted to give them a gift in return."

I want you to share your food with the hungry
and bring into your own homes those who are
helpless, poor and destitute.

Clothe those who are cold
and don't hide from relatives who need help.

If you do these things,
God will shed His own glorious light upon you.

He will heal you; your godliness will lead you forward,
and goodness will be a shield before you,
and the glory of the Lord will protect you from behind.

—Isaiah 58: 7–8

12

. . . .

Chevron's Clare LeBrun

Restoring Yosemite's Splendor

To many people across the U.S., the Chevron name simply conjures up an image of the corner gas station. But residents of the San Francisco Bay Area recognize the company as one of the largest corporate names in the country. Huge petrochemical plants dot the Bay Area fed by the 1.4 million barrels of oil and gas the company produces each day. The refined petroleum is sold to twenty-eight thousand outlets in the U.S. and a dozen foreign countries in the form of gasoline, diesel, and aviation fuel. Chevron's chemical facilities are in fourteen states and France, Japan, and Brazil, and the firm mines for coal and platinum throughout the Midwest, South, and western U.S. With operations so vast and so concentrated on handling natural resources by pipeline, barge, and tankers, it becomes an easy target for the public and press to point at when citing examples of harm to the environment. Yet Chevron places a very high importance on being a good ecological steward. In the 1992 annual report, one of the primary stated corporate objectives was to "Give high priority to environmental, public and governmental concerns." In fact, beginning in 1992, all operating divisions of Chevron were required to develop and implement strategies aimed at meeting specific environmental protection goals.

Clare LeBrun joined Chevron in 1980 in the ortho chemcial division as a writer of horticulture books. After her assignment in that department ended, she moved to the consumer affairs office in the company's San Francisco facility. "I don't know what it is about Chevron people," she says, "but they seem to have a very deep, personal sense of caring for the environment. Maybe it's because our products, if handled improperly, could damage the ecosystem, but more than any other need, I've noticed Chevron employees volunteer for environmental issues without a second thought."

In the summer of 1987, tremendous forest fires swept through the area northeast of San Francisco. From the very first day, many Chevron employees volunteered to help the forest service. Many of them backpacked into the deep woods; others made reconnaissance trips to provide valuable information on what assistance was most urgently needed and where it should be sent.

In the fall of 1988, the rangers of Mendocino National Forest asked for help from Chevron employees in arranging a weekend work camp to clean up areas of this once-pristine wilderness. "I was a real skeptic at first," LeBrun recalls. "How on earth was I going to be able to coordinate a hundred people with feeding, lodging, and access via a dirt logging road—all in the dark?" However, Clare did put the word out to her co-workers. The response was overwhelming, and she remembers being "enthralled" at that first work weekend at Mendocino. "This was not an 'I' project'; this was very much a 'we' campaign both in the planning and the execution," she says. One hundred and fifty people showed up for that first fall weekend of hard physical labor repairing trails, clearing downed trees, laying erosion-prevention material in preparation for the winter rains, and building check dams; one crew did nothing but cook. Chevron helped the economy of the tiny town of Lakeport at the park's entrance by paying for the team's shovels, axes, and food, which were to be acquired locally.

The weekend was so successful that the employees decided to return for a similar trip the following spring and again in October 1989. The spring trip involved planting trees and went very well, but one week before the planned October foray, the area was hit by the devastating earthquake that destroyed so many homes, freeways, and buildings throughout the San Francisco area. "We had to cancel that trip because everything was so disorganized," remembers Clare. It took weeks for the disruption caused by the earthquake to subside and for things at Chevron to return to normal. With the Mendocino effort on hold, Clare LeBrun was searching for another volunteerism project for herself and her colleagues. It wasn't long before she was introduced to the Yosemite Fund.

Uncovering a Need

Initiated in 1988 by the National Park Service, the project's primary goal was to restore the black oaks that once dominated Yosemite's woodlands. Over the last century, tens of thousands of majestic black oak trees have been destroyed to make way for park buildings, trails, parking lots, or roads to accommodate the increasing number of visitors. Well-intentioned fire prevention methods have also taken their toll in black oaks. "Oaks need a lot of sunlight to thrive," says Yosemite Park restorationist Kristin Ramsey, "and they depend on the natural occurrence of fire to clear out the dense, shady forests. By suppressing fires over the years, we've allowed conifers to take root and grow; now, those pines are competing for sunlight and crowding out the oaks." Chevron had been approached by the park service for financial assistance with the Yosemite Fund and in the mid eighties had given it a $250,000 corporate donation. When she discovered the fund's needs in 1989, Clare LeBrun suggested an employee volunteerism project to clean up Yosemite.

"It sounds like it was very easy, but it really wasn't," Clare recalls today. She had to assuage the liability fears of executives and staff attorneys. Then project approval from both the park service and corporate management had to be secured. But release forms were finally printed, and management said, "Go for it. Let's do it!" "Once word of our project got out, there was no stopping it," Clare remembers. "It took on a life of its own." They called the program Project Yosemite.

Clare talked to every coordinator of the Mendocino project, and they loved the idea. It was to be an ambitious undertaking requiring fifty workers, ten supervisors, and a ten-person cooking crew for each of the eight weekends selected in 1990 and the seven weekends in 1991. The program was employee-driven from beginning to end, with the rangers establishing the exact work to be completed, prioritizing the tasks, and providing training to the supervisory crew who would travel to Yosemite a day ahead of the other volunteers. "Yosemite is a really sexy place" declares LeBrun. "People want to go there if they've never been there before, or if they've gone every weekend of their life. The response was so overwhelming we had four times the number of volunteers we could handle." She set up a strict registration procedure to handle the demand.

Coordinating the Logistics

When she first hatched the Project Yosemite idea, Clare LeBrun had no concept of the time, energy, and patience it would take to coordinate such an undertaking. She had to demonstrate complete fairness to her co-workers, regardless of their rank or whether they were close friends or unknown employees at a distant facility. For example, when she accepted an employee on a work trip, they were allowed to bring one guest. Period. It didn't matter if a colleague in the next office had twin teenage sons who adored Yosemite—only one could come. She also had to carefully balance the geographic source of volunteers. "This wasn't a Bay Area project," Clare says. "I wanted it to be open to Chevron employees from throughout California." Generally, the staff in her San Francisco office would receive her trip announcements via internal mail long before employees in a work area hundreds of miles away. So Molly Rights, a colleague with considerable computer expertise, designed a software program that prorated blocks of space on each trip specifically for each of the fifty Chevron work areas around California. Clare would only deviate from that allocation for last-minute cancellations.

The printed announcement flyers showed a special telephone number to call for complete trip details. Employees' social security numbers, supplied on the trip reservation forms, enabled

Molly's program to compile a data base of participants who could be easily traced if they were transferred or promoted to different locations. Reservation forms required first, second, and third choices of weekend and were time-stamped as they came in. As each work weekend approached, Clare would prepare and send out information packets to participants explaining the rules, times, what was expected of them, and what to bring; each packet contained a map and directions, a liability release form, and car-pool details. She imposed a one-trip limit until everyone who wanted to go had done so, unless that person was willing to vol-unteer the extra time to become a supervisor.

"I remember people being so anxious to get on a weekend work trip that they'd come in to the office at 6:30 A.M. on the day registrations were accepted and slide their application under the door," recalls David McMurry, Chevron's environmental contri-butions counsel.

The first work trip occurred over Earth Day weekend. Employees from across the state of California converged on Yosemite after work on Friday. This was sometimes an arduous task in itself: the park was a four-hour drive from San Francisco, six hours from Bakersfield, and a grueling eight-hour road trip for employees in the Los Angeles/Santa Barbara area. The Bakers-field people brought a chuck wagon with them. "I didn't even know what a chuck wagon was," admits Clare. "It was huge—big enough to cook for three hundred people, so we ate really well." Friday nights were typically quiet, with people eating en route and arriving at different times. Clare would meet the arrivals per-sonally and show them around the campground. Dawn would break on Saturday to the rich aroma of breakfast being prepared. Everyone would meet at 7 A.M. and enjoy the chuck wagon breakfast together. At 8 A.M., the park rangers would arrive and conduct a brief history lesson of the park and give instructions on the tasks to be accomplished. Suitably fed, trained, and inspired, the Chevron volunteers would start their work day. Boxed lunches were provided to avoid wasting the time to return to the base camp at midday.

It is hard not to be enchanted by the natural beauty of Yosemite. El Capitan rises from the valley floor as if looking down from heaven to watch over the park's visitors. At night, city folk can see only tiny dots of yellow light scattered across its towering face—the campfires of climbers huddled up for a night's respite from their ascent. The only sounds are those of the gurgling creek broken up frequently by owls calling to each other. During the day it is a common sight to see deer, rabbits, and coyotes—and eagles swooping majestically. Turn a little and the spectacular waterfalls that cascade like ribbons of white silk from the mountaintops captivate the visitor as if time stands still.

Even in this setting, the volunteers' work was far from glamorous. In a typical trip, one team would spend the weekend bent over to weed for hours at a time. Another would plant new black oak seedlings in the area that colleagues had just prepared. When they had finished, another crew would erect sturdy fences around the perimeter to keep park visitors from trampling the young trees. Meanwhile, in other areas, working parties would be raking leaves, clearing brush from overgrown trails, and replanting other plants indigenous to the Yosemite area, such as ferns and raspberries. To protect the freshly propagated transplants from the park's voracious deer population, workers would build screens of natural materials such as leaves and branches around the planting area. When an area is overused, even by walkers, the ground becomes so compacted that oxygen is prevented from reaching the root system, and vegetation, wildflowers—even large trees—will die. "Some of the high-visibility areas had been so heavily trampled that they were bare of anything growing," says Clare. "After we'd cleaned out the weeds, replenished the native vegetation, and mulched each sapling to conserve water, the area looked wild again."

Park rangers would pair people with strenuous and non-strenuous tasks, thus allowing them to attack the really heavy-duty chores in shifts. "There was some real grunt work," Clare says, wincing as she recalls the details. "Everybody wanted to plant trees, but that just wasn't possible. Two of the biggest projects were to weed large meadows by eliminating all non-native vegetation and to remove an old parking lot." The latter proved to be a monster. A large parking area had been used for years with trucks, cars, and campers compressing the asphalt into the ground. Since it had been discontinued as a parking lot, the surface had cracked, and weeds and shrubs—even huge pine trees—had pushed their way up through the crevices. The Chevron team had to remove the undergrowth, often using crowbars to pry up every piece of asphalt and then carry all the waste out by wheelbarrow. "Was that ever backbreaking work?" asks LeBrun, rhetorically. "My husband still has the bruises to prove it!"

The weather was often unpredictable. On their very first weekend work trip in April they had snow. At other times, the sun was almost intolerably hot.

When Clare saw how many people had signed up for each trip—even before the initial visit—she worried about how the park service could accommodate them all. She had been told by the rangers that her groups would not be placed in the public campgrounds, because it would cost the park service too much in lost camping fees. So on their first weekend, they found themselves placed in a very remote campground, accessible by a dirt track five thousand feet up a mountainside. They brought in their own water and rented portable toilets from a local outfitter. After they had spent just four weekends at this tranquil site, a forest fire destroyed it and several acres of adjacent woodlands. For the rest of the year, teams were housed either in a valley campground alongside Sentinel Creek, or in a section of a public camping facility. In the second year, the park service opened up Old Wilderness Campground—aptly named, since the volunteers found no water or toilet facilities when they arrived. Once again, PortaPotties were rented, and the Yosemite Fund built a water tank on a trailer for them.

"I felt like a mother hen sometimes," Clare laughs. "I'd spend half the week on the phone making sure the park rangers, PortaPotties, or shuttle bus for our work teams were all arranged; then I'd spend my weekend ushering people on and off buses and telling them not to exhaust themselves but to enjoy the scenery as they worked."

By 5 P.M. on Saturdays, the volunteers who just a few hours earlier had been the energetic Chevron work crews would drag their tired, aching bodies back to the base camp. The cooking team, "the unsung heroes," according to Clare, would have prepared a veritable feast in the chuck wagon. "Dinner wasn't sloppy joes," she says. "They'd serve us barbecued beef and pork chops and grilled fresh fish." The cooking crews were so enthusiastic about their volunteer duties that many of them took vacation time so they would be able to arrive at Yosemite and set everything up in time for the group. After a hearty alfresco meal, someone would light the campfire, and groups of people who had never met before but who shared the same employer and love of the environment would enjoy the fellowship. Before long, a guitar would be produced, and this group of sore but happy volunteers would sing long into the clear, crisp mountain night. On Sunday morning, everyone would again meet for a hot breakfast and then work, usually on less strenuous tasks, from 8 A.M. to noon. After bidding farewell to their newfound friends, they would make the long drive home, having to report for work just a few hours later, on Monday morning.

Every participant received a custom-designed Project Yosemite T-shirt, and the only way to obtain one was to have completed a weekend work camp. They became quite a status symbol back at the Chevron offices. A group photograph was taken on every trip, and each employee received a framed copy of it above a plaque of appreciation, signed by the company's vice chairman.

Reaping the Rewards

The employees who went begged for the opportunity to return. "Chevron was always getting beaten up in the press," LeBrun recalls. "This project made employees feel so good that the company would do it. People would return to work so energized that I know their productivity increased the next week—you could see it." Grace Freasier, a marketing assistant in the Chevron Products USA office in San Francisco, agrees. "Project Yosemite was just wonderful," she gushes. "I've lived in California since 1962 and had never been to Yosemite before." After experiencing the first work weekend, she went on all but two trips over the next two years, often as a supervisor, cooking crew member, or last-minute fill-in. Grace recalls meeting "the nicest people" from other work areas around the state. "By Sunday you'd feel like your family just got a little bigger," she says. But her favorites were the park rangers, whom she came to know quite well through her frequent visits. "They love the park so much, their love of it and of the environment rubbed off on us. They taught us so many things, like how to walk across a meadow so as not to cause damage. They taught us, as visitors, to take ownership in that park." Grace confesses that her work trips raised her environmental consciousness so much that she now yells at people she sees dropping trash in the street. "I feel great that Chevron encourages volunteerism," she says. "It promotes goodwill among both employees and the public. The cost to the company is nothing compared to the increased employee morale, networking opportunities, and positive public image. It makes me feel good to work for a company that supports such work."

Contributions counsel David McMurry agrees. "Project Yosemite changed a lot of peoples' minds," he states. "It wasn't some slick public relations operation dreamed up by the marketing people. It was employee driven, by volunteers who showed, regardless of their rank, how many people really care." McMurry noted that there were times when a secretary was a work trip supervisor over a corporate vice president, "But on those trips nobody had any rank or talked about who they were back at the office."

Clare LeBrun made five of the eight weekend work trips in the first year and two the next season. "By then," she admits, "I was starting to burn out." So she trained her backup person to take over the final few weekends. "It was such a beautiful partnership between employees and rangers, it produced lasting friendships," she says. "It was a 'total win' situation: Yosemite, Chevron, the employees—all benefited from Project Yosemite."

As the tourists left and autumn's chilly winds sent waves of blazing red, yellow, and orange leaves to earth, the Chevron team collected acorns from the mature black oak trees of Yosemite. "It's called 'preservation of the gene pool," LeBrun explains. "You don't want to bring oak seedlings from, say, the Napa Valley into Yosemite, because they wouldn't be native vegetation." So the thousands of Yosemite acorns were turned over to a local horticulturist for propagation and subsequent replanting in the Park.

In 1991, Mike Finley, Yosemite's superintendent, sent a letter of recommendation nominating Clare LeBrun and Project Yosemite for the President's Environmental Quality Award. Clare also received an award from Chevron commending her for the project. A review of just the first year's accomplishments shows why. In only eight weekends, Clare and her volunteers

- Planted 120 black oak seedlings
- Removed five tons of asphalt from a fifty-year-old parking lot
- Aerated and mulched 38,000 square feet of compacted soil
- Installed 2,500 feet of fencing
- Collected nearly 10,000 acorns
- Unearthed ceramic and glassware items dating from 1850 to 1930

And when the work teams returned to base camp, the cooking crews

- Scrambled 168 dozen eggs
- Brewed 1,680 cups of coffee
- Cooked 140 pounds of ham
- Marinated and barbecued 245 chickens
- Picked up and delivered 840 boxed lunches
- Hauled 700 gallons of water from the valley to the campground
- Grilled hundreds of fish
- Barbecued so much beef they lost count

By the end of 1992, about eleven hundred volunteers had worked twenty weekends over the three years, contributing about 10,600 hours of work to Project Yosemite. Had the park service had to pay for this, just the labor Chevron's volunteers contributed would have cost about $110,000. And despite all the early concerns of injury and liability that almost stopped the project from getting off the ground, the only injury during those 10,600 work hours was a bee sting.

Would Clare LeBrun do it again? "Absolutely!" she instantly affirms. "And there are not many things I'd do differently." She gazes into her coffee for a long moment, and then this transplanted East Coaster who had never set foot in Yosemite National Park before this project tells of planning the weekend work trips closest to a full moon so people could see the owls at night. She speaks of the hitherto-faceless co-workers who came together as one around a mountain campfire, and of the difference their grandchildren's grandchildren will see in this cherished national heirloom because of the work she inspired. Writing for an article in Chevron's employee magazine, Yosemite Park restorationist Kristin Ramsey says, "You know that song, 'They paved paradise, put up a parking lot'? Well, we're doing the opposite. We're taking out the parking lots and re-creating paradise."

When I am employed in serving others, I do not look upon myself as conferring favors but paying debts.

—Benjamin Franklin

13

. . . .

Boeing's Dan North

Sending Humanitarian Supplies
on a Wing and a Prayer

Daniel North loves helping people. Yet in a way, he felt as if he had missed out on something important. As a young man he saw his friends and fellow church members fly off to perform humanitarian mission work for World Vision in developing areas such as Central America and Cambodia, yet he was always either finishing his education or unable to leave his job and could never join them. Dan joined the Boeing Company in the procurement department in Wichita, Kansas, in 1979 and won excellent reviews for his performance. In 1989, he earned a promotion to the company's sprawling headquarters in Seattle.

His interest in helping the needy, particularly in developing countries, remained strong. As he settled in to his new Puget Sound environs, Dan crossed paths with people active in humanitarian service. From them, he learned a surprising fact: many agencies either warehouse or have relatively easy and cheap access to huge quantities of medical, nutritional, or relief supplies; the problem getting them to the needy is the enormous cost of shipping. For example, a 20,000-pound medical supply shipment from Seattle to Khartoum, Sudan, costs $2.94 per pound, totalling $58,800 for the entire shipment; a 15,000-pound consignment of blood-testing equipment from New York to AIDS-ravaged Kinshasa, Zaire, would cost $68,850; and 10,000 pounds of baby formula from Chicago to Calcutta, India, would cost an agency $20,000.

Dan realized that there was a tremendous need for a more cost-effective way of sending donated goods to where they were so desperately needed. He even expended considerable effort calling small cargo carriers and asking them to transport the freight on a free or discounted basis, but to no avail. In fact, in talking with some agencies he discovered that shipping was often the largest cost in their entire operation. In the spring of 1992, Dan North heard about an incident at Boeing that piqued his interest: apparently, paper is a very scarce commodity in Ethiopia, so when Ethiopian Airlines took delivery of a new Boeing jetliner, they willingly allowed a large quantity of donated books to be carried aboard. What a great idea, he remembers thinking. Several months went by, and Dan noticed another item in the employee newspaper. This time, CSA, the airline of the newly independent Czech Republic, took a shipment of medical supplies along when their crew made a delivery flight from Seattle's Boeing Field to Prague.

When Dan talked to the people at Boeing who had arranged for the cargo to be carried free, they did not paint a very encouraging picture. "The company had spent an enormous amount of time and effort to arrange those two shipments," he says, "and you have to realize, Boeing is in the airplane delivery business, and here they were tying up valuable resources and staff collecting humanitarian supplies. That's the agencies' business, not ours." The difficulties encountered were so complex that they managed to put shipments on only two flights in five months, although Boeing was actually delivering airplanes at the rate of one per day in 1992. North realized that this could be the missing link he had been searching for, but first a system had to be designed to facilitate easier handling. He had a challenge.

Much of Dan North's spare time in the weeks ahead was devoted to coming up with such a plan. He spoke with all parties who had been involved in the Czech and Ethiopian flights and with principals of several relief agencies. "I went to the company with a suggested system that would expand the program to many more flights and yet not be disruptive to their normal delivery routine," he says. "And Boeing accepted the proposal on a trial basis." To some, it might seem surprising that a huge multilay-ered corporation would accept a single employee's idea that in-volved changes in one of their time-tested routines. Others, such as thirty-seven-year Boeing veteran Bob Krull, disagree. "The company's mission is customer satisfaction—and commitment to the community," Krull says, "and Dan North simply provided an answer that created the perfect fit. It just made sense." "What I did was consider us to have a worldwide community, not just the Puget Sound area," adds Dan.

New commercial airliners are ordered years in advance, so Dan's first job was to acquire the list of scheduled deliveries for the next twelve months. On that list he could see some obvious opportunities, such as the date when the national airline of a de-veloping country with known hunger or medical needs was scheduled to accept a new jet. Dan pored over the delivery sched-ule—not excluding from consideration an airline from an indus-trialized nation, such as Germany—and then went to see several of the international service agencies in the northwestern United States. "If we could offer you free transportation of humanitar-ian supplies to these delivery destinations, could you use it?" he asked them. Time and again the answer came back enthusiasti-cally in the affirmative.

Once an agency advised Dan of the specific type of freight it wanted to send and the destination it served, he could match it up with the delivery schedule and then approach the airline, for it was, after all, that company's airplane, crew, and fuel that would be used. Since he had no contacts established with the airline community, he would discuss his proposal with the Boeing sales-person who had worked for years with the foreign carrier and was thoroughly familiar with the country's customs and political nu-ances. Once the airline had agreed to carry the shipment, Dan would coordinate the minute details. In many cases, the airline was owned by the country in which it was based, so its officers were obviously delighted, for humanitarian and political reasons, to take tons of donated relief supplies to their homeland. But even privately owned carriers with no financial or ethnic ties to a particular country were often pleased to carry the cargo Dan was arranging.

Dan was given the green light by Boeing in early October

1992. "I figured that if everything went my way, I would be lucky to get the first flight with relief supplies in the air by Thanksgiving," he says. "In fact, it took off just ten days later, on October 22. By Thanksgiving, we'd shipped stuff on six flights!" He recalls the emotion he felt on that brisk fall day when "his" first flight, a TACA Airlines Boeing 737, took off from Boeing Field filled with medicines and other needed supplies for the people in the carrier's homeland, El Salvador. Since then, the program has expanded beyond his wildest expectations, partly because of the simple system Dan established and partly because he is now actively working with the international relief agencies to market Boeing's new service.

Once the airline has agreed to carry the shipment and Dan starts working with them, he rarely gets a full night's sleep. When it is the work day for much of the world, it is nighttime in Seattle. So when managers of a Middle Eastern airline need to check a detail with him from their office at 2 P.M., it's 4 A.M. in Seattle. When an executive in Thailand needs to talk with Dan at 4 P.M. local time, Dan gets awakened at 1 A.M. But North loves what he is doing so much that instead of complaining, he gladly takes the call and has even installed a fax near his bed to facilitate instant day and night global communication at the customer's convenience, even though it means making or receiving calls in the middle of the night. "At first, I thought I could handle one or two flights a month as a voluntary service without it affecting my real job at Boeing," he says. "But before I knew it, the idea had grown so quickly that we've never done fewer than three flights a month, and in just the first ten months we've done thirty-five flights." Finally, a vice president of Boeing came to see the guy behind this service that was making so many people proud. The exhausted Dan North said that he just couldn't see how such a frenetic pace could continue without his job performance suffering. The vice president made an immediate decision and offered to create a new position for Dan to be the full-time relief project coordinator. It was the proverbial offer he could not refuse.

The system is now finely honed: Dan contacts a relief agency with a specific upcoming delivery destination. The agency specifies the size and weight of the medical supply load for that flight. After going through the sales department to seek airline approval, which is almost always given, Dan coordinates with the agency for collection and delivery of the freight to Boeing in "ready to ship" condition. Boeing then loads the cargo onto the aircraft, and Dan checks to ensure all the required documentation is completed. When the airline takes delivery, the cargo is on its way at six hundred miles per hour to a nation of hungry, sick, or otherwise needy people.

The types of goods shipped and the generosity of the airlines still never cease to amaze Dan North. "Thousands of books were destroyed when a hurricane devastated the tiny island nation of Fiji," he states, "So Air New Zealand just agreed to take fourteen thousand pounds of books on their delivery flight to Auckland, where Fiji's flag carrier, Air Pacific, will shuttle the books on to Fiji." He rattles off a veritable United Nations of airlines that have made similar missions of mercy: Hungary's MALEV took delivery of two Boeing 767 jets and loaded each of them with forty-five thousand pounds of food for war-torn Croatia; South African Airways carried medical supplies to a hospital in Swaziland aboard its new long-range 747-400; and Poland's LOT ferried clothing and medical supplies to Eastern Europe.

"Two of the flights literally brought tears to my eyes," Dan admits. "Condor, the charter subsidiary of Germany's Lufthansa, took medication and food to Munich then trucked the supplies to Romania, where it was taken to the orphanages I had seen in such dreadful condition on television. The other was a Malaysian Airlines delivery where they took relief supplies to Cambodia—which closed the circle from where I wished I could do something to help those people after my friends went there so many years ago."

North is happy to work with any organization, provided they meet two criteria: they must be a tax-exempt, nonprofit agency, and they must demonstrate the ability to deliver the supplies to the intended recipients from the airport at which the delivery flight lands. "There are three legs to this stool," he explains. "First, from the agency to Boeing—that's the agency's responsibility. Next, we work with our customer, the airline, to get the freight from Boeing to the destination airport—say, Budapest, Hungary. But quite often, the most difficult and most expensive leg is that last hundred miles—say, from Budapest to a remote mountain village in Romania. I have to see evidence that the agency has the resources to make the final leg, or all the freight will sit in the airline's terminal in Budapest, causing disruption to them."

Obviously, an important part of Dan's job is creating the least possible inconvenience and expense for the airlines. For that reason, he rarely asks for more than forty-five thousand pounds to be carried, because any more than that starts to add considerably to the fuel cost of the flight. He also never—with one exception—asks an airline to make a stop en route to pick up or drop off the cargo, since such an interruption costs tens of thousands of dollars and is enormously disruptive.

The one exception was when Air Seychelles, the flag carrier of the tiny island nation in the Indian Ocean, took delivery of a Boeing 757. Two cooperating charitable organizations, Friends of the West and Samaritan's Purse, needed desperately to get ten thousand pounds of medical and school supplies from Seattle to Somalia. Air Seychelles agreed to drop off the cargo in Nairobi, Kenya, whence it was flown by a United Nations relief flight to neighboring Somalia. "As it turns out, Air Seychelles was planning to start a new airline service to the Seychelles from Nairobi, using that very aircraft," says North, "so they were able to gain some good public relations by stopping off there with the relief supplies." That was the first, and only, flight on which Dan has accompanied his life-saving cargo. Upon arrival in Nairobi after the exhausting flight from Seattle, he took a tiny Cessna piloted by a Swedish UN worker on his final leg to Mogadishu. He witnessed firsthand the awful conditions under which the people were living and saw how vital the service was of the agencies he dealt with daily. "Seeing the tragic conditions of those people has imprinted on my brain forever how lucky we are in the U.S.," he says. "But it also showed me that my being in Mogadishu does absolutely no good. I can sit in my office in Seattle and do much more to help those in need around the world."

And so that is what he does. By day from his office, by

night from his home, Dan North is a one-person department on whose door there is never a "Closed" sign. This quiet, sincere young man's idea is already, after just one year, sending supplies that are saving the lives of tens of thousands of people on a flight a week. Asked about his dreams, he replies, "My first goal has already been achieved. But from here on my dream is to show that this is not a flash-in-the-pan idea but that it is an ongoing program. Then I want to expand the shipments to wherever there is human suffering in the world by strengthening that last leg in the delivery chain. To perhaps help establish a worldwide network of freight forwarders who could quickly and cheaply get our arriving cargo to where it is really needed."

"It's made a fantastic difference to our ministry of helping the needy around the world," says Louise Short, Africa coordinator for Friends of the West. "Before Dan came along with the Boeing project, it was just too expensive to ship by air, and it took so long to ship medical supplies by sea that many lives were lost during the transit time. Now that we're able to ship medical and literacy supplies with Boeing's customers we've been able to help tens of thousands of people in need. In just the first year, we have shipped to Romania, Bosnia, Somalia, Uganda, South Africa, and Albania."

In an industry that has seen massive layoffs due to the financially beleaguered airline industry's new-aircraft cancellations, it is refreshing to see a company look beyond the bottom line and far beyond its local community. It is also enlightening to meet an employee so unabashedly happy and proud in his job. "I am so lucky, because I get to meet the great people in this world: those who actually do the humanitarian work. And I really believe I have the best job there is in the Boeing Company," he says. There are probably a few thousand children in Romania, peasants in El Salvador, and well-fed residents of Somalia that would agree with you, Dan.

What good is it, my brothers and sisters,
if you say you have faith but do not have works?

Can faith save you?

If a brother or sister is naked and lacks daily food,
and one of you says to them,
"Go in peace, keep warm and eat your fill,"
and you do not supply their bodily needs,
what is the good of that?

So faith by itself, if it has not works, is dead.

   —James 2: 14–17

14

· ·

Merrill Lynch's Bill Schreyer

Sharing Christmas with
Ten Thousand Friends

Christmastime, to paraphrase Charles Dickens, is the best of times, the worst of times. For Christians and Jews alike, the Christmas and Hanukkah season is a time of joyous celebration, of parties and the joys of giving, and receiving, gifts. But as some lonely people, especially the elderly "empty nesters," see all those around them in a festive mood and receive myriad messages of family togetherness on television and in stores, they sink into a deep depression. Indeed, one of the real tragedies of the Christmas season in America is that while it is a time for celebration and love for many, it is also the period when suicides are at their annual peak.

William A. Schreyer has been an active supporter of voluntary community service for most of his life. By 1980, he had risen almost to the top rung of the career ladder at Merrill Lynch, Pierce, Fenner & Smith and was based at their world headquarters at One Liberty Plaza in New York's financial district. One day, his driver was telling him about a report he had heard describing the plight of many senior citizens: alone at Christmas, too poor to afford a telephone, and therefore unable to talk to their distant loved ones. Long after the subject had changed, Bill Schreyer's mind kept coming back to the conversation. As his hectic schedule shuttled him between meetings in New York and

Merrill Lynch offices around the world, he just couldn't put that picture of those sad senior citizens to rest. Finally, he decided, it was time to do something about it. But what? There was no way that giving money to them would be spent as it was intended, and it was impractical to pay for telephones to be installed in their homes just for Christmas Day. "Wait a minute," he thought. "We can't take phones to them, but why not bring them to our phones?"

"Our business relies on telephones," says Stephen L. Hammerman, vice chairman of Merrill Lynch. "We have whole floors filled with desks and telephones." All of which, Bill Schreyer knew, would be sitting empty on Christmas Day. So he did what the company is famous for in its investment division: an intensive research study, this time to determine whether such a service would be of interest to the senior citizens and also whether other employees might be willing to donate time on Christmas Day to help him run the project. He quickly discovered that the answer to both questions was a resounding yes. The project was a go.

Bill called his idea Christmas Calls, and as the 1980 holiday season approached, he put the finishing touches on the program. It was decided that it would be too burdensome for Merrill Lynch to handle the seniors' invitations directly, so the company contacted agencies in the New York area that work with them continually, such as the welfare department and the Salvation Army. These agencies were responsible for selecting the people who were legitimately in need of the service, and then it was up to them to arrange for bus transportation to and from One Liberty Plaza. Once there, Bill arranged to give every senior citizen a desk and one hour's unlimited worldwide use of a telephone. They could make as many calls as they liked, for as long as they wanted, to any telephone number on the planet during that one hour. It was an offer unlike any they had ever seen before.

On Christmas Day, Bill Schreyer was at the office before dawn. Soon afterwards, an employee volunteer showed up, and then another, and another, until by nine o'clock on Christmas morning, eight staff members had given up spending the day with their families in order to make it special for others. As the senior citizens arrived, one of the volunteers would warmly greet them and then escort the grateful guests to their assigned offices. Many of them were unfamiliar with the telephone system—especially with the complex international dialing codes—so the Merrill Lynch employee would stay and dial the number until the caller was connected with the right person. Then the employee would leave the room to allow complete privacy. The project was an un-reserved success, and the one hundred senior citizens, many with tears of joy, profusely thanked the volunteers as they were helped back onto the buses for the ride home. The only question the em-ployees had for Bill Schreyer that Christmas afternoon was, "When can we sign up to do this for next year?"

It didn't take a year for the word to get out to other em-ployees about the Christmas Calls program, and long before the next Christmas there was such an increase in volunteers that a de-lighted Bill Schreyer increased the number of invitations to addi-tional agencies. Each year saw more employee volunteers wel-coming an ever-increasing number of senior citizens. Soon, employees were calling from Merrill Lynch branch offices asking if they could offer a similar service to senior citizens in their local communities. "Of course you can," said an obviously happy Schreyer. By Christmas of 1992, just twelve years after that first Christmas Calls project in which one office with 8 volunteers opened its doors to 100 seniors, Merrill Lynch operated the pro-gram in 120 cities in 13 countries. It took over 1,000 volun-teers—600 in New York alone—to help the 14,800 senior citi-zens with their calls.

Many employees celebrate their Christmas meal and fam-ily gathering on Christmas Eve, and then the entire family helps out on the Christmas Calls project the next day. "The concept is such a simple one," said one volunteer. "A lot of people need to make calls but don't have the ability to. We have the phones and provide the ability. We also have a lot of people with big hearts." Stephen Hammerman remembers times when it would not be en-tirely truthful to say he was happy to be there. "I'd show up in the dark at 6 A.M. on Christmas Day and stand around in the bit-terly cold, deserted street, and I'd think to myself, what on earth am I doing here?" he admits. "And then the first busload would come along, and I'd help all those dear people to their phones— and I'd be warm for the rest of the day."

Each year has been different, according to the Merrill Lynch volunteers. Employees in the company's Little Rock, Arkansas, office were stunned when a group of elderly nuns called Mother Teresa in Calcutta, India, and got through, taking a moment on that sacred Christian holiday to greet the woman who has given her entire life to the suffering poor. Another man had had no contact with his aged mother for fifty years until he used Christmas Calls to reach her in London.

As the decade of the eighties came to a close and the Iron Curtain crumbled into oblivion, another set of opportunities became available for U.S. immigrants to finally contact their loved ones back in Eastern Europe. "I remember a woman who called her relatives in Minsk after the Berlin Wall fell and Russia was opened up again," recalls Hammerman, "and for the first time, she got through. As she left the office an hour later, tears were streaming down her face. She turned to me and smiled appreciatively as she said, 'Only in America.'" Stephen Hammerman adds that he personally received an unexpected benefit from Christmas Calls. Last year, as on many Christmases, the story of their project received press coverage; the Associated Press dispatched a short story on the program with a photograph and a quotation from Hammerman. A few weeks later, Steve received a letter from a person in Australia with the same last name who had read about the Christmas Calls program—and seen Hammerman's quote— after his local Australian newspaper had printed the article from the AP newswire. As it happens, both men had spent some effort tracing their family trees, and they discovered that they are distantly related.

Not everything goes according to plan. One year, just as the first buses arrived at the Merrill Lynch headquarters, the entire telephone system failed. Stephen Hammerman was present that day and remembers holding the senior citizens at bay while he quickly summoned the communications department staff to determine the problem. "Whatever it was couldn't be remedied quickly," he recalls, "but they discovered that the phones on several other floors were not affected. So I ran to the original floors, dashed around to every desk picking up the pens and note pads we'd placed there, then ran up to the new floors and redistributed them before returning to the lobby to usher the waiting guests upstairs." "So everything was fine from then on, right?" he is asked. Hammerman's eyes narrow slightly, "Sure it was," he growls, "because I told the communications people that if that happened again, I'd kill them. I lost ten pounds that day!"

For all the happiness the Merrill Lynch employees see, there are also some sad sights. Some people go to Christmas Calls even though they have nobody to call. With their acquaintances from the nursing home or neighborhood all signing up, they don't want to admit they have nobody to call. So they go along on the bus, sit at a desk, and dial random telephone numbers to keep up appearances. Westina Matthews recalls the time on Christmas Day 1985 when a senior citizen showed up by herself at 2 P.M. She had heard a news report on the radio about Christmas Calls and had left her apartment and come by subway to One Liberty Plaza. "Well, let me get you a desk and telephone to use," offered Westina. "Oh no, I don't need to make any phone calls," the lady said. "I just wanted to be here with all the people."

Christmas Calls is by now a finely tuned operation, especially in New York. Refreshments and cookies are served, and a small Christmas gift is given to each senior. Some company volunteers bring spouses, children, and parents to help out. The oldest volunteer to date was Stephen Hammerman's eighty-five-year-old mother. After helping one guest use the telephone, the grateful lady reached into her purse and gave Mrs. Hammerman, whom she did not realize was the mother of the vice chairman of Merrill Lynch, a one dollar tip.

Some people drop by just to witness the excitement in the air as a global network of calls in a dozen languages are carried on simultaneously. New York City mayors have made it their tradition to visit every year. David Dinkins has stopped in, walked around, and said a few words. But Ed Koch wanted to be more involved when he was mayor, and he always brought cookies for everyone. Sometimes he would even ask to speak to the person on the other end of the telephone, leaving them in shock that the mayor of New York was talking to them. The Merrill Lynch volunteers remember one occasion when Mayor Koch walked in and interrupted a lady's telephone call by taking the phone away from her and saying into it, "Hi there. I'm Ed Koch, mayor of New York City." With barely a moment's hesitation, the voice on the other end barked, "Put my sister back on the phone!"

And so sisters talk with sisters, immigrants call loved ones in the old country, aging fathers talk to transplanted sons a continent away, and grandmothers hear the first words from grandchildren they've never seen. As the final group of seniors receive their gifts, wipe away tears, and board the bus for home, the exhausted Merrill Lynch volunteers turn off the lights and call out to each other, "Merry Christmas! See you next year at Christmas Calls." And if there is any sure bet on Wall Street, *that's* a promise you can be bullish on.

We Make a Living by What We Get.
We Make a Life by What We Give.

—Unknown

15

· ·

American Airlines'
Heather Bell and Jacki Graham

Captains of the Green Team

It is natural that an airline passenger's thoughts are typically focused on many things: safety, weather, delays, the destination—anything *but* recycling. Yet the few hours aboard a typical flight can make a sizable contribution to society's landfills. Consider, for instance, the profile of an average flight, say from Chicago to Orlando. Even before takeoff, the first-class passengers will be offered drinks, inevitably served with disposable paper napkins. As the aircraft climbs to cruising altitude, the cabin crew is busy serving 150 passengers with refreshments poured from individual throwaway beer and soda cans, poured into disposable plastic tumblers accompanied by plastic stirrers and paper napkins. This process may be repeated several more times during the flight. The meal itself, whether the ubiquitous "light snack" or hot lunch or dinner, is served with utensils, salad dressing, sandwich, bread, and cheeses all wrapped in nonbiodegradable plastic or aluminum wrap, with one-time-use plastic knives and forks. Imagine the amount of garbage, even just the number of empty soda and beer cans, that are thrown away after every flight. Now try to envision the total amount disposed of from the 17,700 daily flights of just the U.S. domestic carriers.

Heather Bell and Jacki Graham are flight attendants with

American Airlines. Heather, a former equestrian teacher, started her flying career in 1987 and was based at American's new hub in San Jose, California. Concern for the environment and a love of nature run in her blood: her father was a noted conservationist who successfully lobbied to preserve open space as the San Francisco East Bay saw frenetic development and unplanned growth. In the densely populated suburbs surrounding Oakland and San Jose today, she points with pride at the open fields her father was instrumental in preserving. Heather has more than a casual interest in conservation, and when she is not flying, she teaches university-level zoology lab to students majoring in biology. She is completing her master's degree in endangered species and biology at Hayward State University, near San Francisco. One of her reasons for selecting an airline job was the reduced-rate airfare benefit that enables her to travel the world studying endangered species. She saw a dream come true with a trip to Kenya in 1988 and took a leave of absence from American in 1993 to visit the remote jungle regions of Zimbabwe to study the almost-extinct pangolin.

After flying for almost a year, Heather told a senior flight attendant of her concern over the recyclable waste being discarded from each flight. "Forget it!" the colleague replied. "The company won't recycle." Appalled at the volume of trash, Heather called several other company veterans but met with the same ambivalent response. The hardest part of all was getting a fair hearing from American's local management, who wouldn't even give the concept a fair trial.

So in September 1989, obviously believing that matters of conscience override bureaucratic disinterest, this veteran of one year's seniority decided to launch her own recycling program. "Why not?" she asks. "If you really believe in something, just go ahead and do it." A colleague suggested Bell contact Patricia Howitt, a Quality of Worklife representative at the San Jose base. The QWL rep is a voluntary, uniquely American Airlines position best described as a facilitator between management and flight attendants. Howitt personally endorsed the project and suggested a procedure for preparing a formal plan and proposing it to management at the company's Dallas headquarters. This approach was successful, and senior management accepted Heather's idea for a four-month trial at San Jose.

Initiating a Trial Run

She decided to start with the aluminum cans that were thrown away after each flight and sought out the cabin service people who meet and clean each incoming aircraft at San Jose. Her case must have been convincing, as they agreed to keep the empty aluminum cans separate and send them to a recycler. The next task was to get the word out to all her colleagues—not just the flight attendants based in San Jose but those who work flights that operate *to* or *through* the city—potentially every flight attendant American has. Heather sent an electronic mail message to all seventeen thousand American Airlines flight attendants in the country telling them about her idea and asking them to voluntarily separate aluminum cans on any flights into San Jose.

To her astonishment, Heather discovered that instead of paying for the cans to be hauled away as trash, a recycler would pick them up and *pay American* as much as ninety-three cents per pound, a pound being only about twenty-seven cans. From the outset, she decided that every penny received should go to charity, not to the company, especially since this was extra work undertaken voluntarily by the flight attendants. "It'll never work," one manager told her. "The flight attendants' union will never go for it." "Flight attendants?" said another, incredulously. "They'll never do something extra without getting paid for it." One attendant challenged Heather, "Is the company telling you to do this?" Heather Bell was undeterred. The startup day finally arrived, and she was ready. On her off-duty time and for days afterward she would stay at the airport, rushing up the jetway to greet each arriving flight. "Welcome to San Jose!" she would gush to the crew. "Have you heard about our recycling program? Did you separate any cans for us?"

As word quickly spread—remember, those hundreds of crew members touching down in San Jose could each easily be stopping in five or six other cities that very day—American's employees overwhelmingly embraced the idea. "Even our ticket agents and baggage loaders would brag about their unique experiment," remembers Heather. "Pretty soon, flights would arrive with cabin staff I'd never talked to before, and the first thing they'd tell us was, 'We've separated all the cans for you, where do you want them?'" Before long, the phone would ring with agents, flight attendants, and employees calling Heather from all across the country, asking how they could help. She'd return from a grueling, multiple-day work stint flying all over the U.S. only to have two or three dozen long-distance telephone calls to return when she got home. Of all those tiring, expensive, repetitive calls Heather doesn't complain a bit, "because one of them was my introduction to Jacki Graham," she beams, "and Jacki became one of the dearest people I've ever met."

Other than their shared love of flying and the environment, it is immediately evident that both women have the same positive, can-do attitude. Jacki is an ebullient, effervescent longtime flight attendant. She applied for the job to win a two-hundred-dollar bet and was hired by American Airlines back in 1979. After fourteen years of takeoffs and landings, bad weather and irritable passengers, many flight attendants are jaded or have already turned in their wings. But not Jacki Graham. When she started flying, she was one of 6,500 flight attendants with American Airlines. Today the company has almost 20,000. Almost 2,000 of them share Jacki's Los Angeles base. She glows when talking about her job and proudly asserts, "I'll wear navy blue (American's uniform) 'til the day I die!"

Extending the Program's Reach

In October 1989, Jacki read Heather's electronic mail message about the San Jose recycling program. She was already a convert to the benefits of recycling at home, so she asked her Quality of Worklife colleague, Patty Humburger, about adding Los Angeles to American's pilot program. Jacki and Heather talked for hours and soon arranged to meet each other. Their rendezvous came at the perfect time: Heather was becoming inundated with the overwhelming response from American employees and stations nationwide; then the calls for coordinating the actual pickups and disposal of the mountains of aluminum cans started coming to her—and she still had a full-time job that kept her out of town several days a week. Jacki's experience, positive attitude, and input were most welcome.

First, they had to decide where to donate the recycling receipts. "I can't believe how much money we have," Heather told Jacki. "We've already made two hundred dollars." They polled the flight attendants and decided on an allocation: 25 percent to the Wings Foundation, which provides relief for flight attendants or their immediate families experiencing severe financial hardship due to illness or injury; 50 percent to local charities; and 15 percent to the Nature Conservancy, which protects the environment and wildlife in six million acres of preserved land in fifty U.S. states and Canada. The remaining 10 percent was earmarked for what Jacki still calls "Heather's absolutely brilliant idea": a flight attendants' disaster relief fund. The program would provide immediate cash grants for flight attendants who had been the victims of a disaster. They subsequently registered the Flight Attendants' Disaster Relief Fund as a tax-exempt charity. The fund has helped colleagues who were victims of the San Francisco earthquake rent temporary housing while awaiting settlement on destroyed homes. It has provided similar assistance to co-workers devastated by hurricanes: fifty-seven flight attendants lost their homes to Hurricane Andrew in Florida and another six had their houses destroyed when Hurricane Iniki hit Kauai, Hawaii, a few weeks later.

Both Jacki and Heather are clearly proud of the funds recycling has provided in this way. "Flight attendants are doers," asserts Jacki Graham. "They are the ones whose volunteer efforts put the money to all those needy causes."

Jacki was preparing the way to introduce the recyling program to Los Angeles, which, unlike San Jose, was one of the largest, busiest bases in the world for American. With the success of the San Jose project and the burgeoning interest from around the country, Heather and Jacki decided it was time to try and get help from the highest echelons of American's management. San Francisco wanted in. Washington, D.C., was asking to be included, and there was a groundswell of public and media awareness in anticipation of the upcoming anniversary of the first Earth Day. "Yet still, the local airport management was like a brick wall," remembers one co-worker. "I figured, I have nothing to lose," remembers Jacki. "I'm one dinky little flight attendant. I don't care about red tape any more. I just want to do it. At this point, I just wanted to stop asking and start doing." It was time to send a letter to American's titan CEO and chairman, Robert L. Crandall.

Bob Crandall has been the pilot of American's growth from a typical large airline of the protectionist sixties to a global mega-carrier today. He has used his acumen to avoid the troubled fate of better-known or larger carriers such as Eastern and Pan Am, and today American is often the pacesetter in technology, fares, and customer service. The frequent-flyer plan is a Crandall invention, as is Sabre, the airline-owned reservations computer used by travel agents. Competitors, employees, and industry watchers variously describe Robert Crandall as tough, visionary, and ruthless. However, "Mr. Warmth" is generally a moniker missing from those descriptions. So how did a diminutive flight attendant from San Jose, California—a low-rung employee with barely two years' seniority—bring herself to write to him?" "I was nervous at first," Heather Bell admits, "but then I thought, wait a minute, why do I feel that way? He's also a person. He has kids, and surely he cares about how we're leaving the earth for them. Besides, this is *good news*." So she wrote the letter, saying that she had waited to see if the idea would work before she troubled him. The truth was, it was succeeding brilliantly; in fact, just before she completed the letter, Heather was notified that she was to receive the Mayor's Award from the city of San Jose.

Robert Crandall's response was positive and immediate: he called the very next day. Within days, Heather received a letter with glowing praise from him and corporate support from headquarters for expansion of the recycling program to any American station where the flight attendants volunteered. By Earth Day, April 22, 1990, Crandall's editorial page in the carrier's *American Way* in-flight magazine directly addressed the environmental issues facing the country. He described the beginning of a major company-wide conservation and recycling program and gave full credit to the flight attendants at San Jose for their initiative and concern.

Once Jacki Graham had contacted recycling companies, put out bids, motivated the staff, and even spray-painted the dumpsters to identify them as aluminum dumps, the huge Los Angeles base started recycling. After working the crowded Los Angeles–New York wide-body flights all week, Jacki stapled the announcements of "Recycling Kick-Off Day" to each employee's paycheck to ensure they were noticed. When the big day arrived, she considered it contradictory to serve soda or coffee in plastic cups at an ecology event, so she brought in hundreds of fresh apples and gave them out to her co-workers. "We decided to do more than cans," Graham remembers. "We wanted to recycle newspaper, white paper, plastic, and styrofoam, too." But to get such a large crew to simultaneously adopt the concept and attend to so many different items, all on a voluntary basis, was too much, and they reverted to just recycling aluminum cans.

Meanwhile, both San Jose and other stations reported problems with the cabin services crew handling the enormous extra work load of all the recyclables. An arrangement was made with Sky Chefs and Caterair, American's primary and secondary caterers, to handle them. The innovative "Good Faith Partnership" called for the caterers to take the empty cans off the aircraft and deliver them to the recycling facility, all at no cost to the airline. All profits from the recycling sales were then split equally between the caterer and American, with total control over the airline's share given to the flight attendants' volunteer recycling committee.

By December 1990, the program had won awards from the California Department of Conservation and the U.S. Environmental Protection Agency along with the Distinguished Service Award from Keep America Beautiful. The recycling program was fully operational at thirteen airports.

In January 1991, Heather Bell was forced to make a decision between running the recycling program and continuing her studies for a master's degree. "Like any good mother, I had to let go," she says. "This project took more than one person could do, and I really didn't want it to be known as 'Heather's program.'"

Jacki stepped in and offered to take it over. She reviewed the allocation of charitable donations, and employees were contacted for new feedback and suggestions on how the money should be distributed. Since the third year, the proceeds have been divided equally, with 25 percent each going to the Wings Foundation, Nature Conservancy, Flight Attendants' Disaster Relief Fund, and local charities chosen by each participating crew base. "The fact that every single penny goes to the charities they choose is what makes the flight attendants so good at this voluntary effort," says Jacki. Graham now assumed the unpaid role of motivator, trainer, and project spokesperson. She traveled as far away as Munich, Germany, to study the airline recycling plan that is state law in that environmentally strict country.

In the three years following the program's inception, American had hired seven thousand new flight attendants. They learned during training that the company encourages recycling on each flight, but they didn't know where the money went or how important a role they shared in that decision. Jacki produced electronic mail or printed flyers to continually communicate and motivate them, passing on new information when it was received from other stations. For instance, when she was notified of the allocation of each base's 25 percent to local charities—Los Angeles's support of the Living Free Animal Sanctuary, San Francisco's contributions to AIDS charities, Honolulu's HUGS Foundation for abused children—she passed the good news around the nation.

The increase in the program's productivity was impressive. During 1990, American's flight attendants recycled 226,000 pounds of aluminum cans. In 1991, that figure grew to 390,000 pounds of cans. By 1992, over 463,000 pounds of aluminum—representing over 12.5 million actual cans—were kept out of landfills by the volunteer efforts of American Airlines' cabin attendants.

Expanding the Program's Scope

Excited at their success with aluminum cans, employees started asking what else they could recycle. It didn't take long to expand the program. At the company's Nashville hub, oil from maintenance vehicles is now used to heat the automotive shop, while freon from service trucks is purged and reused. The airline's two huge crew bases at Chicago's O'Hare and the Dallas–Fort Worth airports obtained baling machines and now recycle all the polystyrene plastic drink glasses, coffee cups, and snack trays that were formerly sent to landfills. There are still some details to be settled, since they now have a mountain of compacted recycled polystyrene and can't find a source for it. "I have to write to Al Gore about that," says Jacki. Flight attendants at New York's La Guardia airport created a library with used books and magazines they found on the planes, and they donate the thousands of unused soaps collected from their many hotel layovers to the needy.

Kathi Gumph, a flight attendant from Colorado, presented a one-hundred-page proposal that packaged food unopened by passengers be given away instead of thrown away. (It had been cheaper for an airline to discard the tens of thousands of unopened packets of butter, crackers, and so forth, than to pay the salaries and fringe benefits of employees to look through the post-flight trash to save them.) In October 1992, American initiated the volunteer food recycling program at its crew bases in Dallas, Chicago, and Honolulu. "Despite the original skepticism at Kathi's proposal, we were able to prove to the company that we could do it," says Jacki Graham today. "We give all the food to Second Harvest Food Bank, and in just the first nine weeks we gave them eight thousand pounds of food from Chicago alone."

In the spring of 1992, Heather and Jacki proposed their gutsiest idea yet. Not far from American Airlines' hub at the Nashville, Tennessee, airport was a forty-three-acre tract of environmentally endangered land called the Couchville Cedar Glade. The property is home to the only known colony of the Tennessee coneflower, *Echinacea tennesseensis*, and twenty-seven other plants listed as either rare or endangered by the state of Tennessee. Allowing the land to be sold for development would be an environmental tragedy, they agreed. They approached the Nature Conservancy, the international nonprofit conservation organization that manages ecologically significant land by preserving and protecting its plants and wildlife. The Nature Conservancy agreed to manage the Cedar Glade if it was purchased, but it had only raised forty thousand dollars from seventy-seven other corporate and individual donors to date. It was time to call headquarters again. Despite the severe financial losses that made 1992 the worst year in airline history, with the industry losing billions of dollars, the company agreed to their proposition: the flight attendants' volunteer recycling program would buy the land for the Nature Conservancy, but since they didn't have enough money at the time, American Airlines would give them a $200,000 interest-free loan to do it, repayable as the receipts came in from recyclers in the future.

On May 15, 1992, Heather and Jacki were joined in Nashville by Chairman Robert Crandall and Executive Vice President–Operations Robert W. Baker as they presented a $200,000 check to John C. Sawhill, president of the Nature Conservancy. It was the largest corporate gift American had ever made and the first time land had ever been bought for the Nature Conservancy by an employee group. "This generous gift from the employees of American Airlines is a tremendous boost to our efforts to protect this rare habitat and its even rarer inhabitants," said Jeff Sinks, Tennessee state director for the Nature Conservancy. "Our purchase of these properties is a significant accomplishment in the world of conservation." American employees saw this event as just the beginning of a partnership with the Nature Conservancy. One month later, they launched Teamwork for Nature day when hundreds of employees and their families converged on selected sites in Florida, Texas, Illinois, California, and Tennessee for a work day to clean up Nature Conservancy preserves.

American Airlines now recognizes the importance of environmental responsibility in terms of economics, ecology, and employee morale. "We want to be an environmental leader. It's the right thing to do, and since most of our customers agree, it's good business as well," says Robert Crandall. An environment department has been formed, based at the Dallas headquarters but responsible for getting their message to every station. A person has been added to the staff to coordinate all employee volunteer recycling programs, taking an enormous administrative load away from Jacki Graham. The company invested $166,000 to purchase 14,000 recyclable-waste containers, can crushers, compactors, and recycling dumpsters for the thirty thousand employees at the home office. It estimated a $73,000 income in the first year from recapturing and selling to recyclers those items previously wasted. Half of the money will go to offset the initial capital investment, while the other 50 percent of recycling income will go to local charities. American expects to save $21,000 per year in disposal costs and keep 20 tons of aluminum cans and 980 tons of paper, the equivalent of 17,000 trees, out of landfills each year.

The two flight attendants who made environmental awareness part of American's corporate conscience continue at their frenetic pace. Jacki Graham's can-do attitude was evident recently when she borrowed $5,000 to buy equipment expanding Los Angeles's recycling abilities. "We've made $1,500 in just eight months," she glows, "all of which will go to Christmas charities chosen by the L.A. employees." She continues criss-crossing the continent as a full-time flight attendant (L.A. to New York is her favorite route, but you'd better fly first-class if you plan to meet her). She spends "easily one full day a week" in her unpaid job overseeing the recycling program. "Miami will call with a question, then someone else will complain that the recyclers haven't picked up their dumpster. We've even caught another airline's employee stealing the cans from our dumpster," she says. "Then there's the mail. I answer every letter personally." Most correspondence is complimentary or contains suggestions, but occasionally there's a complaint. Although rare, the complainers almost always have the same beef: "We do all the work, so we should get the recycling money." Jacki is well prepared for those people nowadays, telling them, "We collected $40,000 last year and have twenty thousand flight attendants. That comes to two dollars apiece. If the money is more important to you than all the good we're doing for charity, here's your two bucks."

Jacki's volunteer spirit extends beyond her flying career. She takes in abused, abandoned, and dysfunctional animals. The current Graham household census is "down to" seven cats, a dog, and regular visits from raccoon and possum families. She makes food baskets for Wings Foundation's needy applicants, maintains the books for the AIDS Research Network, and also flies around the country helping new stations that want to start recycling. Occasionally a member of the cabin crew will notice they've been teamed up with her to work that flight and will make effusive remarks like, "I've heard so much about you and have always wanted to meet you." A clearly embarrassed Jacki Graham brushes off the celebrity status and downplays the major role she played—and continues to play—in American's recycling program. "Flight attendants are like a silent sorority," Jacki muses. "They're some of the lowest rungs on the corporate ladder, and yet they will work until they drop for something they believe in. We pride ourselves on our recycling program being a total volunteer effort—and it always will be."

Heather Bell may have been mentally engaged in biology books and physically engrossed in the African jungle recently, but she still cares deeply for the project. Dubbed "American's First Lady of Garbage," Heather still spends many hours working on American's program and talking to flight attendants from other airlines in the U.S. and Canada, who call her for advice on how they can initiate similar recycling efforts. "I feel proud of our flight attendants for their volunteerism—especially after what some people said about them initially," she says. "I get such a rush seeing something good like this happen. I just know I'll throw myself into another project soon." She laughs as she remembers times when passengers, seeing her name tag, would recognize who she was. Then she tells of the occasion when she boarded a flight and was teamed with a senior flight attendant whom she had never met before. In the few minutes before passengers boarded, they introduced themselves, and then the senior set the ground rules: "American has a new voluntary recycling program," she told Heather. "It's a really great idea. In fact, because of it we now recycle our trash at home. So I'm just telling you, *this* will be a recycling flight, OK?" Heather thought that would be just fine, but she could only nod her assent as the tears welled in her eyes at the realization of how far her idea had come.

But if someone who is supposed to be a Christian
has money enough to live well,
and sees his brother in need and won't help him—
how can God's love be within him?
Little children, let us stop just saying we love people;
let us really love them, and show it by our actions.
Then we will know for sure, by our actions,
that we are on God's side, and our consciences will be clear,
even when we stand before the Lord.

    —I John 3: 17–19

16

. . . .

Apple Computer's
Elizabeth Armstrong

Matching Hi-Tech with Human Needs

October 17, 1989, had been a glorious fall day across the entire U.S. In the East, the leaves from the Carolinas to Canada had turned a spectacular array of orange, red, and gold, but by evening, millions of people had turned from the autumnal splendor to their televisions for the 8 P.M. start of baseball's World Series game three. In the central and mountain states, many workers left a little early to ensure they would beat the traffic and be home in time for the game to begin. But to those on the West Coast, particularly Californians, this was the *really* big game, pitting two cross-bay rivals, the San Francisco Giants and the Oakland Athletics, against each other. The A's had won the first two games in the best-of-seven series, but this day was the first in the Giants' Candlestick Park, where the fans were sure to give their home team an advantage. For those Bay Area residents not lucky enough to hold one of the sixty thousand tickets to the game, they had a choice of leaving work early to watch it at the many bars and restaurants having parties or leaving work even earlier and getting home before the start at 5 P.M. local time. Commuters listened intently to their car radios as they endured rush-hour traffic jams on their way home.

Elizabeth Armstrong had not been lucky enough to leave work early. She was an area associate ("There are no secretaries at

Apple") for Apple Computers in one of their many mid-rise office buildings in the company's home town of Cupertino, California. "I was pretty much at the bottom rung of the career ladder," she recalls. "I'd been with Apple for about two years and was the inside backup person supporting five people in the marketing department." She decided to take advantage of the unusually quiet office that evening to catch up on a project she was working on.

As people around the world tuned in to the beginning of the pre-game show, they witnessed an event that kept them transfixed to their sets. At 8:04 P.M. Eastern and 5:04 P.M. Pacific time, the ground started to shake violently. The polished superstar network reporters stood open-mouthed: this was not on their cue cards. Television cameras captured the crowd suddenly go from happy anticipation to bewilderment and then to fear as pieces of concrete cracked and fell from the stadium. Sixty million viewers in the U.S. and many millions more around the world watched ABC sports commentator Al Michaels suddenly say, "We're having an earth—," as the screens went dark.

Elizabeth Armstrong will never, ever, forget 5:04 P.M. on that day. As her building suddenly started to shake violently, she looked out of the window. "You could see the ground swelling and buckling," she recalls, "so I ran away from the windows and sat on the floor in the center of the building, next to the conference room." As the earthquake became even more violent, she saw the floor-to-ceiling plate-glass windows explode into a million pieces and crash to the floor. An associate grabbed her and literally dragged Armstrong to the stairwell, where they ran down four flights of stairs. As they passed each floor, they saw windows smashing and filing cabinets crashing to the ground. Doors flew off their hinges, and huge cracks opened up in the masonry walls before their eyes. They saw daylight and dashed towards it, only to find they had run out onto the loading dock. "We took a flying leap off the dock," she says. "I was never so grateful to be in that parking lot as when I landed right then." In fact, it was only after she landed safely on the hard macadam surface that Elizabeth realized she had been walking around her office with no shoes on just before her rapid exit.

The earthquake, which measured 7.1 on the open-ended Richter scale, had its epicenter at Loma Prieta, high up in the Santa Cruz mountains and just five miles from Armstrong's office. Its effects were deadly and devastating across an area that measured hundreds of square miles. In San Francisco, some 40 miles north, apartment buildings collapsed and exploded in flames as gas lines were severed. As commuters streamed across the Bay Bridge, which links San Francisco with Oakland, the upper deck broke open and crashed into the water far below. In Oakland itself, the double-decked Interstate 880 collapsed, killing forty-two motorists as their cars were crushed by tons of steel and concrete from the upper deck. Oakland's airport lost 3,000 feet of runway, and the busy San Francisco International Airport was closed for thirteen hours after the control tower's huge windows shattered and the ceiling fell in. Throughout the mountains from San Francisco to Monterey, towns were completely cut off as roads, telephone lines, and water and electricity feeds were severed. The shocks cracked windows 225 miles to the northeast in Reno and swayed skyscrapers in Los Angeles, 400 miles to the south.

"We really had no idea how bad it was," Elizabeth declares, "but after the rumbling stopped, we realized that we had no purses or keys to our cars and homes, so we cautiously made our way back into the building and back up four flights of stairs." The scene was surreal. "There was so much dust in the air it was hard to see anything at first," she says. "But as our eyes became accustomed to the conditions, we saw piles of books, telephones, computers, and file cabinets, all piled on top of each other on the floor." Amazingly, the only injury was a minor head wound to one employee.

Elizabeth drove the short distance to the apartment she had just moved into a few days before, only to find more bad news waiting: the apartment complex was deemed unsafe to enter. As the tenants started to gather, she was pleased to see Jim, a co-worker at Apple and her next-door neighbor. They had just gone on their first date, and Elizabeth was happy to have a familiar face to share the excitement with. They sat on the lawn, and as the sun started to slip behind the mountains, they began to realize how

bad the earthquake must have been. Smoke from burning buildings could be seen in every direction; the sirens of emergency vehicles filled the air, and helicopters from medivac units, the
National Guard, and television stations criss-crossed the sky. "It
felt eerie not knowing what was going on in our own community," she recalls. "Then Jim remembered he had a generator and
portable television in his storage garage." He quickly retrieved
them, and soon a crowd gathered around to glean every scant detail of the disaster. As evening turned into night, one of the emergency services brought food and blankets to the hundred or so
residents gathered on their apartment building's lawn. That was
a night Elizabeth Armstrong will never forget: sleeping on a blan-
ket under the stars feeling the ground beneath her rumble with
frequent aftershocks as she was lulled into sleep—and often jolted
awake—by the screaming sirens of rescue vehicles.

The next morning, the tenants were allowed to briefly
enter their apartments. Jim's was a scene of total devastation.
Everything from the refrigerator to his enormous book collection
was on the floor. To her surprise, Elizabeth's apartment right next
door was relatively unscathed. "I lost a bookshelf, and found the
coffee table had upturned and fallen on the book my roommate
had been reading just the night before. It was titled *Apple's
Earthquake Preparation Guide*." Fred Stauder, a friend who was
also an Apple employee, stopped by, and the three of them helped
clean up Jim's apartment while watching the continuous local
news coverage.

Mobilizing to Meet a Need

As the hours passed, they noticed two recurrent themes in the
news broadcasts. One was of families who had been separated by
the earthquake and, with telephone service interrupted, were
desperately trying to find out if their loved ones were alive and
safe. The other was of long lines of people in worst-affected areas
waiting to fill out forms at emergency facilities to either get help
or offer their services to people who needed them.

"There's no way they can process all that raw data manu-
ally," said Jim, "especially when people offering the very help oth-

ers are needing might be a half mile from each other yet never make the connection without telephone service." Elizabeth had an idea. "Why don't we offer to supply them with computers and teach them how to store and retrieve all the needs and offers of help?" she asked. A few minutes later, she was calling the mayors' offices, police, and television stations in the worst-hit areas. To her astonishment, they acted as if her offer was not helpful. "We don't need anything like that," one bureaucrat told her. "We have everything under control." As live newscasts continued to be shown on television, it was obvious that was not the case. "Being Apple people, we didn't believe them anyway," says Armstrong. Her next call was to the Santa Clara County Volunteer Agency, and they jumped at the offer Elizabeth was making. "It sounds very interesting," they told her. "Do you mean that Apple could help us in a couple of weeks?" "No," rejoined Elizabeth. "We want to help *now*." It was time to round up the troops.

Armstrong made a sweep of the nearby Apple offices, dozens of which are located in adjacent mid-rise commercial buildings along Cupertino's DeAnza Road. She gathered about ten interested employees, many of whom followed her with their own laptop computers. Elizabeth realized that she would need the company's blessing to devote the time, equipment, and manpower she had in mind, so she called the administrative assistant to John Sculley, Apple's CEO and chairman. "I told her we needed uninterrupted use of the conference room and lots of computers," she says today, "and almost immediately I got the word that we had the complete blessing of the company and could count on any additional support we needed through the community affairs department."

The large conference room became their command post—dubbed the Epicenter—and Elizabeth arranged for telephones, fax machines, and copiers to be installed immediately. As the technical people volunteered, they were charged with designing a software program that could be large enough to accommodate the numerous needs and offers of specific equipment and services, yet simple enough for tired, confused emergency workers unfamiliar with computers to use easily. Armstrong continued calling radio and television stations, the Red Cross, and other service providers offering them the Earthquake Database Project. Meanwhile, Anne McMullin, coordinator of Apple's Employee Volunteer Action program, acted as a recruiter to bring more volunteers on board. Tom Voss was able to get the company to donate ten brand-new Macintosh computers, right off the assembly line. Word of the project spread through Apple like wildfire, and soon there was a small army of volunteers from throughout the company.

The software experts finished their work in record time. They had designed a program that they thought could store information on all the needs that a victim of the earthquake might have: carpenters, plumbers, electricians, doctors, veterinarians, interpreters, help with insurance claim forms, ways to call their relatives with word of their safety, and so forth. They tested the program, and it worked fine. It was now time to load it into as many computers as they could find. Elizabeth sent messages to all Apple employees via electronic mail and voice mail, asking them to lend the project their personal computers and to come in to the Epicenter anytime during the day, night, or weekend to help load the names of services, volunteers, and contacts into the data base. "Over 250 employees donated their own computers," she recalls. "I've never seen anything like it. People would drop by, see we needed help with something, and still be there eight hours later." She remembers contacting radio stations and finding out that literally thousands of citizens from throughout the Bay Area had called in offering their services wherever and whenever needed. Suddenly now, those stations had an outlet for those volunteers, and each station faxed long lists of names, telephone numbers, and skills offered to the Apple command post.

The Office of Emergency Services called and requested help; so did the Red Cross of Santa Cruz and Santa Clara Counties. Then the San Mateo County Red Cross called. As word spread via the emergency broadcasts, the media picked up the story, and they publicized the telephone number Elizabeth had installed in the Epicenter, along with voice mail to take messages if the lines were busy. "That first weekend we received ten thousand telephone calls," she remembers. "It was just incredible." But it was also rewarding. A person would call in offering his portable generator, and in seconds, the Apple volunteer would find a person whose house in the mountains had no power and who desperately needed electricity.

Apple volunteers with loaded computers were dispatched to the agencies who asked for help. Just getting there was often no mean feat, as many roads were still impassable days after the earthquake. Santa Cruz is a fairly large town nestled between the mountains and the Pacific Ocean just twenty-five miles from Cupertino. But those twenty-five miles over the mountains were some of the most treacherous anywhere in the world after the earthquake. "All access to Santa Cruz was closed," says Elizabeth. "The only way you could get there was with the Red Cross convoy of emergency vehicles that made periodic forays across what was left of the steep mountain roads."

Holly Frederickson Weber volunteered to go, and she joined the convoy. There was such devastation along the way: beautiful hillside homes had slid into the ravine, utility lines were broken, and trees lay scattered in every direction like a giant game of pick-up sticks. The road had buckled and was impassable in places. Some of the mountain communities were without water and electricity for several weeks. In nearby Watsonville, 333 of the little town's buildings were totally destroyed. When she finally arrived in Santa Cruz, there was such a need for Holly's services she did not leave for two weeks, entering ten thousand records while she was there.

Elizabeth Armstrong worked twenty-hour days on the Earthquake Database Project. "I had no idea when I first suggested the concept that I'd be managing the whole project," she says, "but my manager was so understanding, he gave me two weeks to devote to it full-time." Volunteers—and calls for help—continued to come in. Even competitors Hewlett Packard and Digital Equipment Company allowed their employees to give their time and talents to the project. In just four days, the Earthquake Database Project grew from four employees to over two hundred volunteers serving in sixteen locations in seven California counties. They served in a huge geographic area fanning out over a 160-mile radius from Cupertino.

Other employees continued to stop in to the Epicenter and

drop off their personal laptop computers—worth from three thousand to six thousand dollars—and say, "Use it if you need it, and give me a call when you want me to come pick it up," according to a grateful Armstrong. A volunteer would then load it with the software and data base and take it right out to an agency that had called for help. Once on location, the Apple person would train the emergency workers in the field in how to use it. On one occasion, Jim was asked by a television crew to demonstrate how their program worked. "Well, let's say you need a nurse who speaks Spanish," said Jim, picking a random example. "You simply enter those needs here, and...there, you have a Spanish-speaking nurse who has called in to offer her service as a volunteer if anyone needs her." The emergency worker was incredulous. "Wait," she commanded. "We need a nurse who speaks Spanish right now."

Sometimes the volunteers were amazed at the archaic methods the emergency services were using. In Santa Cruz, all the doctors, nurses, electricians, plumbers, and other skilled help that would be needed in a major crisis were listed on index cards. When the earthquake struck, all the card cabinets were thrown to the ground floor, and days later, thousands of urgently needed names were hopelessly mixed up, out of order, on the floor. "It would have taken days, or weeks, to find anything in that mess," says Jim.

Looking Back at the Experience

Despite the twenty-hour days, the life-and-death urgency of the calls, and the enormous stress, Elizabeth will always remember the good things that came out of the project. "One day, our Santa Cruz volunteer handled a call in Spanish: a distraught migrant farm worker had finally made it home to find the house destroyed and no sign of his family. He didn't know whether they were dead or alive, or laying in a hospital somewhere. Cynthia Bacon, an Apple volunteer, punched the family's name into her computer and in seconds assured the man that his loved ones were all safe and gave him their location."

After working day and night on the project for two weeks,

it was time for Elizabeth to return to work. The agencies who had borrowed the computers were welcome to keep them for as long as they had a need, and Elizabeth certainly fielded many telephone calls from them in the ensuing weeks. But the command post was dismantled, and the volunteers who manned it went back to their positions in the Apple, Hewlett Packard, and DEC organizations. It had been an altogether incredible experience for all of them, especially Elizabeth Armstrong. "For months afterward I'd turn white every time we felt an aftershock," she admits.

Several months later, Elizabeth received a telephone call from Anne McMullin, Apple's volunteer program chief. "Are you sitting down?" asked McMullin. "You were nominated for the 1990 President's Volunteer Action Award—and you've won it!" Anne told Elizabeth that she had been invited to the White House to accept the award in person from President George Bush. Armstrong was flabbergasted. She didn't even know she had been nominated. In the weeks between the announcement and the presentation, she felt a variety of emotions. Exhilaration at such an honor and sadness—even guilt—at not being allowed to take Jim, Fred, and the other co-workers who had been so involved with the project. "I felt selfish," she admits. "I couldn't believe I'd won an award for helping people. Is that right?" In May 1990, the big day arrived, and there sat a secretary from California inside the White House for a formal ceremony honoring *her*. "I was so nervous," she confesses, "and I think it must have showed, because when I went up to accept the award from President Bush, Barbara put her arm around me."

Most of the examples of employee voluntary service in this book have been of people who had plenty of time to think their idea through, to refine it, to run it by friends, and then, when the timing is right, to start on their project. The Apple Earthquake Database Project was different. It came about almost as suddenly as the disaster that prompted the idea, and it was launched even before the aftershocks had gone away. "I've always loved helping people," says Armstrong. "I've volunteered for lots of good causes: the Girl Scouts, PTA, Project Russia, et cetera. But the Earthquake Database Project made me realize I've got a lot of management potential in me. My life has never been the same since." She talks about the task of motivating and directing over two hundred colleagues, many of whom were considerably higher up the corporate ladder than she. "You work with them day in and day out, and you wonder what they're really like," she says, "Then you are thrown together and find out that they are wonderful, caring, giving people. I have a much better view of my co-workers now. This project gave me the opportunity to push myself farther than ever before and the confidence to take on new responsibilities at Apple." That is fortunate, because the company also saw abilities in Elizabeth that they had not recognized before, and she has been promoted four times in the four years since the earthquake project.

Jim had left Apple several months earlier, "because I really didn't feel they cared about people," he says. "But seeing the way they responded to this really changed my mind." Elizabeth agrees. "I used to think my hard work just made the company richer," she says, "but now I've seen that they really believe in community service, and they want to build community within the employee ranks, too. Apple challenges us and allows us to grow. They never insist that we fit into their mold. I'm very proud of what I—and all the other volunteers—have done. And I feel especially good about the company and how incredibly supportive they have been of all our volunteer activities."

Elizabeth tells how, after they retrieved all the computers, they still maintained their committee for a year. During that time, they sent a questionnaire to each emergency agency seeking suggestions on how to improve the Earthquake Database Project in the future. "Next time, we're ready to go," says Jim. "We can literally pick up and go to any disaster site in the world and offer the service at a moment's notice." "You don't have to start by helping the whole world," Elizabeth adds. "You just need to help one person, one child, one elderly citizen who's frightened or hungry, and everything will drop into place from there."

The Database Project helped Elizabeth in more ways than she has admitted thus far: all the time and effort in pulling the project together enabled her to become better acquainted with her neighbor, Jim Armstrong, and they fell in love. "The first date, two days before the earthquake, was nice," she says, "but that second date sure lasted a long time. So Jim and I decided that if we could work together day and night under all that stress *and* fall in love during that time, we must be meant for each other. So eleven months later, we got married, on the lawn where we spent that first night of the earthquake."

· ·

Epilogue

I was recently on an overseas flight aboard American Airlines. When the flight attendant came around collecting the empty aluminum cans for recycling, I felt proud of Heather Bell, whose simple idea to help the environment was still working at a forty-thousand-foot altitude on the other side of the world. I've overheard conversations in which comments were made about throwing the key away for incarcerated youths who have committed crimes, and I think about Zanny Shealey's volunteer mission in which his nonjudgmental approach to Atlanta's young offenders has paid such dividends for the kids and society alike. On a recent thousand-mile road trip from Romania to Frankfurt, I drove through the Czech Republic. As I stood in Prague's magnificent Wenceslas Square, the centuries-old baroque buildings framing one of the world's most beautiful marketplaces, I thought of Terri New standing in that very spot fewer than four years earlier and of three hundred thousand Czech citizens holding candles aloft and jingling their keys as they sought to be released from the bonds of Communism. What inspiration, courage, and commitment it took for her to pledge to deliver one million books to the newly democratic people of that nation.

Regardless of our occupation, nationality, or religious affiliation, none of us will live on this earth forever. I have heard pastors say that of all the final conversations they have ever had with people approaching death, they have never heard anybody wish they had accumulated a little more wealth or spent a little more time at the office. But just imagine the legacy people like Dolores Riego de Dios and Tony Mason will leave for mankind. Think of today's kids who will become tomorrow's responsible parents and community leaders thanks to the lessons they have learned from Al Lewis, Mal Stamper, and Maria Alvarez.

Randy Travis recorded a beautiful song called "Point of Light."* The words to part of the song could well have been written for the employees you have met in the preceding chapters:

> There is a point when you cannot walk away,
> that's the point when you become a point of light.
> There are heroes whose names we never hear:
> a dedicated army of quiet volunteers.
> Reaching out to feed the hungry,
> reaching out to save the land,
> reaching out to help their fellow man.
> There are dreamers who are making dreams come
>   true,
> taking time to teach the children
> there's nothing they can't do.
> Giving shelter to the homeless,
> giving hope to those without.
> Isn't that what this land's all about?
> All it takes is a point of light,
> a ray of hope in the dark of night.
> If you see what's wrong and you try to make it
>   right,
> That's the point when you become a point of light.

---

*Written by Don Schlitz, New Don Songs/New Hayes Music, administered in the U.S. and Canada by New Hayes Music (ASCAP).

Go out and volunteer for a needy cause in your community. Whether you become a spoke in the wheel by helping an existing organization or you initiate a new project, as Mother Teresa said, "Just begin . . . one, one, one." Become a point of light in some needy person's dark world.

. . . .

HOW TO GET INVOLVED

A Resource Guide
for Companies
and Individuals

I

. . . .

Why Volunteer?

Never since the idealistic sixties, when the Peace Corps influenced so many Americans to serve the needy, has there been such interest in volunteerism. Why is that so? It cannot be directly linked to the volunteers' careers, for the sixties, seventies, and even the eighties were times when employees at all levels of the corporate ladder generally felt far more secure in their jobs than they do in the nineties. When flag-carrying airlines like Pan Am go out of business and "a job for life" companies like IBM fire eighty-five thousand workers, who *can* feel secure any more? Yet those are reasons for fewer volunteers, not more.

It cannot be attributed to political motivation, for just as President Clinton urges Americans to go forth and volunteer in their communities, so did George Bush when he was president. It was his influence, after all, that caused The Points of Light Foundation to be formed. But for all the rhetoric his party's thousand points of light showered on us, nobody has seen him volunteer for any needy endeavor since leaving the White House. On the other hand, Democrat Jimmy Carter has never seemed to rest since leaving office, with his hectic, constant schedule of such voluntary commitments as building homes with Habitat for Humanity, refereeing peace talks between warring nations, and working on the Atlanta Project. So why are so many Americans volunteering in their communities and far beyond?

Deborah Baldwin wrote in the July 1990 edition of *Common Cause* magazine that the baby-boom generation has "spent the last two decades on the move, like migratory birds on a flight pattern tuned to the ever-changing socio-economic winds." But after the bubble burst for many of them as the final decade of the century opened, "an entire generation has a vague longing to settle down and be a part of something—like a community."

A Gallup poll taken in 1988 showed that nearly 50 percent of respondents were involved in charity or volunteer work, compared to 31 percent at the height of the Me Generation in 1984. Indeed, New York Cares founder Suzette Brooks was quoted in the same *Newsweek* article, "The New Volunteerism," as saying simply, "Volunteering has become trendy."

Maybe it is because of the economy, but statistics through 1992 show that although financial contributions to charities have declined, volunteerism has steadily increased. According to the *Nonprofit Almanac 1992–93* from Independent Sector, a nonprofit coalition of more than 450 corporate, foundation, and voluntary organization members, "In 1991, 94.2 million Americans 18 years of age and older reported volunteering an average of 4.2 hours per week. This represented 51 percent of the population 18 years of age or older. The estimated value of volunteers' time in 1991 was $176 billion, excluding informal volunteerism, such as babysitting for a neighbor. This represented a significant increase from the 45 percent of adults who reported volunteering in 1987."

Volunteer community service is a trait more popular with Americans than with citizens from almost any other nation. Independent Sector reported that while 51 percent of U.S. citizens aged eighteen or older volunteered, only 19 percent of French citizens reported volunteering in a 1990 study.

So we know that voluntary service to people in need seems to be a characteristic that is part of the American culture, and that it is on the rise. But this book is specifically on *employee* volunteerism, which begs the question, Is a customer more likely to do business with a company it perceives as being a good community citizen because of its employee volunteerism?

According to a 1991 study of consumers by Opinion Research

Corporation (ORC) of Princeton, New Jersey, a strong link does exist between a company's specific demonstrations of social concerns and the likelihood the consumer will patronize that business. ORC's then-president, Andrew J. Brown, reveals, "There seems to be a bottom-line impact. Public relations efforts that burnish a company's image as a socially responsible corporate citizen are likely to enhance the company's reputation for providing quality products and for honesty in its relations with its customers. These are essential business characteristics that ultimately translate into profits."

ORC's work shows that some specific social concerns appear likely to have the strongest impact on a company's image for fairness in its relations with its customers. "'Good neighbor' characteristics—showing concern for the environment, for the welfare of the communities in which it operates, for the health of its employees—are essentially important to the public." In Mr. Brown's opinion, "having visible charitable and public relations efforts in a wide range of areas may prove essential for a company when it faces potential public controversy. For example, Johnson & Johnson benefited from its prior social involvement when it battled the Tylenol crisis."

Perhaps the ultimate answer to the question Why volunteer? takes all of the above into account as peripheral, reinforcing reasons. Thus the employee volunteer might answer, It's nice that the president of the United States urges me on, but that's not why I volunteer. It's important to me now that I feel a part of the community, but if that's why I volunteer, I'm doing it all for me and not for those in need. And yes, my family has been hurt by the economy, which means although we give less cash, I do give my time. And I'm proud to be an American, but I don't volunteer out of jingoistic nationalism. I'm happy that my company gets credit for my volunteerism, and I really enjoy the camaraderie of working on projects alongside my co-workers, but there's more: the thrill that I get when the AIDS baby I'm feeding gives me an ear-to-ear smile; the warmth that permeates my whole body when the lonely senior citizen takes my hand after I stop to chat with her during my Meals on Wheels route; the hug I got from my at-risk mentoring student as he beamed with pride after getting the first A in his life.

These are the real reasons people volunteer. And the numbers are increasing, because once you have experienced it, you can never ignore a plea for help again.

2
· ·
Employer-Driven Opportunities

The preceding chapters have focused on a central point: that one person with vision, motivation, and enthusiasm can have a dream, inspire others to conduct meaningful voluntary service, and make something wonderful happen. They demonstrate that one person *can* make a difference.

Not everybody has the imagination and drive of the employees in those chapters, yet many people still want to make a contribution to the community. It is to this kind of employee—the person who wants to be a spoke in the wheel rather than the inventor of the wheel—that this chapter is dedicated. It highlights volunteer opportunities that exist because an employer has selected one or more good causes and has urged employees to help financially and physically. One final point: this is clearly not meant to be *the* list of benevolent corporations, nor is it in any way intended to be judgmental. It is simply a representative description of how the volunteer programs work at USX Corporation, Phoenix Home Life Insurance, Safeway Stores, CIGNA, Texaco, Rohm and Haas, and Aetna Life and Casualty.

USX Corporation

The reader may be surprised to learn that the steel and oil giant USX has no program to encourage employee volunteerism, nor does it have a method of tracking those workers who do participate in community service projects.

However, in 1991, former chairman and CEO David M. Roderick started a program for the company's retirees in the Pittsburgh area who were interested in giving their time to needy causes. In doing so, Roderick may have provided the first case in the country of a retiree volunteerism program being established before one for current employees. "Because of the downsizing we've gone through in the steel industry, many employees took retirement at an earlier age than is traditional. So we actually have more retirees than current employees," points out USX personnel staff manager Richard B. Jacobs.

In less than a year, the membership grew to 350 volunteers, helping with projects as diverse as technical assistance, business-related activities, and manual labor. Retired computer experts set up the new computer system at Pittsburgh's Holy Family Institute. Others volunteer at the local food bank two or three days each month. Another team helps out at the Whale's Tale, a home for abused children. The retirees have completed projects that help the elderly, disabled, and at-risk youth, and have provided tutors for students with literacy problems. The group publishes a quarterly newsletter and holds an annual recognition luncheon.

Although the program is supported by USX, it is staffed, managed, and administered solely by the retirees. The company was so moved by the enthusiasm and accomplishments of the fledgling group that in May 1992 it held the first Volunteer Expo for current employees. The event was held in the expansive lobby of the USX Tower in downtown Pittsburgh and provided local agencies with space to set up information booths. Employees had the chance to walk around the gaily decorated room and talk to the exhibitors that were offering volunteer opportunities of interest to them.

Phoenix Home Life Insurance

Phoenix Home Life was formed in 1992 out of the merger of two venerable life insurance companies that date back to 1851. The firm employs forty-nine hundred agents and staff in 150 offices around the country. The "Corporate Responsibility Policy Statement" encour-

ages community service activities, some of which may qualify for limited company funding, primarily in the geographic areas where
Phoenix's home office and major employee bases are located:
Hartford and Enfield, Connecticut, and East Greenbush, New York.
Employees in these and other areas may also apply for "a reasonable
amount of company time" to engage in volunteer activities, "which
must be matched by at least an equal amount of their own time."
Compared to the thousands of companies that have no stated policy encouraging their staff to undertake voluntary community service work, Phoenix Home Life's policy is generous and offers great
flexibility for employees while being easy and inexpensive for the
corporation to administer.

Safeway Stores

Safeway, in contrast to the preceding example, offers a very high degree of motivation but minimal flexibility. The company has adopted
the Easter Seals Campaign as its primary philanthropic beneficiary,
and each year it devotes a major employee marketing effort to that
program. During the campaign, every edition of *Directions*, the
Safeway employee newspaper, carries stories of individual and group
efforts to raise funds for Easter Seals. There is even a special multi-
page supplement entitled *Parade*, which is entirely devoted to the
company's efforts to support the Easter Seals Campaign. It lists a
"District Honor Roll" and "Chairman's Commendations for
Excellence in Fundraising," both recognizing the employees and
stores who have given the most money to this one charity. It is not
surprising that the February 1992 edition of *Parade* trumpeted the
headline, "Peter Magowan [Safeway's chairman and CEO] Receives
Top Easter Seals Award."

CIGNA

The bulk of CIGNA's philanthropy and community service is centered in the two cities where its principal corporate offices and employees are located: Philadelphia, Pennsylvania, and Hartford,
Connecticut. The company selects a number of projects that it feels
are in accord with its stated goals of improving public education and

maternal and infant health. Employees are then notified of the need for volunteers and read upbeat articles on the various community service projects in *Dimensions in Service*, a monthly newsletter published by CIGNA's civic affairs department. Examples of employee volunteerism include the following:

• CIGNA employees contribute more than a ton of non-perishable food to the Foodshare food bank in Hartford each time they run a campaign. The food is then distributed to homeless shelters and soup kitchens in the area.

• Over one hundred employees participated in the annual March of Dimes Walkathon, raising thousands of dollars for programs to reduce infant mortality.

• One hundred fifty CIGNA volunteers arranged a "We Are the Children" Christmas party for more than one thousand underprivileged children and their parents on Christmas Day.

• Three hundred twenty-five employees gave their time and talents to the My Friend Taught Me tutoring program for 180 students at Hartford's Burns Elementary School. Many employees devote far more than classroom time, often spending evenings and weekends mentoring their students.

• Some workers raised more than $5,500 in a walkathon that enabled them to send Burns Elementary students to Camp Courant, a summer arts and recreation program for disadvantaged youth.

• Ninety CIGNA employee volunteers in Philadelphia run Learning, Friends, and Fun, a weekly tutoring session for second, third, and fourth graders that was spawned by the My Friend Taught Me program.

• CIGNA employees in Philadelphia teamed up with Big Sisters to form a Teen Mother program that matches volunteers with pregnant or teen mothers. The CIGNA staff act as friends, counselors, and role models, urging the young women to complete their education and take responsibility for their future.

• More than three hundred CIGNA employee volunteers, led by a colonial fife and drum corps, marched through downtown Philadelphia to historic Independence Park, site of the Liberty Bell and Independence Hall. They spent the day raking, weeding, removing trash, and beautifying this site of our nation's birth.

The company's "Grants for Givers" policy encourages employee volunteers to request $100 grants for the charity to which they give their time. Since the inception of the program in 1982, more than $200,000 has been given away, a fact that clearly makes the volunteers proud of their company. In 1992, CIGNA learned from employee surveys that they "wanted the ability to give of themselves, not just their pocket books," so the company launched the Power of Personal Commitment Program, which encourages employee volunteerism as well as their financial generosity. In addition to monthly newsletters that list volunteer opportunities and stories and photographs of recent projects, CIGNA recognizes a Volunteer of the Month who receives a $500 grant in the name of his or her chosen charity, and once a year, one of those winners is selected as Volunteer of the Year and awarded a $2,500 personal check and another $2,500 for a favorite nonprofit organization.

Texaco

Texaco uses both of the above approaches—large-scale, company-created programs and encouragement of diverse, employee-chosen projects—with considerable success. For those employees who don't want to create their own projects, the company organizes a program that has everything prearranged, and the employee volunteers simply have to show up and go to work. But Texaco also actively supports local projects in which their employees participate.

Like many companies in the energy business, Texaco felt a need to launch a project aimed at environmental protection. The company started a program called the Texaco Global Releaf Urban Tree Initiative, which targets blighted urban areas and then plants trees there. These are not tiny saplings, but large trees, ready to make an immediate aesthetic and ecological improvement in the neighborhood. Texaco pays for the trees—a hefty $2 million in just the first two years—and employee volunteers plant them and nurture them along until they are fully established in their new home.

The company has brought over seventeen thousand volunteers together to plant over 10,000 trees across the country in the past three years. In a massive one-day event called Spring TreeFest, Texaco employees and their families planted 2,793 trees in just three hours along a sixteen-mile stretch of Houston's Braes Bayou. Texaco's goal is to take the Global Releaf Initiative into every community using their own employee volunteers, not only to plant the trees but to be trained by American Forests (formerly the American Forestry Association) so that those staff can then motivate and oversee groups of private citizens to expand the project in areas where Texaco may not have a significant employee presence.

The company also urges its employees to volunteer in local good causes of their own choosing. Texaco made funds available in 1992 for such volunteers to request grants for the charitable organizations to which they give their time. The list of such employee activities is several pages long, but includes the following:

- Employee volunteers at Texaco's Maysville, Oklahoma, gas plant regularly dress up in clown costumes and visit sick children in area hospitals.
- Employees in the company's Midland, Texas, facility operate a Meals on Wheels route once a week, year-round.
- Texaco employees in Ventura County, California, volunteer as tutors in a literacy program that teaches adults to read.
- Workers in the company's Universal City, California, facility visit a nursing home every Wednesday taking small gifts, candy, and cards—but most importantly, themselves—to the elderly residents.

Rohm and Haas

Rohm and Haas's strong corporate dedication to helping the needy dates back a century and comes from its benevolent founder, F. Otto Haas. It continues today under his heirs, who still control the company. In fact, John Haas, F. Otto's son, now in his seventies, still devotes several hours each week to volunteer activities, according to Carol Pyle, assistant manager of corporate social investment. The chemical giant is based in Philadelphia, where it is considered a major supporter of philanthropy, but wherever Rohm and Haas maintains a facility there is a strong commitment to employees who volunteer in the community. Examples of volunteerism include the following:

• For more than a decade, the company has sponsored a mentoring program that pairs employee volunteers with inner-city disadvantaged high school students in Philadelphia. The project now includes job preparation seminars that help the students prepare for their big step into the business world.

• Rohm and Haas employees in Berlin, Connecticut, launched Project Upbeat, which trained high school students not only to "just say no" to drugs but also to act as role models for their peers. Some 150 high school students are involved in the program, and the employees have seen its effects spreading throughout the community's middle and elementary schools. At a Project Upbeat Awareness Day picnic in 1992, over two thousand students and parents participated.

• David Sutton, an employee with the company's herbicide division, created *Poetvision*, a series of twelve ninety-minute videotapes designed to stimulate the interest of high school students in poetry. The program was so successful, it is now used in 250 schools around the United States.

• Rohm and Haas's Houston employees organize a Houston Handicapped Kids Day, attended by over eight hundred physically and mentally challenged children and their families. The day includes carnival rides, face painters, a petting zoo, and a picnic. A disc jockey provides the musical entertainment so everybody can dance when the sun goes down. At the end of the day, everyone receives small gifts.

• Rohm and Haas employees in Philadelphia have "adopted" the roughly one hundred homeless students who live in two shelters. Three times every week, thirty-eight volunteers show up to tutor the children and provide one-on-one support as role models, mentors, and friends. On weekends and during school vacations, many of the volunteers take the children on educational and cultural-enrichment field trips to museums or the zoo. "We get fifteen thousand kids a year coming through here, and I've never seen a group of children so well behaved as those," said one official after a tour of the Franklin Institute.

Rohm and Haas also has a Dollars for Doers program that encourages employees to volunteer in community service roles and to request grants of up to one thousand dollars for the causes to whom they give their time. In 1992, the company gave five hundred such awards.

Volunteer of the Year awards are given to employees and retirees throughout the country. Each winner receives a one-thousand-dollar check for the charity of his or her choice. "Winning it made me feel really good," says Ben Lerner, who presented his award check to Trevor's Campaign for the Homeless, to whom he had devoted many hours feeding the street people. "The plaque didn't mean that much, but I was so happy to be able to give that check to the campaign. I grew up in Philadelphia and saw those people all my life. Then I went to live in New Jersey and was able to ignore the problems of the city. The volunteer work I have done for the homeless is my way of coming back to my roots to give something back to the community I was raised in."

Volunteers are invited to recognition luncheons and are prominently featured in a lavish, full-color "Corporate Social Investment Report" produced each year.

Aetna Life and Casualty

This large, Connecticut-based insurance company has established certain projects that concentrate on two areas of need: immunization and primary health care for disadvantaged children, and higher education for minority students. Although there is a considerable emphasis on programs and grants that further the corporate goals described above, the company is very supportive of all volunteerism benefiting the needy. Aetna is one of the few domestic companies that does not disqualify volunteerism grants to overseas projects, a case in point being a food program for undernourished children in Chile. In 1974, Chile's infant mortality rate was 97 per 1,000. By 1984, the CONIN (the Corporación Para la Nutrición Infantil) program's intervention had helped improve the rate to 20 per 1,000. The Aetna Foundation also operates a Dollars for Doers program to which employees active in community service may apply for cash grants. Aetna employees' volunteer efforts include the following:

 • Aetna employees and agents in Atlanta adopted the Habitat for Humanity project and built two houses that were then sold to families with limited economic means at below-market value with zero-interest mortgages. "On a Saturday morning, we started with a vacant building lot and a concrete sub-floor. Six weekends later, we presented the keys to a new home to a family," says Don McCarthy, general manager for Aetna's commercial insurance division.

• Carol Krup, a nurse supervisor at the company's Rockford, Illinois, office, helped found Trinity House, an organization that provides emergency shelter and transitional housing for teenage mothers. Krup volunteers regularly at Trinity House, sometimes scrubbing and cleaning to prepare for a new arrival, at other times painting, moving furniture, or just listening and offering advice to the young mothers scared about their babies' and their own futures.

• In Los Angeles, Aetna employees Terry Smith and Gwen Pilot spent a Saturday cleaning up the debris from the riots in south central Los Angeles. These volunteers ventured into the worst-hit areas just a day after the disturbances had ended. "It was an opportunity to show the community, as well as the entire nation, that we were ready to start working toward making things better for everyone," said Smith.

• Employees at Aetna's Milwaukee office dressed up as Easter bunnies and delivered almost two hundred Easter baskets to the young patients at the city's Children's Hospital. To the delight of each child, they found the volunteers had filled the baskets with stuffed animals, games, books, toys, and other gifts. "I'll never forget the look on their faces, their smiles and laughter," said Aetna's Phyllis Eggert.

• In Macon, Georgia, sixty-two employees, decked out in Aetna T-shirts customized for the occasion, participated in the Walk America event to benefit the March of Dimes. They had fun, got some healthy exercise, and raised over $2,500 for their chosen good cause.

• In Enfield, Connecticut, Elaine Gasparini of Aetna's Windsor Customer Service Center spends many hours each month as a volunteer at St. Joseph's Residence, a long-term—care nursing home for the disadvantaged and aged. At meal times, she can be found in the infirmary, helping the sick with their food. At other times, she pitches in wherever she is needed, often spending many hours visiting with residents who would otherwise be alone. Even when she is not at St. Joseph's, she is often helping by running fundraising drives for the home, which relies solely on donations for its operating income. "The work here is so rewarding," says Elaine.

"The residents really appreciate the smallest gestures. Even a five-minute chat brightens up their day."

In 1992, Aetna gave away almost $200,000 through its Dollars for Doers program and another $12,400 in support grants for their retirees' volunteer activities.

3

. . . .

The Company Clearinghouse

This chapter examines employers that differ from those cited in the preceding narrative but still encourage employee volunteerism. Rather than offering a selection of company-sponsored projects, these employers gather information from needy causes that request their help and then try to match them with workers wishing to donate their time and talents. This type of corporate benevolence can prove beneficial to all parties, and it may be operated at a very low cost by the company. It also makes a wider variety of opportunities available to the employees.

Ford Motor Company

In 1990, Ford established ACTS—an acronym for Assisting the Community Through Service—on a trial basis at the company's Louisville, Kentucky, plant and for Detroit, Michigan, employees from the world headquarters in Dearborn. "Our company is so huge, both in employee numbers and geographic distribution, that it is really difficult to launch something on a company-wide basis," explains Bob Reid, Ford's community affairs manager.

The ACTS program invites community service organizations that have a need for volunteers to submit their plans to Ford's community affairs department. Reid's staff then evaluates the organization and what they are trying to accomplish. Projects for the benefit of a specific religious sect, political events, or controversial topics such as abortion or gay rights activities are not permitted. But a diverse array of projects, from one-day events to long-term continuing commitments, are approved and are then published in the ACTS roster of opportunities.

In the early days of ACTS, while Ford was encouraging community organizations to submit their needs, Reid's office sent a brochure describing the program to every employee in the test markets—a total of fifteen thousand workers. Accompanying the ACTS announcement was a questionnaire that asked employees for their input on the concept and for their previous, current, and future interests in community service and volunteerism. Twelve hundred employees responded with completed questionnaires, and all of the answers were entered into a computer.

This data base has been the cornerstone of Ford's voluntary service program. If, for example, a group approaches the company needing twenty people to tutor inner-city children in Detroit or to renovate abandoned houses in Louisville or clean up a polluted river bank, the community affairs office simply accesses the ACTS volunteer data base for employees in the appropriate geographic location who have indicated a desire to donate their time mentoring, renovating, or working on environmental projects.

ACTS produces a regular menu of volunteer opportunities and distributes it to all employees. It also keeps track of the activities that have been matched with Ford volunteers, and even in its very limited pilot phase, it can already point to a large number of successful events: the May 4, 1992, status sheet, for example, lists thirty-one projects that attracted everyone from the one worker who helped the United Cerebral Palsy Association of Greater Detroit to the 262 Ford volunteers who participated in the Paint the Town project. In all, 887 employees responded to the needs identified by the ACTS program in just the first four months of 1992.

Perhaps one reason for the success of voluntary service at Ford is the commitment to that ideal from the very highest echelons of management. "Managers at Ford are expected to be involved in volunteerism," says Bob Reid. "As people work their way up the corporate ladder here, managers realize they have to make community service a part of their function." In fact, Ford's chairman, Harold A.

Poling, is personally involved in a number of projects and serves as co-chairman of the Volunteer Leadership Coalition of Greater Detroit, an organization formed to encourage employee volunteerism from employers throughout southeast Michigan.

Ford has also established a Community Relations Committee (CRC) in most cities around the country where the company has a significant presence. There are currently fifty-eight CRCs, each of which is given a budget by corporate headquarters that is used to motivate employees in their city to undertake local service projects. Each CRC is chaired by a local Ford employee on a voluntary, unpaid basis, and the entire CRC network is coordinated by Bob Reid. His office publishes a handsome quarterly magazine, *Network*, that is distributed to all CRC members. It is filled with news stories, photographs of Ford workers around the country on service projects, and various motivational anecdotes.

The company also recognizes an Outstanding Volunteer of the Year for community service in three categories: active employee, retiree, and youth. The winners are announced each year at the beginning of National Volunteer Week, and each receives a one-thousand-dollar check, payable to a chosen charity. Dick Siegel of Ford's human resources—technical affairs department won the Employee Volunteer of the Year Award in 1992 for the many hours he has donated to the Greater Detroit Society of the Blind. He was matched with a ninety-three-year-old lady and a married senior citizen couple, all three of whom are deaf and blind. Whenever his charges need to visit the doctors, attend Society meetings, or go shopping, Bob drives them there. "It's much more than being a chauffeur," he points out. "It's more like being their guardian. I care about them very much and really do feel like they're part of my family now." Dick learned about the need for volunteers by reading an article in the local newspaper. "It's a good feeling, a proud feeling, to work for a company so supportive of our volunteerism," he adds. "I know a lot of people who wanted to help out in the community but didn't know where to look to become a volunteer. Now, with ACTS, it makes it easy for them to know where the needs are and what is expected of them—whether for a one-day effort or a long-term project."

All in all, Bob Reid is very pleased with the current status of Ford's employee volunteerism program and especially with the direction it is taking in the near future. "I think we're in a better position to see what our people want to do—and are doing—than most companies," he asserts. "We're not about to supplant the voluntary service our staff are already doing privately, but we do practice what we preach about being committed to helping solve our communities' problems, from the top on down. We're providing the channels, the up-front project information, and the easiest way to sign up for the type of work each individual wants to do." Reid also points out that volunteerism also comes from the large number of retirees from Ford, who also receive ACTS program details. By the end of 1993, he expects the ACTS pilot program to be expanded from the initial fifteen thousand employees to an estimated seventy thousand workers in Michigan alone.

Walt Disney Company

It takes a lot of people—about 120,000—to bring That Mouse into television sets, movie theaters, and theme parks around the world. And those people—or "cast members," as the company calls them—are not only wholesome, clean-cut, and positive but also love to volunteer for community service. The Walt Disney Company separates its voluntary efforts into three divisions: Walt Disney Studios, which includes the consumer-products and corporate office staff; Walt Disney Imagineering; and Disneyland. In Florida, the third category would actually be Walt Disney World; in Europe, EuroDisney. A Disneyland employee named Mary Jones, who is now in her eighties, originated the company's volunteer program back in 1983 under the label DCAT: the Disneyland Community Action Team. When cast members in the other divisions heard about the Disneyland activities, they wanted to operate a similar project, and the company ran a contest among all its employees to come up with an appropriate name for such a company-wide program. The winner, an employee from Orlando's Walt Disney World, used wordplay based on Mickey Mouse's ears to call the program VoluntEARS. The name has been used ever since as the umbrella under which all divisions' employee volunteer service projects fall.

Regardless of the location or the division of the company, the VoluntEARS program operates along similar lines. First, an employee-driven, all-volunteer steering committee is formed. The direction is from the community relations department in some instances and from human resources in others. The funding for VoluntEARS differs between divisions. Disneyland uses all the coins the park's visitors toss into the park's numerous fountains and pools—some $20,000 to $30,000 every year—as the sole source of funding. Walt Disney Studios and Imagineering, who don't have such a generous source of income, receive a grant from the parent company.

The steering committee then invites community organizations that need volunteers to contact them with specific details. Each Disney division concentrates most of its activities in the county in which it is located. For example, Disney World primarily serves Orange County, Florida; Disneyland's projects tend to be in Orange County, California; and the Disney Studios and Imagineering divisions generally restrict their efforts to the communities in sprawling Los Angeles County. However, exceptions are made in areas of compelling need, such as when the Disney Studios VoluntEARS sent nearly one hundred people to help clean up in the aftermath of the riots in south central Los Angeles. Similarly, there was a tremendous outpouring of food, clothing, and building supplies for Hurricane Andrew's victims in the Miami area from the Disney World employees several hundred miles away in Orlando.

Organizations who contact the company for help are directed to the VoluntEARS liaison, to whom they fully explain their program and needs. The VoluntEARS committee will generally not participate in an activity for the sole benefit of a specific religious sect, political group, or controversial cause. The entire committee then debates all the requests they have received at regular meetings, usually held monthly. They try to balance the activities they sponsor both by date and category. For instance, if they have participated in six environmental projects in the last six months and have only one project they can adopt this month, they probably would pass on a riverbank cleanup day in favor of, say, taking handicapped kids to the zoo.

Once a project is adopted, a flyer is designed and sent to each cast member in the committee's data base, since that is a proven audience of employees who want to volunteer. The committee also picks a project leader at this time, and he or she becomes the main conduit through whom further training requirements or project up-dates are run. In some cases, the event is publicized to the entire em-ployee base, usually by submitting an article to the internal newspa-per that goes to all staff. Employees are asked to sign up for their chosen activities in advance and are usually welcome to bring family members and friends with them. A week or so before the event, a letter is sent by the VoluntEARS project leader reminding the cast member of the date, time, and location of the activity, and it includes other relevant information such as maps, tools to bring, and sug-gested attire.

When the big day arrives, each volunteer is given a distinctive Disney VoluntEARS T-shirt, and in Disneyland's case, project leaders are given white shirts so any cast member can easily identify them. At the end of the day, the project leader records the names of the VoluntEARS, the number of hours worked, and any other significant information and reports it all to the steering committee, which, in turn, keeps a running account of activities for the year. Each volun-teer cast member receives a very attractive custom-made cloisonné pin with the Disney VoluntEARS logo on it, and for each category of volunteer event they participate in they add to the pin with bars labeled according to the kind of activity: "Environment" or "Education," for example. As the employee volunteers for more events and their pins accumulate multiple bars, it truly becomes a badge of honor for them. At the end of each activity, the project leader writes each participant a personal thank-you note.

Although the preceding paragraphs describe the overall com-pany-wide VoluntEARS program, the projects, employees, and oper-ation of separate Disney divisions are slightly different. Here are some examples from the three divisions.

Disney Studios

The Disney Studios division is located in Burbank, California, and includes the production facilities for television shows and movies along with the Disney University employee training center. The VoluntEARS program has a twenty-person steering committee, which elected Joyce Holiday as their president after she was voted VoluntEAR of the Year in 1993. "One of the things I like most about this is that it is such a grass-roots operation," she says. "It really is employee driven, run by the very volunteers who go into the community to do the work." Joan McCarthy, a volunteer from the community relations department, agrees. "Even though we receive some financial support from the company," she points out, "they realize we get the manpower support from the employees. If management makes a suggestion, it has to go through the steering committee just like all the other ideas. But the company is so supportive and proud of what we're doing."

Much of the day-to-day VoluntEARS work is coordinated by Shannon Ross at Disney University. "Shannon is the very heart of this program," says Joyce, effusively. A questionnaire was sent out to all employees asking for information about their interest in volunteerism. Approximately four hundred questionnaires were completed and returned to Shannon, who entered every name, phone number, and area of interest into a computer. That data base is now the core of the Disney Studios VoluntEARS program. Once a project is approved, a "Project Alert" sheet is prepared, which provides the basic who, what, why, when, and where details and is automatically sent to everyone on the data base. Additions to the volunteer list are being made constantly; at the VoluntEARS booth, set up at a recent corporate employee forum, over two hundred new volunteers were recruited, bringing the list today to over twelve hundred employees.

By offering a diverse menu of projects, the program provides an opportunity for every cast member to find a project of personal interest. In 1992, Disney Studios' first full VoluntEARS year, 2 employees signed up for the food drive for the Burbank Temporary Aid Shelter, and 271 either walked or worked at the Earthwalk fundraiser. All told, in the first year, 540 employees from Disney Studios participated in over forty events for over six thousand hours of service donated. Only two of the projects were fundraising activities, but they garnered an incredible sixty-two thousand dollars in financial contributions.

Projects and events are reviewed carefully. Evaluation sheets are used by the steering committee to elicit suggestions on how to constantly improve the program.

Experts on corporate volunteer programs counsel an employer's senior management on the importance of their own participation in voluntary service projects, and the Walt Disney Company's executives appear to take this challenge seriously. "Mark Zoradi, president of Buena Vista International, was the one who spearheaded our Habitat for Humanity project," says Joan McCarthy. "In fact, he used it as a team-building exercise for several of his executives."

Disney employees are fortunate to have so many resources at their disposal that can help a project. The VoluntEARS steering committee can call on whatever internal sources they need to make an event more successful, from professional artists to video cameras and entertainers. For example, the community relations department contacted 350 children from homeless, abused, or impoverished families through Los Angeles's Fred Jordan Inner City Mission and the Maude Booth Family Center. The kids were invited to visit the Disney Studios for a special showing of *Pinocchio*, after which they were served lunch, given cookies and gift bags, and introduced to famous Disney characters. The VoluntEARS provided the labor to chaperon and play with the children during this memorable day. At other times, the steering committee can propose working jointly on a project with colleagues from another division. Such a cooperative venture occurred in metropolitan Los Angeles for an organization called Caring for Babies with AIDS (CBA). CBA had just built one house and renovated another large building in which they now provide the only residential program in the western United States that cares for HIV- and AIDS-infected infants and children. In preparation for the home's opening, VoluntEARS from the Disney Studios spent two Saturdays cleaning the inside and outside of the building. Meanwhile, the creative artists from the Walt Disney Imagineering division painted colorful full-wall murals of Disney characters in the babies' rooms.

Clearly, the VoluntEARS program has tapped into a wellspring of enthusiastic, eager volunteers at the Disney Studios, and they plan to expand as more needy causes come to the steering committee's attention. "We say no to only a very few projects," says Joan McCarthy. "We're looking to say yes to people, not for reasons to turn them down."

Everyone at Disney Studios has a favorite VoluntEARS story, even though the project is so new. Joan McCarthy tells of an employee, active in community service work, who was transferring from Disney World in Florida to Burbank's Disney Studios, whose main concern was that the California division might not have a VoluntEARS program. Shannon Ross tells of the time she recruited, and was project leader for, twenty employees scheduled to start work at 6 A.M. on a Saturday morning as marshals for the American Cancer Society's Run-A-Thon. "All day Friday, then all Friday night, it rained," she says. "And bear in mind this was June, in southern California, where it never rains. Well, 6 A.M. on Saturday came along, and it was *still* raining torrentially—there were flooded roads, massive traffic jams, and accidents everywhere—and all twenty of our VoluntEARS showed up. I really love this program."

Joyce Holiday concurs. "Although most of our projects are one- or two-day events, I'm involved with a Meals on Wheels delivery service—we call it the Mickey Route—that we do every single Saturday," she says. "It all started when I met a nun who asked for some funding, and now we deliver thirty to forty-five meals every week to senior citizen 'shut-ins.' They are such nice people, and we're often the only people they see, so we try to be really nice to them. They're the forgotten people. We take little extras, like flowers at Easter, and you know, it only takes the tiniest little thing to make their life so special." Joyce tells of the Mickey Route just the previous Saturday, when one regular recipient did not respond to the repeated doorbell ringing. After several attempts, they called for help, and the emergency service found the elderly lady in the spot where she had fallen hours earlier. "She'll be OK," adds Joyce, clearly relieved, "but if we hadn't done that, who knows how long she would have lain there."

Joan McCarthy remembers another occasion when the VoluntEARS made a difference. As soon as the rioting, arson, and looting that had gutted much of south central Los Angeles had subsided, about one hundred Disney VoluntEARS went into the still-smoldering neighborhood and spent the day cleaning, sweeping, and repairing. They probably did as much to repair the residents' faith in mankind as they accomplished in repairing physical structures. "One lady came over to us, literally crying," says Shannon. "'Why are you doing this for us?' she asked. They were all so grateful for what we did, and for how quickly we responded." Long after that day, the cast members in Burbank continued to drop off money, clothing, and food for delivery to the needy in that neighborhood.

Once a year, every employee who has volunteered for any project is invited to a gala "family" event as guests of the company. A top corporate officer then presents recognition awards to the cast members who have made so many people's lives happier. "Last year, chief operating officer Frank Wells was overwhelmed by the volume of projects and manpower we had given," says Joan. "It really makes you feel good about your company when you see how they support this."

It is a credit to the efficiency of Walt Disney Studios and the VoluntEARS committee that they are able to administer the entire program without having to add staff for that purpose. Shannon Ross, Joyce Holiday, Jeff Hoffman, and Joan McCarthy all have full-time jobs with the organization and only oversee the VoluntEARS program as additional duties. They are, in fact, volunteers leading the volunteers program. But their sparkling eyes and obvious enthusiasm as they talk about the success stories of their VoluntEARS projects suggest that they probably would want it no other way.

Walt Disney Imagineering

It is hard to imagine two divisions more different than Disneyland and Walt Disney Imagineering, known in the company as WDI. Employees of the former are gushing, ever so cheerful, always-smiling types, because those are the traits required for jobs that place them constantly in front of the general public. At WDI, even their building is hard to find; hidden away on a side street in Glendale, California, it bears no signs even identifying it as part of the Disney organization.

The Imagineering division builds excitement. Every ride at a Disney theme park—indeed, every Disney theme park itself—was designed and built by the brilliant creative artists and engineers at WDI. Their work is extremely secretive, hence the lack of signage on their buildings: they don't *want* the public to find them. But once inside, the seventeen hundred employees care every bit as much about their communities as their colleagues in the more visible divisions.

"We have no full-time people here putting on our VoluntEARS program," says show writer Ross Osterman. "It's all done on lunch hours or after work." Osterman points out the eclectic group of people that comprise WDI's employees. "There are songwriters, engineers, cartoonists, film writers—over three hundred titles, actually," he says. "So it's kind of hard to pick projects that will capture the interest, and make the best use, of those diverse talents." To make matters more complex, he points out that many employees are constantly shuttling back and forth to Disney theme parks in Tokyo, Orlando, and Paris, in addition to spending time at Disneyland, some fifty miles south.

"The main difference I see between WDI and the other divisions is that anyone can clean up trash or register people at a walkathon," he says, "but our people have such amazing abilities, we want to be in projects where those talents can be used for the benefit of people in need." He gives as an example the recent Glendale street fair that asked WDI to participate. "Anybody could have had a booth with a dunking tank," says Osterman. "But we don't do anything normal here, so our people really got into it and designed interactive musical puppets. They were the talk of the fair. That's an example of how we want to use our special talents in a constructive setting."

"One of the things this division is so good at is telling stories and entertaining people," he adds, describing some possible future projects WDI's VoluntEARS are contemplating. One is the police historical museum and community center for the Los Angeles Police Department. Another is an intriguing request by the Los Angeles Zoo to redesign their animal habitats to provide more natural settings. "It would be really good for us if we could improve the environment for those animals," he muses. In a related request, the L.A. Zoo has been trying to get WDI to design toys that would be durable yet entertaining enough to provide healthy stimulation for their animals. "There's no company in the world that designs toys for zoo animals," says Ross, "so they give an elephant a basketball to play with and it lasts about a minute. That's what's great about the people in Imagineering who spend their whole career designing the stuff we do. We probably have over a hundred employees who could calculate the stress factor an elephant puts on a sphere."

In the first year, Imagineering's VoluntEARS program attracted three hundred employees who worked on twenty projects, donating about three thousand hours of their own time and talents. "The employees have loved having an organized way of reaching out to the community," says Marlo Lee, manager of special services and current president of WDI's VoluntEARS steering committee. Adds Ross Osterman, "We have a core group of volunteers now, which speaks well of the satisfaction level of employees so far." They point out that everything the Imagineering division does is worked on by project teams, bringing the creative thinkers, the designers, the engineers, and then the construction mavens together for continuity from the original dream to the completed "Space Mountain" or whatever the project is. This teamwork has followed through to the VoluntEARS activities. Says Ross, "We did a huge mural down in Mexico, a talent show, a project for the Children's Museum in Los Angeles, and we actually built a maze for a Crippled Children's Society fair, with the aisles wide enough for them to navigate through it on crutches or wheelchairs."

"There's a history of volunteerism in this division," adds Marlo Lee proudly. "And remember, this VoluntEARS program was started 100 percent by the employees, and it's still run that way. It's a real grass-roots concept, not a corporate image thing." That pride and enthusiasm is echoed by people at all rungs of the ladder at WDI. "I saw a sign on a disabled hitchhiker once," says project engineer Susan Toler. "It said, 'I'm disabled today, tomorrow it could be you.' I think about that a lot when I'm volunteering." Tony Hatch, WDI's director of communications, adds, "I think the VoluntEARS program is one of the most important things the company is involved in." Marty Sklar, Walt Disney Imagineering's president, himself an active VoluntEAR, says simply, "I get more out of it than I put into it. I'm really proud of our VoluntEARS and what they do." The closing philosophical thought goes to Marlo Lee: "Our job as Imagineers is to build new worlds; but let's not forget the world we live in."

Disneyland

Tammy McFeggan is the kind of girl every guy wished lived next door. She is tall and pretty and just gushes with enthusiasm and obvious love for her job. In fact, if there were no Tammy McFeggan, Disneyland would probably have the Imagineering folks make one from scratch, because she is exactly the person one would expect to be running the VoluntEARS program in a happy, wholesome place like Disneyland.

Tammy joined Disneyland in 1982 as a part-time employee while still in high school. Her assignments included busing tables and sweeping floors, "but 95 percent of our management staff started that way," she points out. Her personal commitment to helping the needy goes back to her high school days, and it continued after she joined the Walt Disney Company. Tammy's hard work and enthusiasm propelled her up the corporate ladder, and after five years with Disneyland, she was moved into the training and development department. In 1992, she assumed the position of advisor to the VoluntEARS program at the park.

The VoluntEARS are made up of cast members with noticeably different personalities in each division, according to one administrator. Disney Studios' employees tend to be family-oriented, salaried staff. The Imagineering employees are, too, but generally with more technical interests and a little older than the average Disney Studios employee. But Disneyland cast members are mostly hourly workers, with vast swings in seasonal employee numbers, and they are generally younger than their colleagues in the other divisions. An understanding of these traits is crucial to the steering committee when they consider the types of projects to adopt, and to managers as they determine the recognition awards and motivation techniques to employ.

"Disneyland's VoluntEARS steering committee meets monthly, after work," says Tammy. "The committee averages twenty-five to thirty people, most of whom are hourly employees. All projects are undertaken in Orange County, the sprawling suburban county near Los Angeles in which the park is located." At the start of each year, the committee tries to assign quarterly projects in such categories as homelessness, the environment, graffiti removal, and AIDS. Then they invite any organization with a need to submit their "wish list" through Tammy to the steering committee. "What's wonderful about my group (of VoluntEARS) is they don't care how dirty the project is," she says. "Other employee groups might be kind of picky about what they do, but after busing tables in Disneyland our people say, 'You want trash picked up around a pond? Great! You need us to clean up an inner-city lot so a community garden may be planted? No problem!'" Tammy McFeggan smiles and adds, "Our employees are so used to being hospitality-oriented, they're never, ever shy."

Like the Disney Studios, Disneyland maintains a data base of VoluntEARS. McFeggan uses the *Paradox* software and currently has about 1,900 cast members enrolled. The park has a base payroll of 8,000 employees, rising to 14,000 in a busy summer season. "As impressive as that is," she says, "Walt Disney World in Florida has about 50,000 cast members in their peak season." Many of the projects adopted by her steering committee are what Tammy calls "tack-ons," where the event is already under way, or at least organized, and her VoluntEARS provide mass manpower. Employees sign up for events after Tammy sends a "Project Alert" flyer to everyone in the data base, or after reading her monthly VoluntEARS column in the staff newsletter.

Nineteen ninety-three was the tenth anniversary of Disneyland's community volunteerism program. In 1983, 117 volunteers helped on four projects. By 1993, 1,904 VoluntEARS were working on fifty projects—almost one per week. Records show that the cast members have contributed over four hundred thousand hours of voluntary service time to needy causes in the first decade.

The types of project they adopt are far too diverse to be described in this narrative. "We turn almost nobody down," says Tammy McFeggan. "Someone will propose an event, and two or three members of the steering committee will say, 'I think we should hold off on that one because we ran a project like that last month,' and then a chorus of other members will say, 'Oh, but this is such a cute idea, and they really need our help,' and then they'll adopt the project anyway." Even after all these years, McFeggan is still amazed at the wonderful things the cast members do in their free time. "We had a seventy-year-old lady completely organize a country-western dance, and we've had 250 people show up for potato gleaning at the experimental agricultural farm at Camp Pendleton. Another idea that all started with one person's suggestion was where the VoluntEARS adopted a local school in a very poor neighborhood. The children were from homes so mired in poverty that they could not afford to buy school supplies. So the cast members put huge drop boxes in the park and asked co-workers and visitors to donate pencils, rulers, pads—any type of school supply item. In addition to collecting enough school supplies for every student, the Disneyland VoluntEARS ran a fundraiser and turned over five thousand dollars to the school to buy televisions, VCRs, and chairs, which the school's budget cuts had prevented them buying before. At an assembly called for the presentation, one boy read a poem to the VoluntEARS which he called "My Gift to Mickey for Him Allowing Me to Stay in School."

One major advantage Tammy's group has over the Disney Studios and Imagineering divisions is Disneyland itself: many projects involve bringing handicapped kids or disadvantaged citizens to the park. At other times they have sold tickets to special fundraising events inside the park after it has closed to the general public. "Minnie's Moonlight Madness" was a combination trivia contest and treasure hunt for which the VoluntEARS met every Monday for six months to plan. Twelve hundred people paid to participate, and they raised over sixty-five hundred dollars for charity. Another project was planned to coincide with Mickey Mouse's sixty-fifth birthday on November 18, 1993. The VoluntEARS offered a five-hour "ride-a-thon" aboard the "It's a Small World" attraction, with participants lining up sponsors in advance for each hour they could stay on. The proceeds benefited sixty-five hundred underprivileged children worldwide.

Another new fundraising program to be initiated on a permanent basis is the aluminum recycling plan. When the custodial employees clean up the park, they will separate aluminum cans and throw them in retention bins at various backstage locations. Then, twice or three times a week, VoluntEARS will collect these cans from those bins and deliver them to a recycler, from whom the VoluntEARS program will get paid. "We're planning to use the money to pay for seeing-eye dogs for the blind," says Tammy, "At $6,000 to $8,000 per dog, that'll be quite a blessing for the recipients."

Once a year, the entire steering committee is taken out for dinner at an exclusive private club as a way of thanking them for their service. Then the entire VoluntEARS corps—including friends and family members if they have participated in an event—is invited to a gala banquet at the Disneyland Hotel. The evening has music and a theme—such as a sock hop or hoe down, and recognition pins are presented to each VoluntEAR by a senior executive of the Disney organization. The evening closes with a very moving, professionally produced video showing flashbacks of smiling cast members at volunteer events throughout the year.

Tammy McFeggan tells of the instruction she used to give when each new employee, whether starting as a vice president or a custodian, would come through her training class. From Walt's earliest days when he made cartoons, to today when millions of people stream through Disney parks in Anaheim, Tokyo, Paris, and Orlando, "The whole Disney goal comes down to three words," she would teach employees, "and those words are: we create happiness."

With that simple goal ingrained into the very culture of the Disney staff, it is easy to see why so many of them give so much of their time to so many people in need. From the abused child whose face lights up in a smile when Mickey Mouse himself gives her a big kiss, to the lonely senior citizen to whom a Disney Studios employee brings a meal and companionship, to the little boy who wrote a poem to express his joy at now having school supplies—for all of these and ten thousand more, Walt's caring, compassionate cast members *are* creating happiness.

4

Initiating a Corporate
Voluntary Service Program

What if you are an executive of a large company who has read this far and can see the value, both internally and externally, of establishing a program that promotes volunteerism among your employees? Or suppose you are the owner of a small business who wants to encourage your staff to be good community citizens, but you don't have the budget or resources of an IBM? This chapter is a step-by-step guide to achieving your goals in either situation.

The Points of Light Foundation provides corporations with many excellent resources for encouraging volunteerism among their work forces. One superb publication is entitled *Developing a Corporate Volunteer Program: Guidelines for Success*, and it explains what the Foundation calls its "Principles of Excellence in Community Service: A Plan to A.C.T.," which is the keystone of a committed, balanced, workable corporate community service program. It is explained as follows:

Acknowledge that the corporation's community service involvement and its employee volunteer efforts contribute to the achievement of its business goals

* By incorporating in the corporate vision, as expressed through mission statements, credos, or social policy statements, the

recognition that societal and community issues have a direct relationship to the company and to its future success

- By integrating the company's social vision with its business vision, thus making community service and volunteering part of business operations
- By communicating the corporate social vision consistently to the company's external and internal stakeholders
- By communicating to all employees, from senior management to front-line workers, the message that volunteer service is the responsibility of everyone
- By participating in leading the volunteer effort

Commit to establish, support, and promote an employee volunteer program that encourages the involvement of every employee, and treat it like any other core business function

- By allocating sufficient resources to develop, manage, and sustain successful employee volunteer efforts
- By managing the employee volunteer program effectively, that is, with a business plan
- By establishing policies, procedures, and incentives that encourage optimum employee participation
- By using community involvement to contribute to key departmental objectives
- By developing volunteer projects that utilize the distinctive competencies and skills of the company and its employees
- By making a long-term commitment to the program

Target community service efforts at serious social problems in the community

- By surveying employees to determine their interests in working on serious social problems
- By focusing employee volunteer programs so that they address serious, systemic problems
- By conducting regular and ongoing evaluations to determine the impact of the company's employee volunteer programs and

other community involvement programs on serious social problems

Since every organization is different, it is difficult to define the precise order of the various steps that should be taken to establish such a program in your company, but you should do the following:

1. Identify your purpose.
2. Determine employee interest.
3. Establish the structure of your volunteer effort.
4. Define your corporate commitment.
5. Determine your community's needs.
6. Establish employee volunteer recognition activities.
7. Decide how to evaluate success.

1. *Identify your purpose.* Be honest. Why use the company's financial and personnel resources to promote employee volunteerism? Is it to enhance the corporate image, to stimulate employee morale, to address problems in the community that disturb you? There are no right or wrong answers here. But if you don't identify your motivation for creating this program, you are asking for trouble later on.

2. *Determine employee interest.* Depending on whether you plan to launch the program in a limited way, such as with one department or geographic location on a trial basis, or with a bang, with all departments starting the volunteer program simultaneously, you need to sample employee interest first. Some companies use their internal newsletters; others simply send a memo around. Some invite representatives from several departments to come together as a focus group, while other firms send a questionnaire to employees to determine their interest in general or as applied to specific projects.

3. *Establish the structure of your volunteer effort.* Who is going to set this new program up? An outside community service and volunteerism consultant? You? Once established, will it fall under the aegis of human resources, community affairs, public relations—or are you small enough for it to report directly to you? In that event, do you really have enough time to commit to this in addition to all your other duties? The Points of Light Foundation research shows that department managers responsible for employee volunteerism

initiatives spend on average 20 percent of their time managing the program. Do you have an extra 20 percent of each day you could give to help this project grow? How will service events be selected, and volunteers contacted? How about a totally autonomous, self-governing, grass-roots employee steering committee? Could you— would you—let them run with such a program even if they made decisions you might not have made yourself? Will you promote activities in which your employees will work together on specific projects? Or do you plan a clearinghouse option in which the committee will list the activities of various needy organizations and your employees will sign up for their personal choice of projects?

4. *Define your corporate commitment.* The two M's here are *management* and *money.* Studies of employee volunteer groups nationwide indicate an extremely strong link between employee morale and the participation in service projects by top management. Will your CEO and vice presidents go out on community cleanup days, five-kilometer runs, or mentoring appointments with at-risk kids? Will your company include corporate and employee volunteerism as a goal in its mission statement? Has senior management approved the budget and made the financial commitment to support the company's volunteer program?

5. *Determine your community's needs.* Talk to your local Volunteer Center; they are rich sources of information on community needs. If there is no such agency in your town, try the chamber of commerce; the Rotary, Jaycees, or Lions Clubs; the Boy or Girl Scouts; or leaders of the places of worship. There is also frequently a volunteer service office at city hall. Do not forget two excellent sources of information about community needs: the local newspaper and your own employees.

6. *Establish employee volunteer recognition activities.* Employees rarely list "recognition" as one of the reasons they volunteer. Yet a photograph in the staff newsletter showing them volunteering can be a source of pride. The same is true of a letter of appreciation from the CEO or even from a department head. Other tokens of recognition for workers who participate in voluntary service might include

- Certificates of appreciation
- Volunteerism lapel pins
- Nominations for external volunteer awards

- An annual recognition luncheon, dinner, or reception with an address by the CEO or a motivational speaker

7. *Decide how to evaluate success.* As one senior executive interviewed for this book said, "I can walk into any department on Monday morning and tell, just by the increased morale and productivity, who participated in volunteer activities over the weekend."

In a 1992 survey conducted by the conference board for The Points of Light Foundation, companies reported receiving the following indirect benefits from corporate volunteer programs:

94 percent said it "improves the company's public image."
94 percent said it "helps create healthier communities."
92 percent said it "enhances the impact of financial contributions."
85 percent said it "makes working with community government easier."

Respondents reported the following benefits to employees and employee development:

93 percent said it "builds employee teamwork skills."
91 percent said it "improves employee morale."
90 percent said it "attracts better employees because of image of community concern."
86 percent said it "provides training for employees."
77 percent said it "affords one way for the company to keep valued employees."

Respondents reported the following direct benefits to the company's bottom line:

77 percent said it "provides a way to implement corporate strategic and business goals."
74 percent said it "seems to lead to increased productivity of employees."
63 percent said it "has a positive impact on productivity."

The most common way to evaluate the success of a volunteer service project is to ask participants to complete a survey form. In many cases, such statistics as the number of employees volunteering, their total hours donated, the number of projects served, and the total dollars spent are kept on an accumulating basis so that an impressive total community contribution such as "160 employees giving 3,045 hours of their time to 14 community service projects" can be given at the year's end.

At the end of the year, the corporate volunteer program can evaluate the numbers by comparing them with previous years to determine, presumably, that "more is better." They should also compare that year with the overall objectives set at the start of the program. Answer the following: Have the projects worked on and the employees who volunteered for them achieved the results for which the program was established? Has the company's mission been met? Has the community been improved because of their actions? Once you have determined these answers, close the loop. Go back to step one as you set your company's sights on the employee volunteer program for next year. Reexamine your objectives: Are they still appropriate? Should they be fine-tuned? Take a look at your goals now that you've got a one-year track record. Should they be changed for the coming year?

If you are not sure or just don't have the time, do everyone a favor. Delegate this most important task to an employee, a committee, or a community service volunteerism consultant who *can* give it the time it deserves. There are too many benefits of a well-organized volunteer program for the company, the employees, and those in need in your community for your program to fall apart because of poor organization or evaluation.

5

. . . .

Getting Started as an Individual

You have read through twenty chapters of this book and have been inspired and motivated by the stories of people just as busy as you who have made the world a better place through their volunteerism. You are probably asking yourself, How can *I* get started in voluntary service? Assuming that you do not yet have the perfect project in mind, the steps you need to take as a beginning volunteer include the following:

1. Examining your volunteer traits and interests
2. Choosing the ideal project
3. Finding additional volunteers
4. Finding sources of funding and supplies
5. Protecting against legal liability
6. Obtaining free media coverage

Examining Your Volunteer Traits and Interests

It is critically important to ascertain your likes and dislikes before you plunge headlong into a project. If you are the type of person who falls apart when you are having a bad-hair day, for example, it is probably a bad choice for you to enlist in an environmental cleanup project that involves taking a two-day wilderness hike in inclement weather. That is not such a preposterous scenario. One of the people who spent a considerable sum of money to join my group of volunteers to build an orphanage in the Dominican Republic whined and complained endlessly because it was so hot. Now there's a surprise for a tropical country in the month of August!

CIGNA had an excellent quiz prepared for their prospective volunteer employees by Volunteer Centers. It is reproduced below with their permission.

THE "GET READY TO VOLUNTEER" QUIZ

When you think about volunteering, ask yourself the following questions:

• What kind of activities, interests or hobbies do I enjoy and do well? Would I want to use these interests while volunteering? Or, would I like to do something different?

• Are there any causes, interest groups or issues that are important to me?

• What kind of time commitment am I able to make at this point in my life?

The answers to these questions will help you define who you would like to help and your time availability. The quiz that follows will help you decide the style and level of work you would find most rewarding, e.g., direct association with people, the opportunity to tackle and complete a job or the chance to have an influence on other people's lives. It's important to identify what motivates you most so you can choose a position that showcases the best you have to give.

How would you like to spend your time?
(Circle your preference in each category.)

A. 1. Working with friends to pack food in a food bank;
    2. Helping the food bank to develop an inventory system;
    3. Speaking to a group to encourage them to give money that will support the food bank's work.

B. 1. Acting as a "buddy" to a pregnant woman through a maternity care clinic;
    2. Helping to renovate a new building for the clinic;

THE "GET READY TO VOLUNTEER" QUIZ, CONT'D.

3. Chairing a committee to organize a walkathon that will benefit the clinic.

C. 1. Working with others to repair homes for disaster victims;
   2. Finding temporary housing in the community for disaster victims;
   3. Spearheading clothing drives in a five-county area to bring help to victims.

D. 1. Training to be a visitors' guide at a museum;
   2. Helping to mount exhibits at a museum;
   3. Serving on a museum board.

E. 1. Tutoring children in grades K through 12;
   2. Writing a manual for school tutors;
   3. Coordinating all volunteers in the school to plan workshops for volunteers and parents.

F. 1. Assisting in serving meals at a shelter;
   2. Assessing the needs of the long-term shelter residents to prepare them to live independently;
   3. Mobilizing community support that will bring job training specialists into the shelter.

G. 1. Providing companionship to a homebound person;
   2. Collecting medical and legal data to use as referrals for homebound people;
   3. Leading an orientation for prospective volunteers who will visit people in their homes.

Count the number of times you answered "1," "2" and "3."
Determine your preferred work style below.
1.   If the majority of numbers you circled were "1s," you should seek volunteer opportunities that involve working directly with people or in group activities.
2.   If the majority of numbers you circled were "2s," you

should seek volunteer opportunities in which there are challenging organizational needs to be filled.

3. If the majority of numbers you circled were "3s," you
should seek opportunities that allow you to take management
or leadership roles in activities such as problem solving and
fundraising.

This quiz was developed by VOLUNTEER CENTERS, a program of the United
Way of Southeastern Pennsylvania, at the request of the CIGNA Foundation.

Now that you have a clearer focus on what type of volunteer
you are, it is important to know *why* you are embarking on this venture and what you expect to get from it. Above all, be totally honest
with yourself. There are so many needs for voluntary service that it
is senseless to choose a project for the wrong reason. You will get
bored or be ineffective, and that will negatively affect you and the volunteers around you. There are plenty of opportunities for everyone,
so pick a project you will enjoy working on.

Independent Sector published a handy booklet which contains
the following "Guidelines for Volunteers":

1. **Know what you want out of volunteering.** You can volunteer in order to promote a cause, advance your career, meet
   new friends, gain recognition, or simply enjoy the personal satisfaction that comes from helping others.

2. **Check the time** it takes to do a particular volunteer job.
   How does the time commitment fit your schedule and lifestyle?

3. **Think about your skills**, interests, and life experiences and
   how they could be useful in a volunteer setting.

4. **Let your employer help.** Many companies have corporate
   volunteer programs or referral services for volunteer opportunities.

5. **Keep your eyes and ears open** when you are at schools, libraries, churches, hospitals, or civic and art events. They're all
   good places to find out about volunteer needs.

6. **Talk to the director of volunteers** (most larger organizations have one) about your prospective "job" as a volunteer: training, hours, supervision, and mutual expectations.
7. **Be open and honest** about your desire for meaningful and satisfying work and the need to have the acceptance and respect of the staff.
8. Be willing to **give and take honest feedback** in your volunteer job and, when necessary, to be an advocate for change.
9. **Respect confidentiality** in volunteer settings.
10. **Most important of all,** bring your heart and your sense of humor to your volunteer service, along with the enthusiastic spirit which is, in itself, a priceless gift.

Choosing the Ideal Project

By contacting your local Volunteer Center you will open the door to an extensive resource on nearby volunteer needs. The first decision you should make is whether you want to initiate your own project or help out on an existing one. Your predominance of 1, 2, or 3 answers in the above quiz should help you in this regard. The following checklist is produced by The Points of Light Foundation to help volunteers focus on the type of project to which they are best suited.

MY COMMUNITY SERVICE PROFILE

(Check all that apply.)

The gifts that I have to give are

____ Teaching someone a skill or subject

____ Listening to or counseling someone who is troubled

____ Mentoring someone who needs a good role model

____ Calling on people who are lonely

My Community Service Profile, Cont'd.

____ Using my professional skills or hobbies to help others

____ Other _____

_____

_____

_____

_____

The community problems of greatest concern to me are

____ The needs of children and youth   ____ Teen pregnancy

____ Poverty   ____ Health care

____ Homelessness   ____ Mental illness

____ Drug and alcohol abuse   ____ Crime

____ Education and literacy   ____ Hunger

____ The needs of senior citizens

____ Other _____

_____

_____

_____

_____

MY COMMUNITY SERVICE PROFILE, CONT'D.

I would like to work

____ On my own or in a situation where I have a lot of freedom

____ As part of a group that I organize

____ As part of a group that someone else organizes

____ In my own neighborhood

____ Outside of my own neighborhood

____ Through my place of work

____ Through my school

____ Through my place of worship

____ Through a club or organization I belong to

___ With a specific program: _____

_____

_____

**I would like to work up to ___ hours a week
at the following times**

____ Daytime, Monday through Friday

____ Evenings, Monday through Friday

____ Weekends

MY COMMUNITY SERVICE PROFILE, CONT'D.

Through my involvement, I hope to

____ Put my ideas to work   ____ Develop new skills

____ Make new social connections   ____ Feel something real

____ Use skills I don't use on my job

____ Learn more about problems in my community

By now, you should have a fairly clear vision of what general type of project you are best suited for. If you are heading in the direction of starting your own new project, go directly to the next section, "Finding Additional Volunteers." If your focus is as a spoke in a wheel, helping out with an existing program, here are some suggestions on where to find a need for projects in your area of interest:

1. *Check with your employer.* If you work for a large company, ask the human resources staff if there is a person or department that handles employee community service volunteerism. You may even have a community affairs department in your firm. If so, contact the appropriate person, tell them of your area of interest, and ask for their information packet of policies concerning employee voluntary service. You may well discover that they have a policy of paid leave while you are doing volunteer work, or at least matching grants that effectively double your own contributions to your charity. Many companies also have a program similar to Dollars for Doers, described in earlier chapters.

If you work for a smaller company, talk to your supervisor or the president. Many times, small firms are much more flexible than giant corporations, particularly when it comes to donating merchandise. I used to own an office supply company, and barely a day went by when we didn't donate stationery, a nice pen set, or a briefcase to the numerous local good causes that came in looking for fundraising gifts. Since I sold the company, I've asked the two large-chain office supply stores nearby for some small token gifts for nonprofit organizations I've been involved in and have always been refused.

2. *Call your local Volunteer Center or The Points of Light Foundation.* This nonprofit group merged with the National Volunteer Center in 1991 and is the preeminent independent voluntary service organization in the country. The foundation helps the business community build the corporate volunteer programs and works through the media to shape popular attitudes about community service.

3. *Contact the National Association.* If you want to help in specific areas such as AIDS, the homeless, or muscular dystrophy, call the national association and ask for the telephone contact of the closest local chapter to you. Most national associations can be reached via a toll-free number, so call 1 (800) 555-1212 for your organization. If that doesn't work, there is a good chance the association has an office in Washington, D.C., so try asking for them at 1 (202) 555-1212. If you strike out again, ask at your county library's reference desk. When you offer your services to the local chapter you'll invariably be welcomed like a long-lost relative, they'll be so glad to hear from you.

4. *Refer to* Volunteer USA, an excellent book listing hundreds of volunteer opportunities. See the Bibliography.

5. *Ask your place of worship.* Most religious leaders see more needs than their own congregation can possibly address, and they network with other leaders both within their denomination and at interfaith meetings. They can frequently be of enormous help in directing your volunteer efforts.

6. *Contact other agencies,* such as the United Way, county or state social agencies (usually found in the county seat or state capital), city hall, or service clubs such as Rotary, Junior League, Lions, Kiwanis, Jaycees, B'nai Brith, or the Knights of Columbus; all are potential sources of volunteer programs in areas of interest you have selected.

Finding Additional Volunteers

Brian O'Connell, president of Independent Sector, an organization that undertakes regular extensive research on trends in volunteerism and benevolence, reveals that "the most common reason volunteers become involved is because someone asks them to help." Not only can I corroborate that from personal experience but for numerous reasons I urge you not to go it alone unless you plan just the briefest, simplest little project. You will enjoy the companionship, the sharing of ideas, and the dramatic expansion of your network for donated equipment and supplies if you'll just bring more people into your project.

So where do you find them? Ask your friends, co-workers, other members of your place of worship. If you are a member of a service club, such as Rotary, ask your fellow club members. Even if you are not a member, call up the president and tell him or her about your idea. Maybe he will adopt it as a club project, or at the very least will invite you to a club meeting as the speaker, during which you can ask the audience for volunteers.

Think carefully about your project. Who is most likely to be moved by the cause you are addressing? For example, if you decide to collect clothing, formula, and medication for an inner-city home for AIDS babies, what better source of help than the other mothers you see every day at your child's day-care facility? If you are starting an outreach program to find housing and jobs for homeless veterans, why not ask for volunteers at your local Veterans of Foreign Wars (VFW) hall, or at officers and Noncommissioned Officer (NCO) clubs at a nearby military base?

If the sheer logistics of your proposed project seem overwhelming, don't try to figure sources of your help as you drive between appointments; sit down in a quiet place with the television off and the children in bed and start with a blank piece of paper. As you focus your mind on your project, ideas will start coming fast and furiously. Write everything down. You now have a list of probably dozens of potential volunteers who, like you once, are sitting at home because nobody ever asked them to help make the world a gentler place in which to live.

Finding Sources of Funding and Supplies

Here is another reason why it is important to have several people involved in your project. It is of critical importance that a budget be developed, making allowances for unexpected costs and price increases. By involving others in this process, you are less likely to overlook a cost item that could affect the entire project. Once the budget is adopted, it is time to start finding sources for the projected income you have listed in budget categories such as "Foundation Grants," "Fundraising Events," and "Individual Gifts." Having several people involved is also helpful in this phase, since you will be less likely to overlook a potential source of funding.

First check with your employer. As you have read in preceding chapters, many companies grant employees cash donations in the form of Dollars for Doers funds or in support of some similar program. Then talk with your volunteers. If your budget needs are relatively modest, they might agree to outright donations or monthly pledges that meet the entire funding requirement. If you have a project large enough to require an advisory board, don't overlook them as a primary source of funds. There is an old saw about putting board members of a charity to the Three-G Test: the three G's stand for "give, get, or get off," meaning every board member should be expected to either give generously to the organization, have the contacts or influence to get others to do so, or get off the board. I'm not entirely comfortable with this rather brutal, mercenary phrase, but I have sat on enough boards watching members tirelessly debate the most inane points and veto perfectly good suggestions while never contributing a dime to the organization we were all supposedly pledged to support.

Once again, it is useful to sit in a quiet place with a blank piece of paper and brainstorm for sources of funding. Service clubs such as Rotary, Lions, and Jaycees are most likely to grant small gifts—say, one hundred to five hundred dollars—to projects within their community. My Rotary Club immediately gave five hundred dollars—and a dozen volunteers—to beautify the community by planting flowers and shrubs around the signs on the main highways that read, "Welcome to Marlton"; but the club would probably not fund a cleanup of a national park in some distant state. Churches and places of worship are generally most likely to fund a project if it is (1) local or (2) connected with their denomination. If yours is both, get together with the pastor and ask for suggestions on how and through whom you should proceed to get approval.

The object of this book is to highlight volunteerism, not fundraising. So this section is not intended to be a blueprint for finding every conceivable source of financing—there are excellent books devoted exclusively to that topic.

One final point to remember: if you are collecting money for some wonderful project you have put together, the chances are the donations people make—including your own contributions and non-reimbursed expenses—are not tax deductible, according to tax expert Jerry Albrecht. A tax deduction may generally be taken only for donations to IRS 501(c)3 nonprofit organizations. You might want to check with your accountant before accepting thousands of dollars in donations from generous friends who will then claim tax deductions improperly.

Albrecht notes that the 501(c)3 status must be applied for on IRS Form 1023, and the application requires a filing fee of between $150 and $375. "One cannot solicit contributions as tax deductible unless the organization has received acknowledgment from the IRS that their tax-exempt status has been approved," says Jerry Albrecht, adding that "if the organization applies for charitable status within fifteen months of inception and is successful in its application, then all contributions made to the organization from day one qualify as deductible contributions."

Of course, if your volunteer work is for the benefit of an existing charity or tax-exempt organization, your friends and supporters can avoid any problems by making their contribution payable to that organization.

Protecting Against Legal Liability

Some people might use the fear of liability as an excuse to do nothing. Such fears are generally unfounded, assuming that you use reasonable care in all of your charitable activities. "There are at least two relevant and distinct doctrines at work here," says Christopher Rade Musulin, a partner at New Jersey's Wells & Singer, P.A., one of the state's oldest continuous law practices. "For as long as charitable and benevolent activities have existed, a common-law doctrine known as charitable immunity generally insulated organizations and individual participants from liability for civil wrongs. Thereafter, with the advent of liability insurance, state courts gradually abandoned the doctrine as a bar to liability. Generally speaking, in the modern world, the payment of an insurance premium usually provides sufficient protection. Acknowledging this, as long as the organization carries sufficient liability coverage, including liability coverage for directors and officers, the fear of liability should not operate as a bar to participation. It is also the case that, in the final analysis, the participant should always employ reasonable care when discharging her or his charitable activities. This is always the best bet for avoiding liability. In addition, many states have limited either liability or damages by statute where charitable organizations are involved."

The second relevant legal doctrine, also developed from the common law, is referred to as the Good Samaritan rule. "This concept is entirely distinct from the charitable immunity doctrine," says Musulin, "although it is relevant when discussing the fear of liability related to benevolent and charitable activities. It may also serve as an additional or alternative defense against the liability claim. Generally speaking, there is no obligation placed upon a stranger to assist another individual in need. However, once a person volunteers assistance, an obligation arises to employ 'reasonable care.' The most common situation involves assisting a sick or injured person on the street, or attempting to save someone drowning in the ocean. Whenever acting as a Good Samaritan or assisting others in such situations, it is now the standard in most state jurisdictions that the actor must employ reasonable care. As long as reasonable care is used in this, or generally, most any endeavor, liability should be remote."

As an example, Musulin describes a situation in which you are driving on a narrow country road when a car approaches you from behind, travelling at a higher speed. This driver wishes to pass you. In a fit of benevolence, you roll down your window and wave your hand, a clear indication to the second driver that all is safe to pass. However, you fail to observe the tractor trailer in the opposite lane shortly ahead. The second driver passes you and is involved in a head-on collision. Despite your benevolent desires, you failed to employ reasonable care. You will most likely be responsible to the injured parties based on your negligence.

Musulin suggests that an attorney familiar with both the charitable immunity doctrine and the Good Samaritan rule in your state should be consulted if liability remains a serious concern. He also says that, as is the case with charitable immunity, most states have statutes codifying Good Samaritan standards, frequently limiting both liability and damages.

Obtaining Free Media Coverage

Although you are not involved in community service work for the publicity, there is an enormous value in obtaining free media coverage. It reflects well on the company, motivates the employees when they—and their friends and family—see their picture in the local newspaper, and enhances the image of both the media and the community you are serving.

There is probably not a charitable group in the United States that hasn't heard at least one of its members say, "And let's call the press and have them come out and cover it" while discussing an upcoming volunteer project or awards presentation. Similarly, there is probably no well-established service club or charity at which the mere mention of publicity would not produce a tirade by one or more of the members about "the lousy local newspaper that never covers any of our activities." It's not impossible to get free media coverage. But to have any chance of getting publicity for your volunteer project it is vital to understand some media facts of life.

The newspaper you contact is in the *news business*. I emphasize both words for a purpose. First, let's discuss news. You buy the paper every day to get the latest information on matters concerning the nation, the economy, and people in your community. In the case of television, they have to fit all that—plus sports, weather, business news, political events, and much more—into twenty-one minutes of air time. The eight wonderful people who spent last Saturday morning cleaning up the local riverbank just aren't important enough to their hundreds of thousands (or millions) of viewers to justify coverage.

Newspapers have similar limitations, but instead of time, they are limited by space. According to Bernard "Bud" Umbaugh, a thirty-three-year newspaper veteran and director of promotions for Calkins Newspaper Group, "The size of any newspaper is based on the amount of advertising scheduled to run that day. Most daily newspapers strive to average a 50-50 split: 50 percent paid advertising and 50 percent news product. Keep in mind that much of the news product contains information that is scheduled to run every day and takes up much of the 'news hole.' Items such as TV listings, weather maps, stock listings, comics, puzzles, events calendars, movie listings, et cetera. Add to that the 'must type' international, national, and state news, and it's easy to see you are vying for limited 'local news' space."

Umbaugh continues, "It's good news that your organization has adopted a local highway and will be meeting there on a Saturday morning to pick up the trash your fellow man has dumped on you. But the bad news is that your local media is not waiting in the wings to reproduce the photo of you and twenty others bending over to rid the grass of old bottle caps and faded lottery tickets. What they will be willing to do is to publish a short story to tell the 'local world' that your fine organization has adopted the highway, its location, and the date and time of the good deed. This is just an example, but I'm sure you get the point."

When presenting a story to a news organization, it is important to keep in mind the human interest factor. When it comes to photographs, do you think they are more likely to include your photograph of ten stiffly smiling volunteers presenting a plaque to the stiffly smiling Man of the Year? Or an action shot of a couple of volunteers bending over the half-frozen body of a homeless man as they hand him a hot meal on the snow-covered steel grate? The difference is, the second photograph has human interest.

Bud Umbaugh, who authored the booklet *Getting Your News into Print*, makes the following suggestions for increasing the chances of getting your news item published:

1. Always type the news release, date it, and identify the organization and the individual's name who may be contacted, with their day and evening telephone numbers. Use a standard 8½-by-11-inch sheet of paper, double-spaced, with a 1½-inch margin on all sides.
2. Keep it as brief as possible, always on one page, if you can.
3. Avoid flowery language. Just provide the basics and make sure you've covered the Who? What? When? Where? and Why? questions, known as the Five W's.

Umbaugh advises preparers of news releases to check them for what he calls eight priority points: correct grammar, relevance, substance, factual accuracy, creativity, credibility, timeliness, and presentation. He adds that most newspapers assign their news photographers to sports events, breaking news stories, and major local occurrences. You should not expect them to dispatch a staff photographer to a volunteer event or recognition luncheon. However, if your own photograph is submitted with the news release, it will often be published if the space permits. The old guidelines of black-and-white photographs no longer apply; clear color photographs are generally acceptable, but check in advance with your local newspaper. He suggests avoiding Polaroid photographs unless they are exceptionally crisp and well defined.

Given the length of this chapter, you might decide that there is too much involved in getting started on a voluntary service project. That is the very last conclusion I want you to reach. The most important suggestion I can make to you is this: if you see a need in your community, do something to address it. Just get involved. The fine people in the preceding chapters did not let tax deduction rules or preparation guidelines for news releases get in the way of their projects. They just got involved. If you volunteer your time and talents in a field you enjoy, you can always find someone to help you with the details. The real payback is not the tax deduction, nor one's photograph in the newspaper. The real payback for me was when the little girl in a Beirut orphanage reached out from her crib and smiled, for what the nurses say was the first time in many months, when I gave her a teddy bear. Or the time the young boy from the inner-city home my church had just renovated hugged me after taking him to an Eagles football game, saying, "You're my very best friend in the whole world." Go out and be somebody's very best friend tomorrow.

6

. . . .

Directory of Organizations Seeking Volunteers

The following is a list of organizations that welcome volunteers. The telephone numbers shown are for their national headquarters (except where a specific geographic region is noted), and callers should ask for the contact number for their local chapter. This is not a complete list; publications such as *Volunteer USA*, compiled by Andrew Carroll (published by Fawcett Columbine, New York) should be consulted for greater detail. See the Bibliography.

AIDS

The Names Project	(415) 882-5500
National AIDS Hotline	(800) 342-2437
	Spanish: (800) 344-7432
Atlanta area: Project Open Hand	(404) 525-4620
Baltimore area: Moveable Feast	(410) 243-4604
Los Angeles area: AIDS Project Los Angeles	(213) 962-1600
New York area: God's Love We Deliver	(212) 865-4900
San Francisco area: Project Open Hand	(415) 255-2529
Washington, D.C., area: Food & Friends	(202) 488-8278

Alcohol and Drugs

American Council for Drug Education	
(Maryland only)	(301) 294-0600
Campuses Without Drugs	(412) 731-8019
"Just Say No" International	(415) 939-6666
	(800) 258-2766
National Council on Alcoholism &	
Drug Dependence	(212) 206-6770
National Federation of Parents for	
Drug-Free Youth	(314) 968-1322
Students Against Driving Drunk (SADD)	(508) 481-3568

Animals

American Society for the Prevention of	
Cruelty to Animals	(212) 876-7700
Humane Society of the United States	(202) 452-1100
National Wildlife Federation	(202) 797-6800

Children and Young Adults

The ASPIRA Association	(202) 835-3600
Athletes and Entertainers for Kids	(800) 933-5437
Big Brothers & Big Sisters	(215) 567-7000
Boy Scouts of America	(214) 580-2000
Camp Fire Boys and Girls	(816) 756-1950
Covenant House	(800) 999-9999
Fresh Air Fund	(212) 221-0900
International Children's Aid Foundation	(609) 854-4894
NAACP (National Association for the	
Advancement of Colored People)	(410) 358-8900
National Black Child Development Institute	(202) 562-0763
National 4-H Council	(301) 961-2800
Project Concern International	(619) 279-9690
Variety Clubs International	(212) 704-9872
	New York only: (212) 247-5588

Women in Community Service (WICS)   (703) 671-0500
Youth Development, Inc.   (619) 292-5683
Save the Children   (203) 226-7271
                                           (800) 243-5075

National Committee for Prevention of
    Child Abuse   (312) 663-3520
National Council on Child Abuse &
    Family Violence   (800) 222-2000
National Runaway Switchboard
    (Chicago area only)   (312) 880-9860

Children Who Are Missing

Adam Walsh Child Resource Center   (407) 863-7900
Child Find of America   (914) 255-1848
National Center for Missing &
    Exploited Children   (703) 235-3900

Crime and Victim Assistance

Center for the Prevention of Sexual &
    Domestic Violence   (206) 634-1903
National Association of Town Watches   (215) 649-7055
National Coalition Against Sexual Assault (202) 483-7165
National Victim Center   (817) 877-3355

Disabilities

American Association on Mental   (202) 387-1968
    Retardation   (800) 424-3688
American Cancer Society   (404) 320-3333
American Council of the Blind   (202) 467-5081
                                           (800) 424-8666
American Mental Health Fund   (703) 573-2200
                                           (800) 433-5959

Association for Persons with Severe
    Handicaps   (206) 523-8446
COMPEER   (716) 546-8280

Epilepsy Foundation of America | (301) 459-3700
(800) 332-1000
Family Friends Program, National Council
on the Aging | (202) 479-1200
Goodwill Industries | (301) 530-6500
Helen Keller National Center for Deaf-
Blind Youths & Adults | (516) 944-8900
March of Dimes Birth Defects Foundation | (914) 428-7100
Muscular Dystrophy Association | (602) 529-2000
National Alliance for the Mentally Ill | (703) 524-7600
(800) 950-6264
National Association of the Deaf | (301) 587-1788
National Easter Seal Society | (312) 726-6200
National Head Injury Foundation | (202) 296-6443
National Organization on DisAbility | (202) 293-5960
(NOD) | (800) 248-2253
National Spinal Cord Injury Association | (617) 935-2722
(800) 962-9629
Recording for the Blind | (609) 452-0606
Special Olympics | (202) 628-3630
United Cerebral Palsy Associations | (212) 268-6655
(800) 872-5827

Education and Illiteracy

Barbara Bush Foundation for Family Literacy | (202) 338-2006
Christian Literacy Associates | (412) 364-3777
Learning Disabilities Association | (412) 341-1515
Literacy Volunteers of America | (315) 445-8000
(800) 228-8813
National Alliance of Business | (202) 289-2888
National Parent-Teacher Association | (312) 787-0977
Reading Is Fundamental (RIF) | (202) 287-3371

Elderly

The Alzheimer's Association | (800) 621-0379
Illinois only: (800) 572-6037

American Association of Retired Persons
   (AARP)   (202) 434-2277
Little Brothers—Friends of the Elderly   (312) 477-7702
National Association of Area Agencies
   on Aging   (202) 296-8130

Environment

American Hiking Society   (703) 385-3252
Appalachian Mountain Club   (617) 523-0636
Greenpeace USA   (202) 462-1177
The Nature Conservancy   (703) 841-5300
The Sierra Club   (415) 776-2211

Homelessness and Housing

Christmas in April   (202) 326-8268
Habitat for Humanity   (912) 924-6935
The Hope Foundation   (214) 630-5765
                                                 (800) 843-4073
Neighborhood Reinvestment Corporation   (202) 376-2400
Chicago area: The Need Foundation   (708) 352-0393
Philadelphia area: Trevor's Campaign
   for the Homeless   (800) 873-8677

Hunger

Bread for the World   (301) 608-2400
Second Harvest National Food Bank
   Network   (312) 263-2303
USA Harvest   (502) 583-7756
                                                 (800) 872-4366

Suicide

American Association of Suicidology   (303) 692-0985

Veterans

Blinded Veterans Association	(202) 371-8880
	(800) 669-7079
Disabled American Veterans (DAV)	(202) 554-3501
	(606) 441-7300
Voluntary Service Program, Department of Veterans Affairs	(202) 535-7377

Miscellaneous Service Organizations

American Red Cross	(202) 737-8300
Campus Outreach Opportunity League	(612) 624-3018
Fourth World Movement	(301) 336-9489
Junior Achievement	(719) 540-8000
Junior Leagues	(212) 683-5151
Lions Clubs International	(708) 571-5466
Peace Corps	(202) 254-7970
	(800) 424-8580
The Points of Light Foundation	(202) 223-9186
Rotary International	(708) 866-3000
Salvation Army	(201) 857-8822
Volunteers of America	(504) 837-2652
Volunteers for Peace	(802) 259-2759
YMCA	(312) 977-0031
YWCA	(212) 614-2700

Bibliography

"American Corporate Community Service." *Fortune*, Nov. 30, 1992.

Baldwin, D. "Creating Community." *Common Cause*, July/Aug. 1990, p. 15.

Carroll, A. *Volunteer USA*. New York: Fawcett Columbine, 1991.

Carter, J., and Carter, R. *Everything to Gain: Making the Most of the Rest of Your Life*. New York: Ballantine, 1987.

Independent Sector. *Giving and Volunteering in the United States*. Washington, D.C.: Independent Sector, 1990.

Independent Sector. *Nonprofit Almanac 1992–93: Dimensions of the Independent Sector*. San Francisco: Jossey-Bass, 1992.

Miller, A., and others. "The New Volunteerism." *Newsweek*, Feb. 8, 1988.

Mother Teresa. *Words to Love By*. Notre Dame, Ind.: Ave Maria Press, 1983.

O'Connell, B. *The Voluntary Spirit*. Washington, D.C., Independent Sector, 1992.

Points of Light Foundation. *Developing a Corporate Volunteer Program: Guidelines to Success*. Washington, D.C.: The Points of Light Foundation, 1992.

Points of Light Foundation. *Principles of Excellence in Commu-*

nity Service: A Message to America's Business Leaders. Washington, D.C.: The Points of Light Foundation, 1992.

Points of Light Foundation. *Principles of Excellence in Community Service: A Time to A.C.T.* Washington, D.C.: The Points of Light Foundation, 1992.

Salholz, E., and others. "The Empathy Factor." *Newsweek*, Jan. 13, 1992.

Wild, C. *Corporate Volunteer Programs: Benefits to Business.* New York: Conference Board, 1993.

Index